Sybase Developer's Handbook

Sybase Developer's Handbook

Daniel J. Worden

AP Professional

AP Professional is a Division of Academic Press

San Diego   London   Boston
New York   Sydney   Tokyo   Toronto

AP PROFESSIONAL
An Imprint of ACADEMIC PRESS
A Division of HARCOURT BRACE & COMPANY

This book is printed on acid-free paper. ∞

ACADEMIC PRESS
525 B Street, Suite 1900, San Diego, CA 92101-4495, USA
http://www.apnet.com

24-28 Oval Road, London NW1 7DX, UK
http://www.hbuk.co.uk/ao/

Library of Congress Cataloging-in-Publication Data
  Worden, Daniel.
    Sybase developer's handbook / Daniel J. Worden.
        p. cm.
        Includes index.
    ISBN 0-12-763950-0
    1. Database design. 2. Sybase. 3. Client/server computing.
I. Title
QA76.9.D3W666 1998
005.74–dc21   98-6555
                                    CIP

Printed in the United States of America
98 99 00 01 02 IP 9 8 7 6 5 4 3 2 1

To my wife Marie with abiding love and deepest respect.
Being with you makes the difficulties seem smaller
and the accomplishments worthwhile.

Acknowledgements

With any project like this it's impossible to note all the people who helped along the way, but here goes.

At the top of the list are my colleagues and collaborators – Jim Munro and Rick Wattling. Without their contribution this would have been a much slimmer book. Thanks for your in-depth coverage on the administration and programming side. Naturally any responsibility for errors or omissions remains mine.

Yet again, Marie Worden and Ron Heinz have been there for me. The page layout and CD is a result of their painstaking attention to detail and long hours. You guys are the best.

There are several Sybase folks who deserve special mention for their help in getting me on side with the new direction – Ray Vitale, Graham Hainbach and Tina Haley. Your enthusiasm and belief in Sybase is contagious. Also, arigato to Noriko Hayama and Ishibashi-san. I appreciate the time you took with me to explain how Sybase works in Japan.

Thanks to Jim McKiernon for his great work on the Job Monitor program and its multimedia description on the CD.

I'd especially like to thank the AP Professional team, Thomas Park, Vanessa Gerhard and Ken Morton. You were extremely patient with me and I hope the final product proves worthy. Thanks to my agent at Waterside Productions, Carole Mclendon, and last but not least, thank you Alexander and Tristan. You guys were very understanding when Dad had to work on the book instead of spending time with you. I love you both.

Contents

CHAPTER 3

Sybase Server Basic Overview .. *37*

CHAPTER 4

System XI Overview *51*

CHAPTER 5

Sybase Database Objects *65*

CHAPTER 10

CHAPTER 11

CHAPTER 12

Open Client *353*

CHAPTER 13

CT-Library versus DB-Library. . . 375

CHAPTER 14

Using Open Server *405*

Introduction

Thank you for picking up this book. No doubt you are already aware that this handbook is geared toward Sybase SQL Server System XI developers. In fact, the objective from the start was to create a "must have" companion guide for anyone working with Sybase as part of their client/server applications suite.

This is not an introductory-level book. While I make every effort to introduce and explain each aspect of the System XI database engine from the ground up, this book will prove most useful to those of you who have worked with SQL Server for at least the last few years.

If you're new to Sybase applications, may I suggest you find a used bookstore and pick up one of my other earlier books? Those were written primarily for readers working with SQL Server for the first time. And those of you who have read those texts should find that this book builds on the material covered there.

In the past few years, the nature of the client/server market has changed and Sybase customers have changed right along with it.

Wherever I go, I see customers who are familiar with the product, its limitations and benefits. These are people who are looking for ways to squeeze optimum performance from their server, or who are facing enterprise-wide integration challenges.

My basic assumption in writing this book is that you have Sybase-related problems to solve, one of the first being when, why and how to upgrade to System XI.

As a reader, I expect you may want to read through the upgrade-related or System XI features chapters to prepare your site. After that, my main purpose for this book is to serve as a troubleshooting encyclopedia, containing practical, documented tips for dealing with issues not found in the manuals. To support this, I have contacted Sybase developers all over the world and asked them to share their experience with me, so I could in turn share it with you.

I hope you find this book a practical and useful handbook, enlightening you about System XI and, at least occasionally, entertaining. As always, I welcome and encourage feedback. Please feel free to contact me through e-mail at this address: djworden@wordn.com Enjoy the book!

CHAPTER 1 — *The Sybase Story*

For anyone contemplating a commitment, or a renewal of their commitment to Sybase technology in the closing years of the 1990s, I can appreciate your position.

On the one hand, there is the product story. This is one of enabling technology, consistent innovation and a consolidation of offerings into a comprehensive toolset. The integration of Sybase, PowerBuilder and Watcom has brought a formidable selection of technical solutions to the table.

Then there is the management story. Sybase has flitted from one marketing message to another, making it difficult for corporate systems architects and buyers to see the underlying value. Consulting services are pricey and focused more on technology than the return on its application. Last, the financial news has been uninspired to say the least.

It is my sincere hope that in this book I will allay any fears you might have about spending your time and effort on this product suite.

When Sybase first hit the market in the mid 1980s, the technical vision behind the company propelled it to immediate fame and fortune. The Sybase SQL Server had two very important innovations, stored procedures and triggers. Better yet, it was open and could serve as an engine to pretty much any front end client. This was unheard of in the rdbms world at that time and the marketplace wanted it big time.

A decade later, a great many things had changed. Not only was Sybase now approaching a billion dollars per year in revenue, but its competitors had caught up. Having peaked in the mid nineties at the number two rdbms vendor by sales, Sybase has been nudged aside into the number three spot. Or even lower depending on which competitor you ask.

Worse for Sybase, even Oracle began offering a version of stored procedures and triggers, while the company got a black eye in the trades for shipping product before it was ready. The re-architected System 10 product had caused difficulties for customers trying to scale it up into mainframe replacement applications. And to make matters worse, the early System XI had key features that didn't work quite as advertised.

For a great many of us who signed on as Sybase developers and partners during the halycon years, the past few years have seemed somewhat bleak in comparison.

Surviving the Ups & Downs

Problems with Sybase scalability, discovered by customers and trumpeted by analysts had the net effect of bringing to a standstill any glamour in buying into a Sybase solution. Whereas technical management previously endorsed the toolset with enthusiasm, they began to responded with questions and "concerns."

The stock market while posting all time highs, continued to treat Sybase shares as a poor cousin. Throughout 1997 the company traded between the $12 and $20 dollar range, down from its all time high of more than $50 in 1995.

Sybase laid off people, then more people until finally, in April 1998, the long time CEO Mark Hoffman retired to become chairman and turned over the Presidency to Mitchell Kertzman who had moved to Sybase with Powersoft. By June 1998, the stock hit an all time low of $6.50.

Well, that may be interesting, but really, how do such lofty events affect the life of a Sybase developer? If you are focused on the potential outcome of Sybase corporate and the future price of shares, I suggest you skip immediately to the last chapter of this book.

For those of us more interested in technology than the stock market the answer is straightforward. They don't. The news doesn't affect how Sybase fits the system requirements of our various organizations. As you will see covered in this book, the capabilities of these database products speak for themselves.

Getting the Job Done

It was once true that to have experience as a Sybase and Power-Builder systems professional was an automatic ticket to a good project, new work, and a good future. By mid 1996, however, new Sybase customers seemed to be coming on board at the speed of molasses in January. Cold molasses. Up hill, no less. In short, it seems that these days we have to work at it a little harder.

As a systems developer, your choice of tools is one of the most important investments you can make. You want tools that allow you to build the kind of systems you envision. Not mediocre products offered by highly profitable corporations. That in a nutshell is the theme of this book – Sybase offers tools that let you build the kind of systems you want. Whether the company makes any money or not is a secondary concern.

The value of this section is a review of how Sybase got from its initial point in the market to where it is today. I want to look at how events unfolded so we can appropriately emphasize certain aspects of the toolset as critical to developing effective and sustainable Sybase applications.

We Are Here...

The process of moving from start-up to billion dollar enterprise in a decade was not without its disappointments and even failures. Backing products such as Gain Momentum split the company's focus and took critical resources away other projects. Replication server didn't take the world by storm. But the news has not been all bad. Far from it. There are other products quietly waiting in the wings. Like Jaguar CTS and Power J, for openers.

Keep in mind that with well over 25,000 customer sites having installed Sybase products in its first ten years, what fell flat on its face was the **rate** at which new Sybase customers were coming on board. This did not mean that either the company or the products were no longer viable, it simply meant that the nature and focus of the users, and therefore the emphasis of the application of the products changed. A new vision was required to support this change in Sybase reality.

The New Vision

Where once Sybase had focused entirely on its OLTP performance measures and key features like stored procedures and triggers, the new vision under CEO Mitchell Kertzman became one of providing glue to pull organizational data together. Sybase as a database product appealed most to global organizations who needed to move data in and out of other systems. The middleware division of Sybase was targeted directly at this area. GUI applications to service users of all this data could be built using the now Sybase owned tool – PowerBuilder.

Replication server had been a cornerstone of the development efforts in the mid 1990s but the initial products had been poor performers, difficult to administer and lacking in robustness.

Acknowledging that on the database side, the real corporate customer interest was in the DataWarehouse, Sybase began to look for ways to deal more effectively with massive amounts of data. The IQ product was touted as the ultimate solution for managing terabytes of corporate data.

And, of course, there was the front end. With the founder of Powersoft as CEO of Sybase overall, one could hardly expect that the corporate emphasis would exclude PowerBuilder, the darling development environment of the early 1990s. The new vision for PowerBuilder was not only cross-platform, but a total corporate development environment. Object orientation, rapid application development and expanded CASE tool offerings were bundled into the PowerBuilder 5 suite in 1996.

On the Move

Powersoft had masterminded the takeover of Watcom, a compact but well built DOS/Windows based rdbms engine out of Waterloo, Canada. This was the one area where Sybase had no real offering of its own. To support mobile computing, Watcom quickly became SQL Anywhere and a T-SQL capable compiler was added to the product.

Utilities, such as the pipeline and bidirectional replication allowed synchronization of these home and laptop-based databases with corporate data stores under Sybase. Perhaps even more importantly, Sybase could now offer a competitive product to Personal Oracle, something that was simply not possible before the Powersoft acquisition.

The bottom line? With the acquisition of Powersoft, Sybase not only got a new CEO and ownership of a comprehensive front-end development environment, but they also got the final piece in the database puzzle: a small footprint, Windows-compliant rdbms that was compatible with their larger offerings.

Once More Into the Breech

At the time of this writing, (early 1998), Sybase seemed to have consolidated its position, direction, and resources. The net effect of this is to have streamlined its product offerings, to focus on meeting the challenges of specific marketplaces and to tie together its products into an overall solution.

The question becomes: How do you build solutions to organizational problems using these tools? As indicated in the Introduction, I wrote this particular book with the experienced Sybase developer in mind. I recognize that you already understand conceptually how stored procedures work, what you're looking for now is a source to help you debug the frustrating things when they do not work in reality.

The typical application I kept in mind was primarily someone upgrading to Sybase XI. I see 'System Eleven' as being the new four dot nine dot two. Remember that great release from years back that had terrific performance, great reliability, and... *sniff,* but perhaps I'm growing too nostalgic. Come to think of it there actually were a number of compelling reasons for the rearchitecting of the database engine that came out in System 10.

What's really exciting about this is the move to Adaptive Component Architecture. I'm not being biased about this; I believe Sybase is back on its technical feet and has a new direction that can get folks to sit up and take notice.

Basically, I see Adaptive Server as the release Sybase standardizes on for all their customers for the next few years. Adaptive Server 11.5 includes all the cool OMNI stuff which used to be priced separately. Even if System XII comes out (?!), being somewhat triskadekaphopbic I certainly wouldn't recommend they release a System XIII! As we'll discuss in later chapters, there is more than enough in the current release of the product to keep any database technophile working and tweaking away.

Beyond the database product itself, let's look at the products the company offered going into 1997 and define which ones we will cover as part of this developer's handbook.

Sorting Out the Products

Of course, we have System XI as the database engine of choice, but internally Sybase defined several categories under which the database was positioned. Workgroup Products, for example, include the Windows NT, Novell and OS/2 version of Sybase System 10 and XI. The version previous to System 10 was 4.2.2.

In this book I will be using examples extensively from Windows NT, Unix, and SQL Anywhere. The Novell and OS/2 versions of Sybase are not seen by anyone I know as real growth areas and, in fact, I wouldn't be surprised to see them dropped from support in future releases.

The DOS or stand-alone version of the product is, of course, Sybase Adaptive Server Anywhere. This is a relatively small footprint version of the database product which runs under Windows 3.x, Windows 95, Windows NT (3.5.1), Netware 3.11 and up, and

OS/2 2.11 and later. Interestingly, the minimum specs for the product is a 386 with 8 megs of RAM. So if you are planning to use examples from this book at home, you don't necessarily have to upgrade the machine in the den. (Performance of the multimedia demo on the machine is going to be pretty unattractive, but whatever...)

Larger-scale rdbms solutions include offerings for the tier one ports to Solaris, HP-UX and AIX. These are the platforms for which Sybase develops and ships first. Secondary platforms include such vendors as Sequent, DataGeneral, and Pyramid.

Typically, Sybase does not lag far behind in releasing second tier platform versions, although in some cases they may choose to never release a specific version. I'm thinking of a particular case I came across where the DataGeneral Aviion series of servers did not have a version 10.0.2 release supported. To be fair, many of the bug fixes contained in 10.0.2 were incorporated into a 10.0.1 EBF (Emergency Bug Fix) release specifically for the Aviion.

The main point I'm trying to make here is that while Sybase products cover a multitude of platforms and versions, your life as a developer can be greatly affected by the exact version of a specific release running on a particular platform. DBAs have long been familiar with the nasty little bugs which can generated by an outdated bios on a controller card, for example. These are often the cause of incompatibilities and difficulties which plague a Sybase site. (Not more than any other rdbms vendor, but then not many fewer either!)

Sybase and Microsoft

Okay, let's deal with this issue. Sybase and Microsoft were technical and marketing partners for almost ten years. In late 1995 they got a corporate divorce and are fighting over custody of SQL Server. This analogy actually works as I will explain.

Microsoft's 4.2.2 version of SQL Server is basically the same code line as the 4.9.2 version of Sybase SQL Server. Obviously the MS version worked on the Intel platform whereas the Sybase version was supported by various Unix vendors and Novell.

With System 10, Sybase changed the internal architecture of the SQL Server product. The creation of a syb_backup process and the addition of a new systems procedures database are just two examples of the extent to which changes were made.

With SQL Server 6.0, Microsoft began to tinker with changes to their server and with version 6.5 significant differences began to emerge. SQL Server 7.0, otherwise known as Sphinx will only accentuate the differences over the common ancestry of the two products.

My company, WNS, has been developing solutions for customers using both Sybase and Microsoft SQL Server since 1991. In many cases, it was a coin toss or a customer leaning to determine which one we would use (after the NT version came out). Recently, I have been hearing things about the Microsoft version of the product which is causing me to rethink using SQL Server 7.

Of course, you wouldn't use the Microsoft product if you had any kind of range in the platform on which you wanted to deploy your solution. Microsoft is committed to NT which, while a useful tool, is not the one-size-fits-all solution it is sometimes made out to be.

With that said, I have some concerns about the new version of Microsoft SQL Server which is pulling us back to the Sybase side of product continuum. Specifically, I believe that Microsoft is committed to providing support for Visual Basic for Applications natively within SQL Server. This means you could write stored procedures in either T-SQL or VBA. It makes sense that

Microsoft would want their database product to support another SQL variant than the one owned by Sybase.

The impact of this change is subtle but significant.

Even during the dark days of System 10.0.1, few argued with the quality and caliber of the Sybase development teams. They may not have gotten everything right the first time, but they knew (and know) onions from leeks. The optimizer is a solid, high-performance piece of programming and at various times has been the envy of other database companies.

Microsoft, on the other hand, is known for their breadth of features and not so much for their compact code.

If Microsoft rewrites the database kernel to accept VBA as well as T-SQL, I have little confidence that its performance will scale beyond a workgroup or department. To address these needs, Sybase offers Adaptive Server Anywhere, which is not only cheaper and smaller, but runs on Netware or on the desktop, including Microsoft's Windows CE.

In short, I don't see Microsoft SQL Server and Sybase addressing the same markets with the same products as has been the case since the separation of the two camps a few years ago.

The problem from a customer, buyer, or developer's standpoint is the confusion over the use of the name SQL Server. In the minds of many people SQL Server is the Microsoft product and Sybase is the database from Sybase. By mid-1997, Sybase decided to address this issue head on by releasing Adaptive Server as part of the Adaptive Component Architecture.

To be fair, this wasn't just a cosmetic name change. The Adaptive Server, while built around the System XI kernel, is a very, very different beast than the Microsoft SQL Server – which by extension means it's different than Sybase 4.9.2.

At a glance, there is the support for specialty datatypes, the built-in DirectConnect to other Sybase engines, Java in the database, and support for asynchronous stored procedures. Add to those services the ability to truly tune the kernel for performance and we are talking about a completely distinct product, one that I am convinced has a legitimate and significant role to play in the development of relational database solutions. We'll cover the architectural features of the Adaptive Component Architecture and Adaptive Server in more detail later in the book.

For our purposes, I will try to minimize the use of the term SQL Server in favor of referring to the server product as the Sybase database engine or simply the server. However, based on years of treating the two products interchangeably, I will probably slip a few times. If I specifically mean the product from Microsoft, I'll refer to it as the MS-SQL Server; otherwise, it's all Sybase to me.

Management Changes

As the general manager of a systems solution company, I have had to do business with many different technology companies. At this level you quickly discover which firms are "open for business," and which are resting on past achievements or market forces.

There is a tendency among people who work with technology to overlook the importance of sales, marketing and management to the success of any organization. I do not intend to get on a soapbox here; I simply want to point out that other factors have been operating in the way the Sybase name is perceived. Most of us working with Sybase see it as a functional technology rather than a synonym for corporate or managerial excellence.

Without being unduly negative, I think it's fair to note that Sybase, having grown to its current size over a six or seven year period, had some problems internally. These problems affected the way the company provided service to existing customers, as well as products and the general perception of the company in the marketplace. The net effect of these problems was to create doubt in the minds of even the most committed Sybase developers about the viability of the company.

The good news for us is that by Spring of 1998, very real changes were in place within the Sybase organization. Excellence and its opposite most often start at the top. Mitchell Kertzman brought in John Chen from Siemens-Nixdorff to share in the responsibility of running the company. From what I hear, Mr. Chen runs a very tight ship and this is a change from what had become standard operating procedure.

There is a new standard being demanded from staff within Emeryville and this is likely to ripple out to the rest of the Sybase organization over time.

Linda Gladdin, an ex-Sun employee has taken over responsibility for the Partner organization. Sybase has traditionally been focused more on selling and supporting products through its own offices. Speaking as a partner with Sybase, I can tell you that pricing, provision and support of products through the Partner channel has at times been unnecessarily difficult. Ms. Gladdin has taken charge of these issues and already changes are making themselves felt.

Of course, there are many seasoned Sybase managers and staff who have been just waiting for a "new broom" to sweep away some of the obstacles to getting the job done. I firmly believe that the Sybase corporation has been through the worst and has marshaled its forces, addressing their weak areas and building on strengths. I expect that all of us who work with the products and people Sybase offers will be seeing a continual improvement. This can only make developing systems with Sybase products even more attractive than it has been in the past.

Chapter Summary

From this chapter you should have gained an appreciation for where the Sybase corporation comes from, its evolution, and emphases for the future. Specific issues such as System XI and Microsoft were addressed as well as the financial performance of the company from late 1996 to present.

From a developer's standpoint, this information should be useful because investment in a skill set takes serious time, energy, and presents no small opportunity cost.

As we get into the specifics of how, where, and why Sybase products work, I think it's important to have confidence in the fundamental viability of the toolset you have chosen.

From this chapter you should have gained a sense that the news is not all bad and the future for Sybase developers is hardly bleak. In fact, change is already being made in the products and organization itself. We should be able to look forward to a renewed sense of place with Sybase and Adaptive Component Architecture.

On that happy note, let's move on.

CHAPTER 2

Adaptive Server Architecture

Unified Field Theory

Sybase has long been accused of producing too many confusing and poorly integrated products. This may be the necessary, but unwelcome result of Sybase's growth by acquisition strategy. To their credit, the products acquired in the feeding frenzy from MDI and Powersoft were individual leaders in their market segments.

The challenge was how to integrate these and make the whole more than the sum of the parts. A skim through the Sybase product catalog can quickly become a frustrating experience. Sybase has made strides in recent years to define a well-constructed integrated marketing plan for its products.

Unfortunately this veneer of integration runs only skin deep. It's useful for explaining the products and their capabilities, and more clearly defines the role and market niche for each component in a customer friendly way. So as a communication tool the integrated marketing strategy seems to have been successful.

There was, however, a bold but perhaps naive bunch of customers who actually believed that the products should work together and share something beyond the same letterhead. To their vindication and great relief, Sybase has finally released a technical architecture for integrating the various products. This includes defining the common components and interfaces between the various product options.

Sybase refers to this blueprint as the "Adaptive Component Architecture." Under this plan each significant Sybase server product has a place and a defined interface to the user or customer and each other. Interfaces to third-party database server products have also been defined in this model. Before getting too carried away I should warn you that although the faces are familiar, the names have all been changed. I can only speculate that this is to protect the innocent.

The most obvious name change is that the SQL Server name is no longer a part of the vocabulary. The new name is "Adaptive Server Enterprise." The initial release is version 11.5. Don't be confused by this change in parlance. This is the next System XI release. This observation is not made to diminish the new features and capabilities that are included in this release; I merely want to orient you to the new Adaptive Architecture terminology. Sybase seems to have finally divorced itself from the ill-fated Microsoft alliance. Unfortunately, for Sybase customers Microsoft has been ceded the SQL Server name. Now that Sybase has finally resigned itself to this fate they've made a clean break in adopting the Adaptive Server terminology.

The core of the new Adaptive Architecture is still the data engine contained in the "Adaptive Server Enterprise" product. We'll step through the other components and features of the architecture one at a time.

Optimized Data Stores

Under the Sybase Adaptive Component architecture not all servers are created equally. In a move counter to the "universal" server concept of one server fits all, the Sybase products are oriented toward optimized functions. Not surprisingly these functions relate to areas where Sybase has individual products providing these functions. Sybase breaks these services into four distinct areas.

- OLTP – This area is obviously related to traditional transaction enabled business applications. The emphasis is on small, predictable workloads and maximum system throughput. Obviously this is the domain of the Adaptive Server Enterprise product. (Or the product formerly known as SQL Server.<g>)

- Decision Support – This is often referred to as data warehousing or data marts from an implementation perspective. The workload is nonscheduled and hard to predict. Data are primarily read with infrequent updates or additions. The individual queries come in all shapes and sizes – from itty-bitty to great-biggy. Although the Adaptive Server product can perform reasonably well in this role, the Sybase IQ product is positioned as the product best optimized for this task.

- Mass Deployment – Sybase coined this term to refer to personal databases. These products are intended to provide data service and storage for individual or small workgroup applications. In some situations this can also involve remote or disconnected users using laptop computers. Although these products can participate fully in replication networks their emphasis is on individual as opposed to enterprise requirements. Sybase has positioned the SQL Anywhere product in this space.

- Complex Data Types – These areas demand specialized datatypes and operations to support very specific operations. The stereotypical application in this area is geographic information systems in which database information is intrinsically related to some spatial dimension such as latitude or longitude. Operations such as mapping or relocation actions are intuitively required to benefit fully from these systems. Lately image datatypes had been touted as falling into this category. This is, of course, beyond the simple blob image type carried along attached to a row record. Sybase recognizes that these applications require special capabilities that would not necessarily easily fit within the confines of a "universal" server.

In Sybase's new terminology, products that serve data in these various areas are referred to as "data stores." Customers are encouraged to choose the "data store" implementation or combination that best meets their specific requirements. This leaves the customer with flexibility to obtain the best requirement fit possible. Each Adaptive Component data store is intended to optimize its operations and data storage methods to best service its intended customers. Customers should be able to access these stores and migrate data appropriately between the various storage systems as required.

Obviously, in order to make this work, the various data stores must conform to certain standard and well-defined interfaces before this is practical.

Common Language Processor

This is the architectural component that ensures that all of the data stores provided speak the same language. This specifies the detailed syntax and semantic definitions that each compliant application must implement. This is, of course, the lowest common denominator form of this function. The various specialized engines may also incorporate distinct terminology to achieve the required functions. This is the user interface to the Adaptive Component Architecture.

Once again before we get too carried away in describing what's new we need to understand what's the same. The common language for the data stores is still the traditional Transact-SQL, which has been in use since the first release of SQL Server. Sybase has been working diligently to bring together the various family members around this one consistent language element for a long time. The Adaptive Server specification establishes this mandate more formally. The new releases of all the Adaptive Component products now realize this standard. The common interface makes using and supporting the various server products more accessible and reduces retraining associated with using specific products in the various required niches.

If the wary traveler sticks to the common syntax of T-SQL, all of the logic and scripting created for a specific Adaptive Component can be ported to any other compliant platform. This makes the logic component much more reusable and allows developers to focus support on a more condensed code line. This means that any T-SQL script or stored procedure that is created for the Adaptive Server Enterprise will function as expected in the decision support and mass deployment products such as IQ and Adaptive Server Anywhere.

Those inclined to be cynical may observe that Sybase had been very close to realizing this goal in previous releases of these products. So this may not be more than fresh paint on an old house. New in the Adaptive Component Architecture, however, is the full fledged embracing of standard components based on Java-Beans, ActiveX, and CORBA standards. So objects created in these environments can run natively on any of the data store platforms. In addition, these components can be distributed to other application tiers are required to fulfill a specific application vision. Again these components once developed can be reused many times in any of the server or middle tier environments. In the initial release the Adaptive Server Enterprise product only provides native support for JavaBeans components. The ActiveX and CORBA support is included in the product plans for future releases.

Internally, the server products provide a Java virtual machine that executes the component logic. The component can access the stored data using the JDBC interface in manner similar to an external program. This implementation is much more standard than the Oracle Cartridges model. For developers, this allows them to choose a single language and programming model on which to implement any of the client presentation, business, or data access layer components. In fact, components developed in this model can be rehosted on different tiers at various times depending on the individual requirements. This provides a high degree of flexibility in application deployment and usage. Of course, the Powersoft development products will support developing component objects to this specification.

The Common Language processor then provides a consistent interface and method for accessing data whether by T-SQL or using object methods. It also provides flexibility in deploying data storage to the product or data store that best fits the requirements of the information and in using objects to implement application services on any tier that proves useful.

This feature, although very helpful and much needed, does not provide the level of data and location transparency that's desired. This is provided by another component of the overall architecture.

Component Integration Layer

The Component Integration Layer provides the glue that holds the overall architecture together. If we were to categorize this function from the perspective of the older or existing product line this would appear very much like the OmniServer product. This provides an Open Server type of framework that can dispatch queries or requests formed using the common language syntax and dispatch it for execution on the appropriate data store. This would apply whether the component was a native compliant

Adaptive Component or a third-party data engine such as Oracle. This becomes the central hub of the database activity, the touchstone of integration.

For natively compliant applications such as Adaptive Server Enterprise, this layer can be effectively bypassed, resulting in improved performance; that is, providing requests can be fulfilled from within a single server. If the request requires data from other places such as legacy data or Oracle, then the request is parsed into the appropriate form for that engine, obtained, and translated back into the appropriate format before returning it to the requestor.

Common Management Component

In the process of integrating many different specialized components into a single service, this architecture has increased the overall complexity and support requirements. When this is contrasted with other product offerings implementing the "universal" server it becomes apparent that certain support issues need to be addressed to ensure that management costs don't become prohibitive. Sybase has defined the "Common Management Component" to address these system management issues. It appears as if the SQL Monitor technology would be the cornerstone in implementing these services.

Within this component, data management and security functions are defined. Each of these defined services can be deployed to any Adaptive Component-compliant data store. Beyond the data stores the management functions can incorporate other middleware products such as dbQ (recently discontinued) and NetImpact Dynamo (recently renamed PowerSite). This provides a mechanism for implementing policy-based management schemas. This should provide a more consistent application of enterprise rules and processes.

A Product for All Seasons

So what? What does this provide that wasn't there before? How is this better or worse than other products that you might consider?

Existing Sybase customers who are using multiple products in various roles can easily improve their efficiency and reduce the maintenance activity by upgrading to Adaptive Components and utilizing the common management and language items. The good news is that this upgrade should be free as part of the regular product upgrade cycle. There is no particular reason why customers should shy away from this upgrade. We've put the System 10 experience in our past and more recent experiences have not been nearly as painful. The underlying products are familiar and mature despite the name changes.

Another reason for adopting this architecture is the added application deployment flexibility that it provides. The Sybase SQL Server product cut its teeth implementing early client/server applications. In that function it was ideally suited to two-tier implementations where a significant portion of the business logic was contained within the database. This provided a mechanism for tightly coupling the data and business logic. This allowed business or logic changes to be implemented in the data server and shared with all the application clients reducing system administration. Sybase's competitors scrambled to implement these same features. The migration to three-tier and n-tier application architectures has to some degree diminished this requirement. Business logic has been implemented in specialized application servers. There have also been costs as developers have been forced to learn the intricacies of the various middleware products in addition to the data server and presentation services. In many cases these each require a specialized programming language and in some cases programming model. By implementing a consistent object programming model on all the application tiers the developer is provided with maximum flexibility in deploying a specific application function. Using the standard object languages such as Java business logic can be recast to any application tier desired. This can even be dependent on specific deployment situations within an enterprise rollout. The developer only has to be adept in one programming language or model.

Another advantage which plays to a traditional SQL Server strength is performance. By providing flexibility to deploy applications to optimized data stores best suited to a function and the flexibility to deploy in various geographies an ideal performance profile can be created. Decisions can be made based on available processing power and available bandwidth among other factors, providing many opportunities to customize the delivery. This is in addition to the high degree of tuning that can be accomplished within the data store component.

At the present time these capabilities are unique in the market and can add significant value to the overall development exercise.

Adaptive Server Enterprise Features

Beyond the general architectural specifications Sybase has released the Adaptive Server Enterprise product as the first tangible product of the overall architecture. So it provides an opportunity to review the features and specifications of the product replacing the System XI server.

As I mentioned the Adaptive Server Enterprise product looks to the casual observer just like a Sybase System XI SQL Server. It's not surprising then that the product adapts quite well to various data management roles between on-line transaction-oriented services and batch or decision support roles. The new Adaptive Server Enterprise product provides improved mechanisms for segmenting resources to the various workloads and application requirements that a single data server must support. This provides some incentive to consolidate various data sources and applications into a single server that may have been dispersed for performance reasons previously. Like System XI the new server incorporates named cache spaces and object or database binding to these resources. This provides a mechanism to improve the predictability of application performance by guaranteeing memory resources. In addition, each cache space can be configured for the optimum I/O block size. This is augmented with the ability to configure specific cache replacement policies by named cache space. This allows the best caching strategy to be chosen for various data objects. This again improves the overall ability to maintain consistent system response.

New with Adaptive Server Enterprise is the ability to configure affinities between the processor resources and specific applications or user processes. This ensures that a certain portion of the overall processing capacity is always available to the assigned tasks. This again helps ensure that predictable results can be obtained. This is the processor equivalent to named cache spaces. Of course, to use this feature effectively, the system must be implemented in an SMP environment. In addition, the overall network load is distributed more equitably to the various database engines that are available.

Other processing improvements have also been incorporated. One of these features is an optimized descending index scan. In previous releases doing a descending index scan required an additional data sort to provide the result set. In Adaptive Server Enterprise the index can be scanned in reverse order to obtain the proper result and eliminate the sort step. The new server supports "asynchronous transactions" generated using a messaging engine. For many applications this transaction processing mode is much better suited to their requirements than the better known synchronous transactions. The engines provide a much improved structure for performing parallel queries.

These parallel enhancements can be used in other functions such as loads and backups. Each of these features can quite effectively improve the overall system throughput. This is in addition to enabling the server to create indexes in parallel, dramatically reducing the time required for this function.

There are additional enhancements in the security and recoverability of the system. The "roles" within the Sybase server have taken on an improved functionality. This includes the ability to create generic roles and assign permissions and ids to these roles as required. These assignments can be changed dynamically as the application processing changes. The standard security environment can be augmented with third-party products such as DCE, Kerberos, SSL, and public key products. There is also a proxy service available to improve security integration with the various other application layers.

The server includes additional support for high availability configurations with failover capabilities. This includes improved support for "point-in-time" recovery. The DBCC function has been improved to provide for on-line service at up to 1 GB per minute. The results are saved in a system table for later retrieval. This allows for much higher availability and improves the product's ability to service VLDB requirements.

Other enhancements to the auditing system have been made to reduce its impact on the performance of a system when auditing is enabled. The server can also provide access from the management environment to the SQL statements that are currently active. This provides for improved debugging of in-flight performance problems.

The new server provides support for "extended stored procedures." This provides the mechanism to safely access non-SQL functions external to the server implemented in any language or tool required.

In all, the new product provides a range of desirable features that many existing customers have been requesting. This continues to build on the strengths of the existing System XI product and addresses many of the shortcomings. In most ways this product is technically the best general-purpose relational data management product available for Unix and NT platforms.

That's not to say that this comes without a cost. To obtain the best results with the product or the new architecture, the customers, developers and database administrators must carefully determine how to implement the available features to their best advantage. Other products are available that require less implementation effort, but lack the flexibility to easily customize to specific circumstances or performance requirements.

Summary

Anyone who has purchased a new car is aware of the fact that the hood should only be opened by a factory trained technician. There is nothing in there that the owner can adjust, set or fiddle with. Of course this has advantages and shouldn't be dismissed as entirely undesirable. However, what you get when you drive it off the lot is what you're stuck with. There are other individuals who are always looking for that last ounce of performance or reliability (like a hardcore hot rodder). If your disposition or requirements lean toward this, then the Sybase products and Adaptive Server Enterprise are the vehicles for you. With trained and experienced hands you can obtain performance and reliability that just cannot be duplicated with other products.

CHAPTER 3

Sybase Server Basic Overview

In this chapter we will look at how Adaptive Server relates to its environment, specifically the box on which it is running. This is a non-platform-specific discussion, focusing more on how SQL Server has been implemented across all platforms and introducing the basic structure for all versions of Sybase.

Many of the people I meet with these days have been using Sybase for some years. This chapter is meant more as a refresher of the basics than as an in-depth review. You should gain some insight into aspects of the server hithertofore (I have always wanted to use that word in a sentence!) unexplored. At the same time, it seems only fair to have a chapter which covers the overall architecture and SQL Server concepts at a glance for those who are relatively new to the technology.

The Big Picture

Sybase SQL Server was intended from the beginning to be an open, easy-to-integrate product. Where other vendors were selling database engines with proprietary toolsets, Sybase was selling an open set of libraries for anyone to write applications. The general topology in which Sybase operates looks something like this:

FIGURE 3.1. Sybase interpretation of client/server architecture.

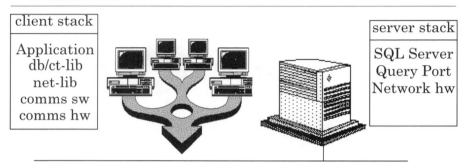

client stack
Application
db/ct-lib
net-lib
comms sw
comms hw

server stack
SQL Server
Query Port
Network hw

Client/server connectivity is managed between the two machines with stacks or layers. These are made up of products from many different vendors. On a workgroup server alone, for example, the hardware might be from Compaq, the operating system Windows NT from Microsoft, and the server software from Sybase. Additionally, there are client-side vendors such as Chameleon, FTP, and Novell who provide communications software that might have to coexist with the operating environment, the net libraries from Sybase and the application vendor.

To the user, the application connects to the database and requests and obtains data. However, for each transaction, the request comes from the user to the application; the DB-Library call is made which looks for network services to be brokered by Net-Lib which in turn passes the request to the communications software. CT-library is the System 10 and XI specific set of libraries from Sybase, which are discussed in much greater detail in their own chapter.

In terms of the overall process, though, SQL Server manages the user connection on the server side by picking up all packets addressed to a dedicated query port. In this way, the server platform forwards all SQL Server requests to the Dataserver, and processes regular network traffic as appropriate.

SQL Server is a multi-threaded application, meaning that it presents one process to the operating system and manages all user connections and jobs within that one process.

Typically, SQL Server manages its own RAM and disk resources as well, though this may differ somewhat from platform to platform. Unix for example provides raw disk to SQL Server, whereas workgroup releases for WinNT and Novell allocate files for SQL Server databases.

FIGURE 3.2. **The SQL Server's relationship to its environment.**

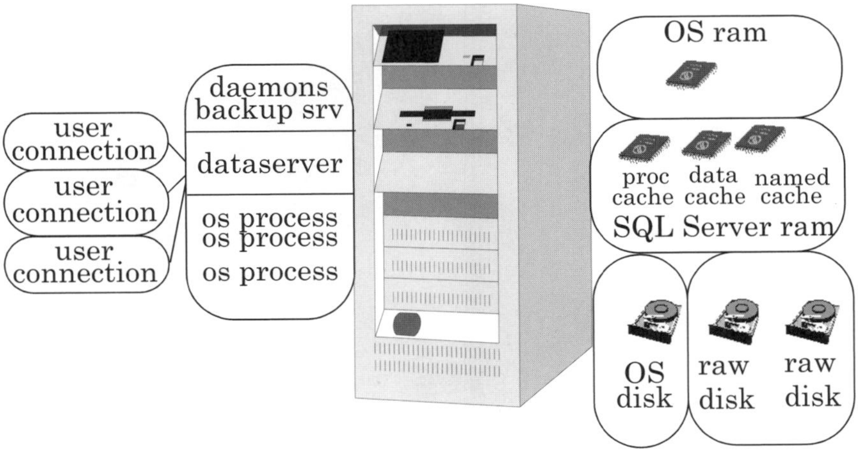

For each server, the overall architecture should resemble that shown in Figure 3.2.

Dataserver

The Dataserver process which makes up SQL Server manages user connections and parses requests for data. Each request is parsed first for syntactic accuracy, then it is optimized and finally compiled and executed. The relationship of these components is represented in Figure 3.3:

FIGURE 3.3. **The Dataserver kernel components**

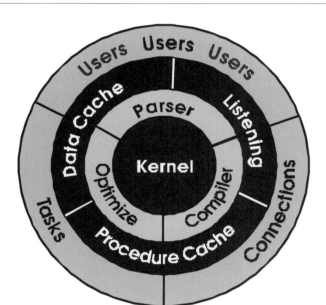

The parser rejects any requests for nonexistent objects, badly formed SQL statements and checks for access permission.

The optimizer determines which query plan should be used, including which indexes to use to minimize the amount of I/O necessary to satisfy the request.

The compiler takes the query and plan and turns it into machine code prior to executing it. Executed queries remain in cache while stored procedures have their own cache. This means that the time required to execute either a query or stored procedure for the second time is greatly reduced.

The parser only looks for errors in statements or permissions, while the optimizer is cost based. The cost is determined by the amount of disk access that must be performed in order to satisfy the query.

General rules of thumb for the optimizer include such things as an index will only be used if less than 25% of the table will be returned as the result set.

Caching of data and procedures can greatly affect query performance, as it is always faster to retrieve data from memory than from disk. As described in more detail in Chapter Four, the new release of Sybase gives developers and administrators much greater control over the use and configuration of cache.

Disk Devices

When looking at the SQL Server architecture, it is important to understand the role of logical devices.

SQL Server operations do not access hardware devices by their operating system names. Instead, the hardware must be declared to SQL Server in the form of logical devices. These logical devices refer to underlying hardware devices. The logical device names are used by all database creat/alter statements, as well by dump/load operations. System 10 supports direct naming of files for dump and load; earlier versions did not.

The master device is an important concept, because all of the system's databases are created there when SQL Server is first installed. Systems procedures have their own device, sysprocsdev introduced with System 10. This is a handy improvement over previous versions in that stored procedures can now be added over time to become larger than the initial data device size. The master device may not be extended without a rebuild of the server and reload of the master database which, while not rocket science, is a reasonably tricky and dangerous activity.

The data devices installed by System XI are the master device and sysprocsdev. If you have the option you should install them as raw partitions and on disk slices which you do not anticipate to be either busy or accessed by any other systems administrators.

As soon as you have installed your SQL Server, you should immediately create at least one user disk device in order to have a place to create user databases.

The Systems databases

Four main systems databases are created as part of the default installation of System XI, these include master, model, tempdb, and sybsystemprocs (see Figure 3.4).

FIGURE 3.4. System XI default databases.

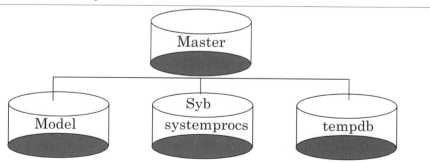

The Master Database

The term master database can be a bit confusing when first introduced, because it is installed on the master device. The master device holds the master database, tempdb, and model. Although tempdb may be extended onto different devices, the master database is not.

It is a very bad idea to create user databases on the master device because recovery of a master dataase is a much more complicated procedure than a regular database.

As mentioned, the master database holds all meta data about the server and its users. The systems administrator, sa, is the owner of the master database.

The Model Database

Since model is copied when a new database is created, any standard users, groups, database-specific stored procedures or datatypes are kept in model.

Only one user at a time can create a database, since model is in use while the database is created.

Tempdb is used extensively by applications such as the Smart Stream Financial Information System. There are several reasons for this. First, tempdb can be much larger than a user database, allowing developer's to build large tables made up of results from different databases. Second, every user has permission to create tables in tempdb. For purposes of extracting and manipulating data from tables where a user has select privileges only, tempdb can be used to hold results sets while they are being used.

Additionally, it is possible to extend tempdb onto faster disks, special devices or in cache, thereby increasing the performance of operations which incorporate tempdb.

User Databases

Sa must grant a user permission to create or alter databases. This protects the SQL Server environment from having a bunch of databases created without regard for placement or performance.

When a user does create a database, they become the database owner and have all permissions to create users and selectively grant or revoke permissions for operations within their database.

By default, a database is created on the default device (typically master). Normally, the database is created on a logical device and the log specified on another, separate device.

```
Create database mydatabase on c7t1d0s4_data=100 log
on log_dev= 10
```

(The size is specified in megabytes.)

Segments

Segments allow SQL Server database owners to move indexes, tables, logs, and large datatypes such as image or text onto discrete disks or disk areas.

Three segments are set up when a database is first created: system, logsegment, and default.

The logsegment contains the record of database transactions which affect the physical data, i.e., update, delete, insert. A log segment can only be used for logs, and it is always recommended that a specific log segment be created for any database on a separate disk from the data. The system segment holds all of the systems tables and information about the database.

The default segment is where all user database objects are created unless an additional segment is created and a table or index is told to use that segment explicitly.

Segments are highly useful for managing the allocation of space and for spreading data out across multiple disk devices, a process known as striping.

If you wish to ensure that no one can create a table which eats up all the available disk space, you would create a small segment and make it the default. That way, any table created without explicitly naming another (nondefault) segment can only be as large as the default segment.

Additionally, developers need not know that the database logs, indexes, and data are stored on separate devices. To create a table on a segment other than the default, the segment name must be specified in the create statement. For example,

```
create table Monster( Name char(20), Size char(10))
on Scary_Segment
```

This will create a table named Monster on whichever disks have been included in the definition of Scary_Segment.

Master Systems Tables

An integral part of a relational database management system is the feature which holds system information in tables exactly as user data is kept.

The master database of SQL Server has systems catalogs which are tables named as above. Sysservers, for example, holds the names of all servers that the local SQL Server needs to be aware of for access remotely.

- `syslogins` holds the names and passwords of anyone allowed to connect and use the SQL Server. sysconfigures holds the descriptors for the local SQL Server, including memory configured, number of databases, locks, and so on.
- `sysdevices` identifies the logical disk and dump devices which have been declared for access by the server.
- `sysusages` describes the allocation of the master database on the master device
- `sysdatabases` describes the names and options of any user databases which have been created, as well as the other systems databases.

User Databases

Within each user database, there are additional systems tables, specifically, tables which control access and objects within that database.

- `syssegments` holds the description of all default and additional segments defined for the database, where sysobjects lists all tables, views, procedures, etc., that have been created within that database
- `sysprotects` is the table that holds information about the permissions which have been granted or explicitly revoked from users for particular objects.

Logins, Users & Security

Since SQL Server manages its own user population, it has its own security routines. Being a user of a platform where SQL Server runs does not give you access to SQL Server, you must have a login. (The stored procedure sp_addlogin name, password is used to accomplish this.)

Additionally, each database has to set up the login in order for that user to be able to use that particular database. A login alone will not allow you to use a database and do anything useful.

Different levels of security or access are provided by each database owner. Security can be granted and revoked for select, update and delete for particular tables, and execute of specific stored procedures.

To make administration easier, users may be placed in groups and permission granted or revoked from the group. Remember, while they may be different than any other environment you've encountered before, Sybase administration procedures are the same from one SQL Server platform to another.

To illustrate graphically how permission and access is granted to specific database users, check out the diagram shown in Figure 3.5.

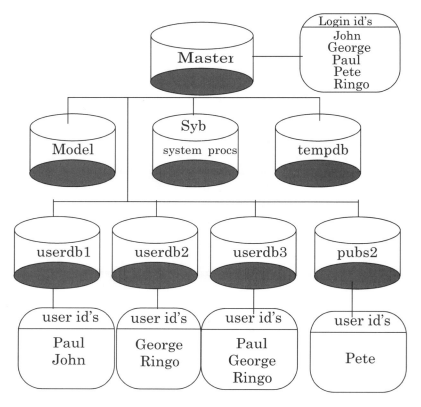

FIGURE 3.5. Relationship of Login and database user id's

The only database which Paul, George, and Ringo can access is Userdb 3. George and Ringo may use database 2 where John and Paul have access to database 1. George may have all rights in database 3 yet select only in database 2.

Each of them, John, Paul, George, Ringo, and Pete must have valid logins in the master database in order to become users of any database. By default they become members of the group public but they can become members of any other single specific group through the sp_changegroup procedure.

Permissions are specified with the `grant all to public` style syntax.

Summary

This chapter should have provided you with a solid refresher or in some cases a good introduction to the basics of the SQL Server structure. For many of you I suspect this was a bit of a sleeper, but I find it generally worthwhile not to assume too much. On the other hand, if you're like me you sometimes find it necessary to look up the systems tables layout because you want to do something to the data in those tables. For those of you with lots of Sybase experience, I'm hoping you will get a chance to refer to the systems table layouts provided in this chapter.

By covering the basic terminology and concepts in this chapter, this handbook should be of more relevance and value as a standalone source of information on Sybase.

The key points here cover the way Sybase has been architected to take over certain functions such as memory, disk and network management from the operating system on which it runs.

From this chapter forward we get into more depth on the specific features and functions of System XI.

CHAPTER 4

System XI Overview

New & Improved...

Okay, I'll be the first to admit that all too often we hear that something is the latest & greatest, new & improved (as opposed to old & tired?). However, when it comes to System XI, I have to say that I think the new and improved label fits pretty well.

It is unfortunate that so much negative press has surrounded both the System 10 release and the fortunes of the company on the stock market. When it comes to the actual technology these things are red herrings...they distract us from addressing the real issues, specifically, the question of 'does this thing work and how well?'

In this chapter, I would like to take an open-minded approach to System XI. Yes, I expect that we should look at the historical problems of the Sybase engine, and also factor in real-world findings about the first few releases of System XI. The point remains that the product has been generally available now since 1997 and frankly I think it's about time the jury came in.

We Have a Verdict...

The bottom line? Sybase System XI is a successfully rearchitected product which works in production environments. It addresses the very real problems encountered with System 10. It keeps all the good features and functionality introduced with 10, *but* also brings performance back in line with the 4.9 version. In short, it works.

System XI Specific Features

You will be specifically interested in moving to System XI if any of the following major functional requirements fit your situation:

- More than four CPU engines on database server
- Very large database (VLDB) environment
- DSS or DataWarehouse requirements
- Busy but more or less stable physical data model
- Problems with existing System 10 environment
- Still using version 4.9
- Underutilized DBA expertise/time

In my opinion if any of the above criteria apply to you, then you should be seriously evaluating *when* not *if* you will be migrating to System XI. The last point is meant somewhat tongue in cheek, as I have not met many dba's in a production environment who weren't as busy as a rooster in the hen house. Whatever your utilization, System XI provides some very serious tools for configuring your specific server environment, and if you have the expertise around, this upgrade is a great way to put it to work.

The corollary to this is that if none of these things apply to your environment, I would suggest you move to a System XI test environment. That way you can determine if you are actually going to get much in the way of benefits from the upgrade.

For those interested in just keeping up, take heart, System XI is not the scariest of upgrades and it does contain lots of new stuff.

What's New?

The following specific areas were addressed in the System XI release:

- Better use of RAM through User-defined Caches
- Increased number of tunable server parameters
- Better feedback from the optimizer for query tuning
- New options for tuning queries
- Improved support for multiple CPU engines
- Introduction of housekeeper task
- Changes to transaction log management
- New systems procedures, tables, and commands

There are, of course, many subtle or minor changes to the release, though for our purposes it should be appropriate to just hit the highlights. If in our coverage of what's new in System XI you don't find something that is exciting or applicable to your environment, the detailed list of changes is unlikely to do it for you either.

It Works!

Perhaps the most exciting thing about System XI from our point of view is that in most cases it provides a pretty serious performance increase right out of the box. That's right, folks, the OBE (out-of-box experience) is relatively pleasant.

The relative part of this is a reminder that I like to make to all systems people from time to time. We're talking about a piece of information technology here, circa the last half of the twentieth century. That means that, like teenagers, even a well-behaved program is still going to pose its share of challenges and awkward moments. I suggest we keep our expectations in line with reality to avoid disappointment. Like the commute to work, it works best when you have it to yourself, most of the time the trip is uneventful and occassionally you end up fuming in traffic. As I've already indicated, by and large this is a functional and robust piece of code.

System Architecture Changes

The System XI engineering team made some interesting assumptions when they approached how this version of SQL Server was going to work. The resulting features include new systems processes. When you now do an sp_who on a quiescent SQL Server you see the results shown in Figure 4.1.

FIGURE 4.1. System XI processes

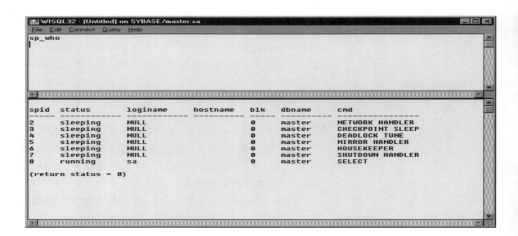

In this figure, you see the output from an sp_who on a System XI server with no other users. The network handler, and mirror handler, checkpoint sleep processes should be familiar from previous versions of Sybase. They manage the user connections at the query port, synchronizing data changes across mirrored disks and writing dirty pages to disk respectively. The select is, of course, the execution of the actual sp_who procedure.

More interesting is the deadlock tune, housekeeper, and shutdown handler. These are examples of System XI specific changes to the internal operation of SQL Server in ways you as a developer will encounter. (After all, who doesn't do an sp_who on at least a semi-regular basis?)

Shutdown Handler

The shutdown command has been enhanced in System XI to manage backup servers as well as the SQL Server. Shutdown with nowait issued by sa is still a pretty dramatic way to bring the system down, but the regular shutdown command now waits for the backup server to complete any dumps or loads prior to actually shutting down the SQL Server.

Deadlock Tuner

In previous versions of Sybase all transactions checked for deadlock contention as soon as a lock was requested. For applications which are unlikely to deadlock (batch operations, or single-user database situations for openers), this deadlock check adds to query overhead. In System XI you can now specify the deadlock checking to begin only after an application has waited 500 ms or more to be granted a lock.

This makes sense; why check for deadlocks if your application has been granted a lock immediately? In this new scenario, the overhead is taken up only in the event that the application is waiting for a lock to be granted. Usually, this will be a result of select or exclusive locks having already been granted to another application, however, in that case it makes sense for the application to check to see if a deadlock condition exists at that time.

Housekeeper Task

The housekeeper task is a System XI innovation that makes better use of idle CPU time. Specifically, in situations where SQL Server has no user tasks to execute, the housekeeper task takes advantage of the idle time to clean dirty pages out of cache and into disk. These are known as "free writes."

This is one way the SQL Server engineers have configured System XI for better performance in that the overall workload (user tasks, systems tasks) is leveled on an opportunity as well as scheduled basis.

In earlier releases of SQL Server you would specify the maximum amount of recovery time you wanted your server to endure on a restart. Once sufficient data changes were cached to meet or exceed that limit, SQL Server would begin the checkpoint process regardless of how much user activity was being requested.

With the introduction of the housekeeper process, SQL Server is now on the lookout for opportunities to "clean house" (hence the name I guess!) which resets the cache until more user activity generates changes to the data.

The overall effect of the housekeeper task is to take better advantage of available CPU cycles, decrease recovery time and level the duration of the checkpointing process.

Tunable Parameters

A number of features in SQL Server can be set in keeping with the requirements of your environment. These include:

- Data caches
- Memory pools
- Definable I/O sizes
- Isolation levels
- Lock escalation
- Selectable network engines

These features provide significant options to you as a developer or administrator in tailoring your environment to enhance slow, frequently performed queries.

Data Cache

As we will discuss in greater depth in the configuration chapter, one of the major new features of System XI is the data cache, named cache spaces and memory pool features. These features relate specifically to the behavior of data pulled into ram as a result of a query. In previous versions of Sybase cache was configurable only in terms of its overall size (memory allocated to SQL Server) and the split between procedure and data cache.

The new approach allows infinitely more control over the way your server handles specific situations. For example, you can now isolate an area of cache for specific databases or objects (see sp_cacheconfig in systems procedures for syntax). The concept here is that you can load frequently used lookup tables, or entire databases such as tempdb into ram. This means that the physical I/O occurs essentially only once on startup and from there on is read from ram. For VLDB environments this can provide dramatic improvements in query execution times!

Memory Pools

Within caches, memory pools are defined to allow reading and writing of larger block sizes. The default size for reading and writing data within SQL Server has been 2k, the size of a page. For table scans however, you can benefit from grabbing as much of the table as possible in the fewest possible bites. To do this you define a data cache with a memory pool defined as up to 16k.

Memory pools are defined and take effect dynamically, which means they can be managed for any given application load or time without having to restart the SQL Server.

Definable I/O Size for Transaction Logs

One of the other new systems procedures introduced with System XI is the sp_logiosize proc. For reasons similar to those surrounding memory pools, this procedure affects the size of the I/O blocks used by the transaction log.

LRU & MRU Buffer Replacement

You can now determine whether you want to have data pages from your query read in at the top or bottom of the buffer. Like the old FIFO (first in, first out) or LIFO (last in, first out), you can now select which pages in the buffer get discarded in favor of the data pages from your query.

The least recently used page is the top of the chain where the most recently used is the bottom. The idea is that you generally want to throw the oldest data out of cache but in some cases you will want your pages at the bottom of the chain. This is described in more detail in the query tuning and optimization chapter.

Lock Management and Escalation

One of the key areas of focus for enhancement of the System XI release was in the behavior of spinlocks. Spinlocks are generated by the SQL Server kernel which keeps new processes from accessing resources until released by whichever process got to the resource first.

In keeping with the use of Sybase in multi-processor environments, sp_configure can now be used to define the table lock spinlock ratio, page lock spinlock ratio, and address lock spinlock ratio parameters beyond the default of 20 rows for table locks and 100 for the other two.

This improves the usage that different processes make of multiple CPUs. Details can be found in the chapter on implementing and configuring your SQL Server.

As well as making improvements to the internal lock mangement process, you as a developer can now set when your query will attempt to acquire a table lock.

In previous versions of Sybase you either locked the entire table for the use of your query with the HoldLock option, or waited until 200 pages locks were acquired at which point SQL Server attempted to lock the table on its own. You can now set the number of page locks acquired by SQL Server before escalating to a table lock for any given table, database, or for the entire server instance.

Multiple Network Engines

For some SMP environments you can migrate client connections from engine 0 (the first CPU running SQL Server) to the least utilized engine. The net effect of this change is to allow more concurrent user connections as new engines are added to the server.

Query Monitoring & Optimization

Anyone who has been writing stored procedures or dynamic sql and submitting it to SQL Server can attest to the terse nature of showplan and statistics session options. With System XI, a number of new set options have been provided to help you tweak your queries for better performance.

Set Showplan Output

I could go on for a while about what the new set showplan output looks like, but you might prefer to have a look at it yourself (see Figure 4.2). I think you'll agree that it is of considerably more utility than previous versions.

FIGURE 4.2. Showplan output in System XI

```
QUERY PLAN FOR STATEMENT 1 (at line 1).
    STEP 1
        The type of query is SELECT.
        FROM TABLE
            authors
        Nested iteration.
        Index : aunmind
        Ascending scan.
        Positioning at index start.
        Index contains all needed columns.
        Base table will not be read.
        Using I/O Size 2 Kbytes.
        With LRU Buffer Replacement Strategy.
au_lname                                        au_fname
---------------------------------------------- ---------
-----------
Bennet                                          Abraham
Blotchet-Halls                                     Reginald
```

Showplan always told you what type of iteration was being used and which, if any, index was being accessed. With the updated version it now lets you as a developer see exactly how much memory is being used by your query; specifically, the I/O size and buffer replacement strategy described earlier in this chapter under the LRU and MRU buffer strategy comments.

As well as showplan improvements, a number of set commands have also been added, including forceplan, prefetch, stats subquerycache, and table count.

Forceplan makes the optimizer join the tables in the exact order specified in the query. The prefetch option sets the large I/O option to on for the session. The stats subquerycache tells you how the subquerycache was used were subqueries where part of the executed statement. The table count option specifies the number of tables to be optimized during one join query.

Other Enhancements in System XI

A number of relatively minor changes are introduced with this release. Of course, if your site is one affected by the changes, it may not seem small to you! However, compared to the scope of some of the other System XI features, they do not seem tremendously significant and are noted only briefly here.

Dumps and Backups

System 10 database and log dumps are upgradable to System XI. This means that after migrating your server to System XI, should you need to restore a database dump from the earlier version of Sybase, you can now do so. The dump files are upgraded on a database-by-database basis as needed with the exception of the master database.

Backup server senses tape device characteristics. It is no longer necessary to predefine a tape backup device for such characteristics as read, close, append, I/O size, and so on. Backup server checks the specified device to determine if it matches an internal list of devices; if not, the Backup server checks the backup_tape.cfg file for device configuration. Once found, the dump proceeds. This feature applies only to Unix-based servers.

Update in Place

For anyone updating tables with new information, the update-in-place model has been a bit of a holy grail – desirable, but difficult to get your hands on. In previous versions of Sybase it was difficult to get only the changed contents of a column written to a table. Instead, the update process was really one of delete and insert, which placed tremendous performance limitations on massive update operations.

Of course, it was possible to perform updates in place in earlier versions of SQL Server. However, given the restrictions on nulls, requirement that the row length not be changed, and so on, the changes made in System XI should prove a performance boon to anyone who does frequent update statements.

Identity Column Changes

The identity column introduced first with System 10 allows you to create a table containing system-generated values which uniquely identify each row. Some enhancements have been made to the way identity columns are handled by System XI including the ability to define the precision of identity columns, reserving a certain number of column values for a given operation and the ability to create a unique index by including the identity column in the index key.

Summary

System XI follows through on the rearchitecting of the Sybase database engine which began with System 10. However, at last you can now really scale SQL server and take full advantage of multiple CPU engines. Undeniably, this was a sore point with System 10.

The real advantage to System XI is one of performance as well as scalability. As mentioned earlier in this chapter, people have consistently found four to six times performance improvements over System 10 and performance which was just as fast as version 4.9.2.

Added to that are the new tunable parameters, which means you can tweak your server and queries to take maximum advantage of your database engine and server platform. For VLDB, and DataWarehouse environments this capability is vital since we all know that the user appetite for data is insatiable.

From reading this chapter you should have a good sense of exactly what has been introduced with System XI. You should also be able to use this description to determine which elements affect or interest you most. With that you should now be in a position to read on and research how best to make these changes work for you.

CHAPTER 5

Sybase Database Objects

In this chapter we look at the citizens living in the land of Sybase, particularly the database objects in user databases. All relational databases have tables, and Sybase is no exception. It used to be that stored procedures and triggers were esoteric, exotic, and obscure, now it seems that every rdbms on the market is saying "Me too! I've got procs, I can do triggers!"

Here we don't particularly want to get in to too much detail on the specific syntax for creating database objects. At least not yet. Instead, I'd like to take you on a tour of the Sybase database and introduce you to the specific forms of rdbms flora and fauna which exist here.

As you are no doubt familiar, the installation procedure of Sybase SQL Server allows you to install an optional pubs2 database. This is the database containing the database objects typically referenced in Sybase documentation and training materials. I'll be using pubs2 in this chapter just so you can use your own servers to verify that these objects actually do exist.

First Contact

In the introduction I mentioned that this was not an introductory book, and I promise that as we move further into the text, the examples will become more demanding and interesting.

To ensure this book stands on its own, however, I think it makes sense to do this one chapter from the ground up. If you've never been to SQL Server before, Billy, then stay aboard. On the other hand, if you're an old pro, you may want to skip ahead to the next chapter.

Meta Data

All relational databases have as an article of faith the construct that all systems data is maintained in tables, just as user data is kept. This means that SQL operations can be performed against the tables containing meta data which is data about data.

In the Sybase arena, the systems table containing data about database objects is called sysobjects (see Figure 5.1).

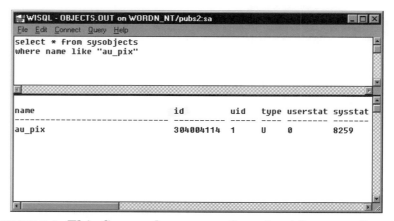

FIGURE 5.1. This figure shows sample output from a select against the sysobjects table.

Sysobjects contains the meta data on all objects maintained in a particular database. Each database has its own sysobjects table and you can use this systems table to get useful information about any given object.

However, to do this, you need to establish the object id number. This is the key value on which other useful systems tables are linked. We'll get into that a little later in this chapter.

One of the key concepts in this chapter is getting you used to the idea that it's okay for you to muck around a bit with the systems tables. Maybe you end up limiting yourself to cool selects. Fine. But as a developer there will be times when you need to go after down-and-dirty object descriptions and this is where we introduce how to go about just that.

Normally, of course, you would simply use the sybase supplied systems procedure to get info about objects or a list of objects. Namely, sp_help. Figure 5.2 shows the useful output sp_help supplies when invoked.

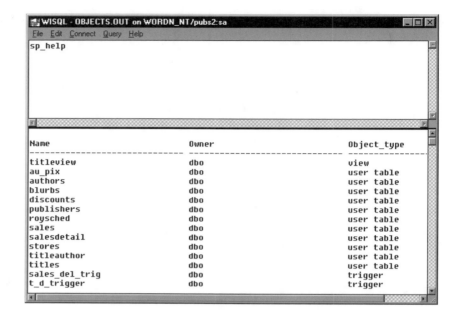

FIGURE 5.2. Output from the sp_help systems procedure.

Notice the handy object type description. Very nice. The author of the stored procedure went to the bother of formatting the output to include a text translation of the rather cryptic values contained in the type column of sysobjects. For example, if you really want to know how Sybase stores object level meta data, look at the sample query shown in 5.3.

FIGURE 5.3. The contents of the type column in sysobjects

Meta Data Object Naming Conventions

As you can see in figure 5.3, there are some pretty strange naming conventions. Like many systems which were originally developed in the Unix environment, some conventions are just tradition. Perhaps it's unfortunate, but that holds true for Sybase as you get down into some of the naming conventions behind the scenes.

The definitions of the types are:

- D = Default
- P = Procedure
- R = Rule
- S = Systems Table
- Tr = Trigger
- U = User Table
- V = View

Is it just me or does Tr seem really awkward? In the first place, it is upper and lowercase, and since the default install of Sybase SQL Server is case sensitive, it makes a difference. But more than that, S and U cover the tables, so they had to make it Tr so we wouldn't confuse a trigger with a table?

In any case, those are the values and will be for some time to come. Like any convention, like it or not you end up following it if you want to do selects on sysobjects.

Having listed the various objects, I would like to acquaint you with their role and characteristics.

What Is an Object?

This section gives you a quick overview of each of the objects within a Sybase database. I will give you a description of what it is used for as well as the inherent restrictions associated with the object. In addition, the syntax and options are supplied. With any luck at all, you'll come back to this section whenever you need to look up some pesky characteristic like, "How long can a stored procedure be?"

Keep in mind that in the Sybase world an object doesn't have properties and methods, isn't necessarily encapsulated, or possess any of the other aspects of the object-oriented world. To the database engine an object is simply a thing which exists within it. So if you were looking for the beginnings of an object oriented database – sorry, no dice. That being said, look for some interesting new extensions to Adaptive Server Anywhere 6.0, including Java in the database. That looks like the direction Sybase will take to include object-oriented extensions in its database – through inclusion of a Java Virtual Machine as part of the rdbms kernel.

Let's remember, the characteristics of the objects we do have are rather interesting in their own right. And when it comes to building client/server applications, many of them are highly useful.

As they say at the races, you can't tell the players without a race card, so in this section, let's introduce you to each of the database objects.

Default

This is the value automatically added to a column where an explicit value was not defined in the insert or update statement. This is used where most values in the table are the same, but differences must sometimes be accommodated. State of residence for a regional library may almost always be the home state, but you wouldn't hard code that into the application, right? There can be one default per column, defaults are not applied retroactively but may be applied only to future updates when created with the future only clause. Typical syntax to create a default looks like:

```
create default dflt_address as "MA"
```

Once you successfully run this syntax through isql (or whatever client application you use to issue sql to the server), you will find you have a new object in your database, specifically a default. Very nice. Until you bind it to a column, however, it's just going to sit there taking up space.

This is useful since you can essentially reuse the default for many columns in the database. To bind a default to a column you use the systems procedure sp_bindefault.

```
sp_bindefault dflt_address, "employees.table"
[future only]
```

The systems procedure then applies the default value MA to any row inserted or updated without an explicit state in the SQL statement. The future only clause is used when you wish the default to be applied only on newly inserted rows.

Rule

Rules are a column-level method of ensuring data compliance to a specified format or values. You may make a list of allowable values or you can exclude certain values. Rules are used to ensure that values like zip codes are correct or that a SQL statement attempting to insert incorrect values is rejected, even though it may be syntactically correct.

The syntax to create a rule is:

```
create rule zip rule as
@zip in ("AB", "AK", "AL", "CA", "GA", "LA")
```

In this case the only values that can be successfully inserted into the zip column have either five or nine numeric digits. To ensure the nine-digit zip code had a hyphen in the SQL statement you have to include it in the rule definition surrounded by quotes. That indicates to the server that to accept the nine-digit postal code the insert statement actually has to submit five digits, a hyphen and four digits. This can make life interesting for multi-developer applications if the folks working on the front end are not made aware of the exact requirements of the database. Most of the time you would use a rule to ensure either five or nine digits and let the application worry about format.

In some cases, however, format is integral to ensuring valid data. To accommodate Canadian postal codes, for example, the data must be stored as letter, number, letter, number, letter, number. To create a rule covering this you would add the following syntax:

```
create rule nafta_rule as
@zip = [A-Z][0-9][A-Z][0-9][A-Z][0-9]
```

Because there are only ten provinces (and two territories) the first letter designates a specific region. The syntax below demonstrates how you specify upper- and lowercase letters for some valid Canadian postal codes.

```
create rule wild_nafta_rule as
@zip=[N,n,V,v,L,l,M,m,][0-9][A-Z][0-9][A-Z][0-9]
```

You can combine and, or, not operands to create multiple formats and ranges for allowable values. This means that business rules can be incorporated into the back end to ensure data integrity by a number of methods.

Stored Procedures

The proc is the single most significant database object of the Sybase database engine. It lets you program the server and invoke precompiled SQL from a client application by name supplied with parameters as necessary. Systems procedures are stored procs supplied with the server when installed. As a Sybase developer, you are going to be working a lot with procs, unless you're involved in some N-tier project with a need to develop an application portable across multiple database vendors. Sybase stored procedures are not necessarily compatible with Microsoft SQL Server procedures nor are they necessarily compatible from one version of Sybase to another. Yikes!

Version 4.x of SQL Server had a restriction of 64k per stored procedure. This was changed with System 10 to 16 MB as the maximum size of a proc. As well, System 10 included support for some data definition language support within a stored procedure, such as create and drop objects, etc.

System XI didn't change any of the supported aspects of stored procedures over System 10. However in the early releases of XI (version 11.01 and earlier) customers complained of spontaneous procedure combustion and incredible procedure degradation, meaning that procs which worked fine in System 10 didn't work at all, or performed very poorly after a server upgrade to System XI. This was due to the compiler overhaul which was done in System XI to provide better performance.Unfortunately, I don't have a rule of thumb to help you identify likely culprits prior to the upgrade.

Creating Stored Procedures

The syntax to create a very basic stored procedure includes:

```
use pubs2
go
create proc sp_myproc as select name,type from
titles
go
```

To execute this stored procedure, at the isql command line you invoke the procedure by name.

```
sp_myproc
go
```

This provides a result set including all of the names and types for all books listed in the titles table.

Stored procedures have some interesting characteristics. For example, they inherit the permissions of their creator rather than their executor. This allows the right to execute procedures to be granted to a specific user which gives them access to database objects they otherwise might not have. This highly useful feature allows stored procedures to ensure data integrity and security and also makes complex operations relatively transparent to the proc user.

Triggers

Triggers are stored procedure-like sets of SQL syntax which are automatically invoked when delete, insert or update operations are performed on tables. Triggers are the traditional mechanism used within SQL Server to ensure data consistency when cascading deletes are performed. For example, if you want to remove a book from the pubs2 database, and here I mean eradicate any sign that it ever existed, you need to do more than issue the command:

```
delete from titles where book_id = "xyz".
```

In fact, as you look at the pubs2 database, you can see that book data is held in the titles, titleauthor, sales, salesdetail and roysched tables. If you just delete the titles row with the offending title_id, the corresponding rows in the other tables are orphaned. To ensure this can never happen, you use a delete trigger on the titles table. The syntax for this is:

```
create trigger title_del_trg
on titles for delete as
delete titleauthor,roysched,sales,salesdetail
from
titleauthor,roysched,sales,salesdetail,deleted
where titleauthor.title_id=deleted.title_id or
sales.title_id=deleted.title_id or
roysched.title_id=deleted.title_id or
salesdetail.title_id=deleted.title_id
```

But if you are unfamiliar with triggers, you may wonder where this deleted table came from all of a sudden. Within Sybase, whenever an operation which modifies table data is performed two special tables are created, specifically inserted and deleted. These are not actual tables but pointers in the transaction log, but they can be incorporated into trigger logic as if they really existed. When an update is performed, the old row image is stored in the deleted "table" and the new row image is held in inserted (see Figure 5.4).

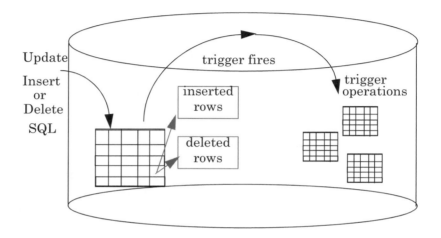

FIGURE 5.4. Trigger Behavior within Sybase

Trigger behavior within a transaction is reasonably complicated. A trigger firing is treated as a nested transaction, so including the rollback command rolls back the entire transaction, not just the operation which fired the trigger. This can make life interesting for developers. You will get more detail on trigger and transaction behavior later. Here I just wanted to provide a working definition and sample of a trigger along with a brief discussion of its characteristics.

Indexes

One of the most important database objects a developer uses when creating applications is indexes. Within Sybase there are two flavors of index, clustered and nonclustered.

The clustered index is the way the data is organized as it is physically stored on the hard disk, whereas a nonclustered index is literally a copy of data held (hopefully) on a different disk. It is only necessary to know about the location of the index when you create it, since it is frequently desirable to separate your indexes from the tables being indexed. This allows queries to separate index search activity onto a separate device from the table containing the rows to be retrieved into a result set.

The main value to using an index is to avoid table scans, a laborious process of reading each row in the table to determine whether or not it satisfies the search criteria specified in the where clause. Indexes allow your query to come up with a "short list" of locations where the desired rows reside and to pull them into a result set with a quick in and out.

Indexes are covered in greater detail in the chapter on performance later in the book. This is because as a developer, indexes give you the greatest single tool for increasing performance of your database applications.

The syntax for creating a nonclustered index follows:

```
create index title_id_ndx
on titles(title_id)
on index_segment_device
```

The unique, ignore_dup_key, ignore_dup_row, and allow_dup_row options allow you to create indexes which massage your data, or at least verify its relative integrity.

For example, if you create a clustered index with the ignore_dup_row option, the resulting indexed table will have cleaned up any duplicate data. To accomplish this, you could use the following syntax:

```
create unique clustered index title_id_ndx
on titles(title_id)
with ignore_dup_row
```

The resulting index will in actuality be a table with only unique rows sorted by title_id. This is a quick and handy way to clean up data you suspect has been updated more than once.

Views

Views are an integral construct in relational database systems. Logically, they are tables, but underneath that appearance, views are SQL syntax which treat a result set as a named table. Put another way, views are referred to in the same manner as tables, but the data is not stored in the view, it's stored in the table or tables referenced by the view.

This is very useful when you want to allow users to access only certain data held in one table. Sybase doesn't allow you to grant select on specific columns within a table, so to restrict access to, say, telephone numbers in the authors table, you would create a view. The syntax for accomplishing this follows:

```
create view private_author
as
select name,au_id
from authors
```

This can get much more complex when you add multiple tables and convoluted where clauses. Most end users really appreciate being able to get to the data they want by way of views rather than having to learn the data model themselves!

There is, of course, some performance overhead associated with using views. However, this is often more than offset in a rapidly changing environment by the ability to drop and recreate view definitions. This insulates users (and even developers) from changes in the data model.

Tables

The most important element of any relational database is the tables held within it. Here I will define the characteristics of Sybase tables, a brief description of the datatypes which make up the tables as well as a few things you really need to know about them. Indexes and associated issues are covered in more detail in their own chapter later in the book.

Tables in Sybase may be constructed of not more than 250 columns, although the number of rows contained is limited only by disk space. More practically, the number of rows will be limited by query performance. The total number of bytes per table cannot exceed 1962, excluding text and image datatypes.

This means you could have 193 columns of 10 bytes each, 19 of 100 or any combination within the two restrictions. It is not necessary to define a primary key when creating a table, but you may choose to define a parent – child relationship explicitly within the create table syntax. To create a table you use the following syntax:

```
Create table my_table
(
```

```
column1 char(10),
column2 int,
column3 money null,
column4 datetime
)
```

For Sybase versions after System 10, explicit integrity constraints may be added to ensure data is not orphaned after a delete without using triggers. This works for a single parent/child relationship and does not allow for large "families" with multiple relationships. This situation is handled by triggers as explained in the example earlier in this chapter. The syntax for adding constraints within the table data definition language is as follows:

```
Create table my_table
constraint constraint_name
{{unique | primary key}
[clustered | nonclustered]
(
column1 char(10),
column2 int,
column3 money null,
column4 datetime
```

This ensures that the named constraint is applied whenever SQL which modifies data in the table is submitted. The elements of the create table statement include the table name, followed by the column name, datatype and whether or not nulls were allowed in the table. Not null is taken as the default, although this can be set for each database.

Datatypes

The contents of each column is governed by the datatype selected when the table is created. The datatypes available with Sybase are listed in table 5.1:

TABLE 1. Table Datatypes and their characteristics

Name	Size	Characteristics
char(n)	1 byte per character	Up to 255 characters, letters, numbers & symbols. Empty space padded with blanks.
varchar(n)	1 byte per character	Identical to char but empty space truncated.
nchar(n)	2+bytes each depends on language selected on install	multi-byte character set version of char(n) datatype. Empty space padded with blanks
nvarchar(n)	same as above	Empty space truncated
datetime	8 bytes: 4 bytes for number of days since January 1, 1900. 4 bytes for the time of day.	Covers January 1, 1753 to December 31, 9999. Accurate to 3.33 milliseconds.
smalldatetime	4 bytes: 2 bytes for number of days after January 1, 1900, 2 bytes for the number of minutes after midnight.	Covers from January 1, 1900 to June 6, 2079. Accurate to 1 minute.

TABLE 1. Table Datatypes and their characteristics

Name	Size	Characteristics
int	4 bytes	Cover whole numbers between 2,147,483,647 and -2,147,483,648
smallint	2 bytes	Between 32,767 and -32,768
tinyint	1 byte	0 to 255 inclusive
float(n)	8 bytes	Holds positive or negative decimal numbers with precision values above 15.
real	4 bytes	Holds positive or negative decimal numbers with precision values between 1 and 15
numeric(precision, scale) System 10 & 11 only	Based on Precision, 2 bytes for 1st value, 1 byte for each value after that.	Precision must fall between 1 and 38 digits. Default is 18.
decimal System 10 & 11 only	same as numeric	same as numeric
money	8 bytes	$922,337,203,685,477.5807 to -$922,337,203,685,477.5808. $symbol required on input to differentiate from float.
smallmoney	4 bytes	Same as money but covers between $214,748.3647 and -$214,748.3648

TABLE 1. Table Datatypes and their characteristics

Name	Size	Characteristics
bit	1 bit	0 or 1, nulls are not permitted
text	min 2k per row	Holds printable character data up to 2,147,483,647 bytes.
		Stores large text files, can point to separate physical storage location.
image	min 2k per row	Holds between 0 and 2,147,483,647 bytes of binary graphic data.
		Stores Binary Large Objects (BLOBS) up to 2 gigabytes per row.
binary(n)	1 to 255 bytes	Stores binary data, behaves like char with empty space padded with blanks.
varbinary(n)	1 to 255 bytes	Stores actual binary values, truncates unused space.
identity System 10 and 11 only	2 bytes minimum, increases with precision, like numeric	Numeric datatype with a scale of 0. System generated values used to uniquely identify table rows.
timestamp	8 bytes	System datatype with a varbinary(8) base. Used for concurrency control.

Smallmoney, smalldatetime, and real (a smaller version of float) were introduced with version 4.8. The multilingual character support for Kanji and other multibyte character sets came with version 4.9. System 10 introduced support for numeric, decimal, and identity datatypes.

Summary

From this chapter you should have gained a quick in-place reference for characteristics of the various database objects held in Sybase SQL Server. The intent was not so much to educate you about any given object, but to give you somewhere to go to look it up at a glance. At least, that's what we've always used this material for prior to this book!

As a developer, referencing object descriptions is especially useful when you are creating applications which use temporary tables. In a relational database app, small is better. Also, depending on which front end you use, such as PowerBuilder, you will no doubt find that an int is not an int and that in some cases it is necessary to go into the specific characteristics of a datatype to ensure your application can bind and manipulate the result set appropriately.

From an administrative standpoint, this information is valuable during capacity planning and data storage exercises.

As a seasoned developer, no doubt you already know the concepts contained in this chapter by heart. On the other hand, it's always nice to have just one place to look it up.

CHAPTER 6

Systems Procedures Reference

As you are no doubt aware, Sybase systems procedures are the means provided with SQL Server for data and server manipulation. With the introduction of System 10 and System XI, many new systems procedures have been introduced, complete with new capabilities and syntax. In some cases, old systems procedures, such as sp_password have been slightly modified in order to accommodate password encryption.

With this chapter, we want to give you a quick but comprehensive reference to any and all systems procedures you could encounter within your SQL Server environment.

Overview of Systems Procedures:

System procedures are located in the sybsystemprocs database (System 10 and System XI) or master database (version 4.x) and are owned by sa, but they can be executed from within any database. If a system procedure is executed in any other database, it operates on the system tables in the database from which it was executed.

Systems procedures can be executed by any user who has been granted execute permission on them. This permission MUST be granted in the sybsystemprocs/master database, so a user can either have permission to execute a system procedure in all databases, or in none of them. Users not listed in sybsystemprocs/ master...sysusers are treated as "guest" and are automatically granted permission on many of the system procedures. To deny a user permission on a system procedure, sa must add him to sysusers and revoke rights to that procedure. The owner of a user database cannot directly control permissions on the system procedures within his or her own database.

All systems procedures report a return status. For example,

```
"return status = 0"
```

means that the procedure executed successfully.

You can create your own system procedures that can be executed from any database. See Chapter Seven for specific examples and descriptions.

sp_addalias

Use to give a user of another database temporary access to the current database as a user setup in the current database (including the dbo). It can be used for granting access to a database without adding a user to that database.

Syntax

```
sp_addalias login_name, name_to_use
```

Sample

```
sp_addalias new_reader, reader
```

If you run an sp_who after an alias user has been added, it will display the person's true login name, such as new_reader, not the name to which they have been aliased. The addalias command simply sets the database access and permissions to the equivalent of the database user. new_reader can have all the permissions and access of the user reader in the database, but new_reader does not masquerade as reader. All activities are still traceable to the new_reader login ID.

sp_addauditrecord

System 10 and System XI only.

Use to allow users to enter user-defined audit records (comments) into the audit trail. Auditing must be enabled and the adhoc records option set to on.

Syntax

```
sp_addauditrecord [@text="message text"]

[,@db_name="db_name"] [,@obj_name="object_name"]

[,@owner_name="object_owner"]

[,@dbid=database_ID] [ ,@objid=object_ID]
```

Sample

```
sp_addauditrecord @text="I gave J. Brown permission
to view the author_royalty table in the pubs
database. This permission was in effect from 9:10
to 11:30 a.m. on 94/12/10.", @dbname="pubs",
@obj_name="author_royalty", @owner_name="dbo",
@dbid=10, @objid=1004733320
```

sp_addgroup

Use to add a group to a database. Groups are used as collective names in granting and revoking privileges.

Syntax

```
sp_addgroup grpname
```

Sample

```
sp_addgroup developers
```

Creates a group named developers.

sp_addlanguage

Use to define an alternate language for the server. It defines the names of the months and days for an alternate language and its date format.

Syntax

```
sp_addlanguage language, alias, months, shortmons,
days, datefmt, datefirst
```

Sample

```
sp_addlanguage french, null, "janvier, fevrier,
mars, avril, mai, juin, juillet, aout, septembre,
octobre, novembre, decembre", "jan, feb, mars, avr,
mai, jui, aout, sept, oct, nov, dec", "lundi,
mardi, mercredi, jeudi, vendredi, samedi,
dimanche", dmy, 1
```

This stored procedure adds French to the languages available on the server. null makes the alias the same as the official name, french. Date order is dmy (date/month/year). 1 specifies that lundi, the first item in the days list, is the first weekday.

sp_addlogin

Use to authorize a new user by adding a new user account to SQL Server.

Syntax

```
sp_addlogin login_name [, passwd [, defaultdb
[, deflanguage]]]
```

System 10 and System XI only.

```
sp_addlogin login_name, passwd [, defaultdb
[, deflanguage [, fullname]]]
```

Sample

```
sp_addlogin marie, bonbon, pubs, french
```

Creates a SQL Server login for marie. Her password is bonbon, her default database is pubs and her default language is French.

sp_addmessage

Not in version 4.2.

Use to add user-defined messages to sysusermessages for use by stored procedure print and raiserror calls and by sp_bindmsg.

Syntax

```
sp_addmessage message_num, message_text [,
language]
```

Sample

```
sp_addmessage 20001, "The table '%1!' is not owned
by the user '%2!'."
```

Adds a message with the number 20001. Since the language parameter is missing, SQLServer assumes that messages are in the default session language indicated by @@langid. Note that it does not overwrite an existing message of the same number and langid. Drop the message using sp_dropmessage first.

sp_addremotelogin

Use to authorize a new remote server user by adding an entry to master.dbo.sysremotelogins.

Syntax

```
sp_addremotelogin remoteserver [, login_name
[, remotename]]
```

Sample

```
sp_addremotelogin PRINCESS
```

This creates an entry for the remote server PRINCESS for purposes of login validation. This is a simple way to map remote names into local names when the local and remote servers have the same users.

```
sp_addremotelogin PRINCESS, john, jad
```

This causes a remote login from the remote user `jad` on the remote server PRINCESS to be mapped into the local user `john`. Note that the local name must currently exist as a user on the local server.

sp_addsegment

Use to define a segment on a database device in the current database.

Syntax

```
sp_addsegment segname, device_name
```

System 10 and System XI only.

```
sp_addsegment segname, dbname, device_name
```

Sample

```
sp_addsegment indexes, pubs2, dev1
```

This command creates a segment named `indexes` for the database `pubs2` on the database device named `dev1`.

sp_addserver

Use to define a remote server, or define the name of the local server.

Syntax

Version 4.x only:

```
sp_addserver server [, local]
```

System 10 and System XI only.

```
sp_addserver srvname [, {local | null} [,
network_name]]
```

Sample

```
sp_addserver PRINCESS, null, GRACE
```

Adds an entry for a remote server named PRINCESS. Null specifies that this server is a remote server and network_name is GRACE. If a network_name has not been specified, it will default to PRINCESS, the srvname.

sp_addthreshold

System 10 and System XI only.

Use to create a threshold to monitor space on a database segment. When free space on the segment falls below the specified level, SQL Server executes the associated stored procedure.

Syntax

```
sp_addthreshold database, segment, free_pages,
procedure
```

Sample

```
sp_addthreshold mydb, segment1, 200, pr_warning
```

Creates a threshold for segment1. When free space on segment1 drops below 200 pages, SQL Server executes the procedure pr_warning.

Note that databases do not automatically acquire a last-chance threshold when upgraded to Release 10.0. Use the `lct_admin` system function to create a last-chance threshold in an existing database.

sp_addtype

Use to add a user-defined datatype.

Syntax

```
sp_addtype typename, phystype[(length)]
[,nulltype]
```

System 10 and System XI only.

```
sp_addtype typename, phystype[(length) |
(precision [, scale])] [, "identity" | nulltype]
```

Sample

```
sp_addtype birthday, "datetime", null
```

Creates a user-defined datatype called `birthday` that is a datetime and allows null values.

sp_addumpdevice

Use to add a dump device to SQL Server.

Syntax

Version 4.x:

　　To add a tape device:

```
sp_addumpdevice "tape", device_name,physicalname,

cntrltype [, skip | noskip], size
```

To add a disk device:

```
sp_addumpdevice "disk", device_ name,
physicalname, cntrltype
```

Note: For Sun SCSI tape drives, use the disk device syntax.

System 10 and System XI only.

```
sp_addumpdevice {"tape" | "disk"}, device_name,
physicalname [, size]
```

Tape devices are assigned a cntrltype of 3; disk devices a cntrltype of 2.

Sample

```
sp_addumpdevice "tape", mytapedump, "/dev/nrmt8",
40
```

Adds a 40 MB tape device. Dump and load commands can reference the device by its physical name, /dev/nrmt8, or its logical name, mytapedump.

sp_adduser

Use to add a new user to the current database.

Syntax

```
sp_adduser login_name [, name_in_database
[,group_name]]
```

Sample

```
sp_adduser new_reader, Dave, readers
```

This procedure added the user with the login name of
new_reader to the current database (pubs) as user Dave and
made Dave a member of the group readers. To log on to the
SQL Server, the user must use the new_reader login name.
However, while within the pubs database, new_reader is not a
valid user. For all activities where you specify a user name within
pubs, new_reader becomes Dave and can be accessed only by
using that name.

Because it is easier to administer users when they are part of
groups, you need to know how to determine what groups are
already on a database when deciding where a new user should
belong.

sp_auditdatabase

System 10 and System XI only.

Use to establish auditing of different types of events within a
database, or of references to objects within that database from
another database.

Syntax

```
sp_auditdatabase [dbname [, "ok | fail | both |
off" [, {"d u g r t o"}]]]
```

ok – successful attempts, fail – failed attempts, both – all
attempts, off – turns off auditing.

d – drop, u – use, g – grant, r – revoke, t – truncate, o – outside
access.

Sample

```
sp_auditdatabase pubs2, "off", "gru"
```

Disables auditing of the grant and revoke commands within pubs2, and execution of the use command on pubs2.

sp_auditlogin

System 10 and System XI only.

Use to audit a SQL Server user's attempts to access tables and views on the server. Audits the text of a user's command batches; lists users on which auditing is enabled; gives the auditing status of a user; or displays the status of table, view or command text auditing.

Syntax

```
sp_auditlogin [loginname [, "table" | "view"
[, "ok" | "fail" | "both" | "off"]]]
```

ok – successful attempts, fail – failed attempts, both – all attempts, off – turns off auditing.

Separate commands must be issued to enable both table and view auditing for a single user.

Sample

```
sp_auditlogin
```

Returns the login names of users for whom auditing is enabled on the current server.

```
sp_auditlogin "joe", "table", "fail"
```

Audits Joe's attempts to access tables on which he lacks permission.

```
sp_auditlogin "joe", "cmdtext", "on"
```

Audits the text of commands executed by Joe.

sp_auditobject

System 10 and System XI only.

Use to audit accesses to tables and views.

Syntax

To audit existing tables and views:

```
sp_auditobject objname, dbname
[, {"ok" | "fail" | "both" | "off"}
[, "{d i s u}"]]
```

To audit newly created tables and views:

```
sp_auditobject {"default table" | "default view"},
dbname
 [, {"ok" | "fail" | "both" | "off"}
[, "{d i s u}"]]
```

ok – successful attempts, fail – failed attempts, both – all attempts, off – turns off auditing.

d – delete, i – insert, s – select, u – update

Sample

```
sp_auditobject publishers, pubs2
```

Displays the current auditing status of the publishers table in the pubs2 database.

```
sp_auditobject publishers, pubs2, "fail"
```

Audits failed attempts to access the publishers table in the pubs2 database.

```
sp_auditobject "default view", pubs2, "fail", "du"
```

Establishes auditing of failed delete and update attempts for all new views in the pubs2 database.

sp_auditoption

System 10 and System XI only.

Use to enables or disable system-wide auditing and global audit options, or report on the status of audit options.

Syntax

```
sp_auditoption {"all" | "enable auditing" |
"logouts"
| "server boots" | "adhoc records"}
[, {"on" | "off"}]

sp_auditoption {"logins" | "rpc connections" |
"roles"} [, {"ok" | "fail" | "both" | "off"}]

sp_auditoption "errors" [, {"nonfatal" | "fatal"
| "both"}]

sp_auditoption "{sa | sso | oper | navigator |
replication} commands"
[, {"ok" | "fail" | "both" | "off"}]
```

enable auditing – enables or disables system-wide auditing. A System Security Officer must set this option to on before any other auditing can take place.

all – enables or disables all options (except enable auditing) simultaneously.

logins – enables or disables login attempts by all users. To audit individual users, use sp_auditlogin.

logouts – enables or disables auditing of all logouts from the server, including unintentional logouts such as dropped connections.

server boots – enables or disables generation of an audit record when the server is rebooted.

rpc connections – generates an audit record whenever a user from another host connects to the local server to run a procedure via rpc.

roles – audits the user of the set role command.

sa | sso | oper etc. – audits the user of privileged commands.

errors – audits errors

adhoc records – allows users to send text to the audit trail. See sp_addauditrecord.

Sample

```
sp_auditoption "sa commands", "both"
```

Establishes auditing of all commands that require the SA role, whether or not the execution was successful.

sp_auditsproc

System 10 and System XI only.

Use to audit the execution of stored procedures and triggers.

Syntax

To establish auditing for existing stored procedures and triggers:

```
sp_auditsproc [sproc_name | "all", dbname
[, {"ok" | "fail" | "both" | "off"}]]
```

To establish auditing for future stored procedures and triggers:

```
sp_auditsproc "default", dbname
[, {"ok" | "fail" | "both" | "off"}]
```

ok – successful attempts, fail – failed attempts, both – all attempts, off – turns off auditing.

Sample

```
sp_auditsproc
```

Returns the names of all stored procedures and triggers being audited in the current database.

```
sp_auditsproc "all", pubs2, "fail"
```

Audits all executions of stored procedures and triggers on the pubs2 database that fail due to lack of permission.

sp_bindefault

Use to bind a default to a column or user-defined datatype. See Defaults.

Syntax

```
sp_bindefault default_name, object_name [,
futureonly]
```

Sample

```
sp_bindefault def_ssn, ssn
```

Assuming that a default named `def_ssn` and a user-defined datatype named `ssn` exist, this command binds `def_ssn` to `ssn`. The default is inherited by all columns that are assigned the user-defined datatype `ssn` when a table is created. Existing columns of type `ssn` also inherit the default `def_ssn` unless you specify `futureonly`, or unless the column's default has previously been changed.

sp_bindmsg

System 10 and System XI only.

Use to bind a user message to a referential integrity constraint or check constraint.

Syntax

```
sp_bindmsg constraint_name, message_num
```

Sample

```
sp_bindmsg positive_balance, 20100
```

Binds user message number 20100 to the `positive_balance` constraint. The message must exist in the `sysusermessages` table in the local database prior to calling. See `sp_addmessage`.

sp_bindrule

Use to bind a rule to a column or user-defined datatype.

Syntax

```
sp_bindrule rulename, object_name [, futureonly]
```

Sample

```
sp_bindrule today, "employees.startdate"
```

Assuming that a rule named `today` has been created in the current database with `create rule`, this command binds it to the `startdate` column of the `employees` table. When a row is added to `employees`, the data for the `startdate` column is checked against the rule `today`. See Rules.

sp_changedbowner

Use to change the owner of a database. *Note*: Do not change the owner of the sybsystemprocs database.

Syntax

```
sp_changedbowner login_name [, true]
```

Sample

```
sp_changedbowner reader
```

Makes `reader` the owner of the current database. To successfully execute the `sp_changedbowner` command, the user specified must have a valid login (created through the `sp_addlogin` command) but cannot already be a user in the database. Generally, the systems administrator would create a database and add a login, then execute the `sp_changedbowner` command to give the new user ownership of the new database and allow the user to use the database. You should note that the name of the database owner is not the name you set using the `sp_changedbowner` command. To grant permissions or use any other stored procedures dealing with users inside a database, the database owner will be known literally as `DBO` after you use the `sp_changedbowner` command. To give a user of another database temporary access to a database as a user currently set up in that database (including the DBO), you would run the `sp_addalias` procedure.

sp_changegroup

Use to change a user's group.

Syntax

```
sp_changegroup grpname, name_in_db
```

Sample

```
sp_changegroup admin, dianne
```

Makes `dianne` a member of the `admin` group. It doesn't matter what group `dianne` belonged to before, she is dropped from the group she previously belonged to and added to the one specified.

sp_checknames

Use to check the current database for names that contain characters not in the 7-bit ASCII set.

Syntax

```
sp_checknames
```

Sample

```
sp_checknames
```

Examines the names of all objects, columns, indexes, user names, group names, and other elements in the current database for characters outside of the 7-bit ASCII set. It reports illegal names and gives instructions to make them compatible with the 7-bit ASCII set.

sp_checkreswords

System 10 and System XI only.

Use to detect and display identifiers that are Transact-SQL reserved words. Checks server names, device names, database names, segment names, user-defined datatypes, object names, column names, user names, login names, and remote login names.

Syntax

```
sp_checkreswords [user_name]
```

Sample

```
sp_checkreswords
```

Reports on reserved words in the current database. The return status indicates the number of items found. Use before or immediately after upgrading to a new version of SQL Server.

sp_clearstats

Use to initiate a new accounting period for all server users or for a specified user. Prints statistics for the previous period by executing sp_reportstats.

Syntax

Not in version 4.2:

```
sp_clearstats [user_name]
```

Sample

```
sp_clearstats
```

Initiates a new accounting period for all users by updating the syslogins field accdate and clears the syslogins fields totcpu and toio. This should only be run at the end of a period since it creates an accounting period.

sp_commonkey

Use to define a common key – columns that are frequently joined – between two tables or views.

Syntax

```
sp_commonkey tabaname, tabbname, col1a, col1b
[, col2a, col2b, ..., col8a, col8b]
```

Sample

```
sp_commonkey projects, departments, empid, empid
```

Assume two tables, projects and departments, each with a column named empid. This statement defines a frequently used join on the two columns.

sp_configure

Use to display or change configuration variables.

Syntax

```
sp_configure [config_name [, config_value]]
```

Configuration Variables:

additional network memory, allow updates, database size, default language, default sortorder id, devices, fillfactor, language in cache, locks, memory, nested triggers, open databases, open objects, preread packets, procedure cache, recovery flags, recovery interval, remote access, remote connections, remote logins, remote sites, time slice, upgrade version, user connections

Version 4.x only: infect ticks, kernel language, media retention, serial number

System 10 and System XI only: audit queue size, cpu flush, default character set id, default network packet size, engine adjust interval, extent i/o buffers, i/o flush, identity burning set factor, maximum network packet size, max online engines, password expiration interval, stack size, tape retention

Sample

```
sp_configure
```

With no parameters, `sp_configure` displays all of the possible options with their current settings and range of permitted values. If you specify the `config_name`, the value of `config_name` appears.

sp_cursorinfo

System 10 and System XI only.

Use to report information about a specific cursor or all cursors that are active.

Syntax

```
sp_cursorinfo [{cursor_level | null}] [,
cursor_name]
```

cursor levels: N – any cursors declared inside stored procedures at a specific procedure nesting level. You can specify any positive number for its level.

0 – any cursors declared outside stored procedures.

-1 – any cursors from either of the above. You can substitute any negative number for this level.

Sample

```
sp_cursorinfo null, author_sales
```

Displays the information about any cursors named `author_sales` declared by a user across all levels.

sp_dboption

Use to display or change database options.

Syntax

```
sp_dboption [dbname, optname, {true | false}]
```

Options:

dbo use only, no chkpt on recovery, read only, select into/bulk-copy, single user, trunc log on chkpt

System 10 and System XI only: abort tran on log full, allow nulls by default, ddl in tran, no free space acctg, auto identity

Sample

```
sp_dboption mydb, "auto identity", true
```

Automatically defines 10-digit `identity` columns in new tables created in `mydb`.

sp_dbremap

System 10 and System XI only.

Use to force SQL Server to recognize changes made by ALTER DATABASE. Run this procedure only if instructed to do so by SQL Server messages. Only SA can execute this procedure.

Syntax

```
sp_dbremap database_name
```

Sample

```
sp_dbremap pubs
```

An `alter database` command changed the database pubs. This command makes the changes visible to SQL Server.

sp_defaultdb

Used to set a user's (or your own) default database on login to the SQL Server.

Syntax

```
sp_defaultdb user, default_database
```

Sample

```
sp_defaultdb reader, pubs
```

From this point forward, whenever `reader` logs onto this SQL Server, the database used will be pubs. This makes it unnecessary to issue the `use pubs` command prior to executing any T-SQL statement or stored procedure; it also ensures that `reader` will not accidentally create user objects on the master device.

sp_defaultlanguage

You can change default options for users, such as the language default they use when they log on to the SQL Server. You would accomplish this as SA with the sp_defaultlanguage procedure, or you can use the procedure to change your own default language:

Syntax

```
sp_defaultlanguage loginame [, language]
```

Sample

```
sp_defaultlanguage new_reader, french
```

Sets the default language for `new_reader` to French.

sp_depends

Use to display information about database object dependencies: the view(s), trigger(s), and procedure(s) that depend on a specified table or view, and the table(s) and view(s) that the specified view, trigger or procedure depends on.

Syntax

```
sp_depends objname
```

Sample

```
sp_depends "marie.authors"
```

Lists the database objects that depends on the `authors` table owned by the user `marie`. The quotes are needed, since "." is a special character.

sp_diskdefault

Use to set a database device's status to default on or off. This indicates whether or not a database device can be used for database storage if the user does not specify a database device or specifies default with the create database or alter database commands.

Syntax

```
sp_diskdefault logicalname {defaulton |
defaultoff}
```

Sample

```
sp_diskdefault master, defaultoff
```

The master device is no longer used by `create database` or `alter database` for default storage of a database.

sp_displaylogin

System 10 and System XI only.

Use to display information about a login account.

Syntax

```
sp_displaylogin [login_name]
```

Sample

```
sp_displaylogin
```

Displays information about your server login account such as your server user id, login name, full name, any roles that have been granted to you, date of last password change, and whether your account is locked.

sp_dropalias

Use to remove the alias user name identity established with sp_addalias.

Syntax

```
sp_dropalias login_name
```

Sample

```
sp_dropalias marie
```

Assuming `marie` was aliased to a user in the current database, this statement drops `marie` as an aliased user from the database.

sp_dropdevice

Use to drop a SQL Server database device or dump device. You must restart SQL Server after you drop a device because the kernel has a process that is accessing the dropped device, and there is no way to kill the process. Restarting with startserver or dataserver frees up the logical device number.

Syntax

```
sp_dropdevice device_name
```

Sample

```
sp_dropdevice tape9
```

Drops the device named `tape9` from SQL Server.

sp_dropgroup

Use to drop a group from a database. You cannot drop a group if it has members. You must execute `sp_changegroup` for each member before you can drop the group.

Syntax

```
sp_dropgroup grpname
```

Sample

```
sp_dropgroup sales
```

Executing this command drops the group named `sales` from the current database `sysusers` table.

sp_dropkey

Use to remove from the syskeys table a key that had been defined using sp_primarykey, sp_foreignkey or sp_commonkey. Note that dropping a primary key automatically drops any foreign keys associated with it. Dropping a foreign key has no effect on a primary key specified on that table.

Syntax

```
sp_dropkey keytype, tabaname [, tabbname]
```

Sample

```
sp_dropkey foreign, titleauthor, titles
```

Drops the foreign key between the tables `titleauthor` and `titles`.

sp_droplanguage

Use to drop an alternate language from the server and remove its row from master.dbo.syslanguages. You cannot drop a language with associated system messages without also dropping its messages.

Syntax

```
sp_droplanguage language [, dropmessages]
```

Sample

```
sp_droplanguage french
```

This command drops French from the set of available alternate languages if there are no associated messages. If there were associated messages, the dropmessages parameter must be used.

sp_droplogin

Use to drop an SQL Server user login by deleting the user's entry in master.dbo.syslogins. SQL Server reuses a dropped login's server user Ids, which compromises accountability. You may avoid dropping accounts at all and instead use sp_locklogin to lock any accounts that will no longer be used. This command will fail if the login to be dropped is a user in any database on the server. Use sp_dropuser to drop the user from a database.

Syntax

```
sp_droplogin login_name
```

Sample

```
sp_droplogin marie
```

Drops marie from SQL Server.

sp_dropmessage

Not in version 4.2.

Use to drop user-defined messages from sysusermessages.

Syntax

```
sp_dropmessage message_number [, language]
```

Sample

```
sp_dropmessage 20002, french
```

Removes the French version of the message with the number 20002 from sysusermessages.

sp_dropremotelogin

Use to drop a remote user login.

Syntax

```
sp_dropremotelogin remoteserver [, login_name
[, remotename]]
```

Sample

```
sp_dropremotelogin PRINCESS, john, jad
```

Drops the login for the remote user jad on the remote server PRINCESS that was mapped to the local user named john.

sp_dropsegment

Use to drop a segment from a database or unmap a segment from a particular database device.

Syntax

```
sp_dropsegment segname [, device_name]
```

System 10 and System XI only.

```
sp_dropsegment segname, dbname [, device_name]
```

Sample

```
sp_dropsegment indexes, pubs2
```

This command drops the segment indexes from the pubs2 database. If you also supply a device name, the segment is no longer mapped to the named database device, but the segment is not dropped.

sp_dropserver

Use to drop a server from the list of known servers. If you try to drop a server that has remote logins, the request will be rejected unless you supply the droplogins parameter.

Syntax

```
sp_dropserver server [, droplogins]
```

Sample

```
sp_dropserver PRINCESS
```

This command drops the remote server PRINCESS.

sp_dropthreshold

System 10 and System XI only.

Use to remove a free-space threshold from a segment. Note that you cannot drop the last-chance threshold from the log segment.

Syntax

```
sp_dropthreshold database, segment_name,
free_pages
```

Sample

```
sp_dropthreshold mydb, segment1, 200
```

Removes a threshold from segment1 of mydb. You must specify the database, segment, and amount of free space to identify the threshold.

Note: You can use the no free space acctng option of sp_dboption as an alternative to sp_dropthreshold. This option disables free-space accounting on non-log segments. You cannot disable free-space accounting on log segments.

sp_droptype

Use to drop a user-defined datatype. A user-defined datatype cannot be dropped if tables or other database objects reference it.

Syntax

```
sp_droptype typename
```

Sample

```
sp_droptype birthday
```

Drops the user-defined datatype named birthday.

sp_dropuser

Use to drop a user from the current database. You cannot drop users who own objects in the database, nor users who have granted permission to other users. If other users are aliased to the user being dropped, their aliases are also dropped and they will no longer have access to the database.

Syntax

```
sp_dropuser name_in_db
```

Sample

```
sp_dropuser marie
```

Drops the user `marie` from the current database; `marie` can no longer use the database.

sp_estspace

System 10 and System XI only.

Use to estimate the amount of space required for a table and its indexes, and the time needed to create the index. It can only be used on tables that already exist in the current database, but the tables need not contain data.

Syntax

```
sp_estspace table_name, no_of_rows [, fill_factor
[, cols_to_max [, textbin_len [, iosec]]]]
```

Sample

```
sp_estspace titles, 10000, 50, "title,notes", 0, 25
```

Calculates the space requirements for the `titles` table and its indexes, and the time required to create the indexes. The number of rows is 10,000, the fillfactor 50%, two variable-length columns are to be computed using the maximum size for the column, and the disk I/O speed is 25 I/Os per second.

sp_extendsegment

Use to extend the range of a segment to another database device, or to extend an existing segment on the current database device.

Syntax

```
sp_extendsegment segname, device_name
```

System 10 and System XI only.

```
sp_extendsegment segname, dbname, device_name
```

Sample

```
sp_extendsegment indexes, pubs2, dev2
```

This command extends the range of the segment `indexes` for the database `pubs2` on the database device `dev2`.

sp_foreignkey

Use to define a foreign key on a table or view in the current database. The number and order of columns that make up the foreign key must be the same as the number and order of columns that make up the primary key. The datatypes (and the lengths) of the primary and foreign keys must agree, but the nulltypes need not agree. To display a report on the keys that have been defined, execute `sp_helpkey`.

Syntax

```
sp_foreignkey tabname, pktabname, col1 [, col2,
col3, ..., col8]
```

Sample

```
sp_foreignkey titles, publishers, pub_id
```

The primary key of the publishers table is the pub_id column. The titles table also contains a pub_id column, which is the foreign key of publishers.

sp_getmessage

Not in version 4.2.

Use to retrieve stored message strings from sysmessages and sysusermessages for print and raiserror statements.

Syntax

```
sp_getmessage message_num @msg_var output [,
language]
```

Sample

```
sp_getmessage 20002, @myvar output
```

Retrieves the message with the number 20002 from sysuser-messages. Note that the variable @myvar must have a datatype of char, nchar, varchar or nvarchar. Because language was not included, the message is retrieved in the language from the @@langid variable.

sp_help

The general sp_help command is one method of getting a list of all the objects held in a particular database. Use to obtain a list of all objects, owner, and type for the current database, including user-defined datatypes.

Syntax

```
sp_help [object_name]
```

Sample

```
sp_help
```

This will output a complete listing of all the objects in the current database, including tables, indexes, views, stored procedures, rules, defaults, and user-defined datatypes complete with their underlying type, length, and null/not null acceptance status.

sp_helpconstraint

System 10 and System XI only.

Use to report information about any integrity constraints specified for a table. This information includes the constraint name and the definition of the default, unique/primary key constraint, referential constraint, or check constraint.

Syntax

```
sp_helpconstraint tabname [, detail]
```

Sample

```
sp_helpconstraint authors
```

Displays the constraint information for the table authors.

sp_helpdb

Use to report information about a particular database or about all databases.

Syntax

```
sp_helpdb [dbname]
```

Sample

```
sp_helpdb pubs2
```

Displays information about the pubs2 database.

sp_helpdevice

Use to report information about a particular device or about all SQL Server database devices and dump devices.

Syntax

```
sp_helpdevice [device_name]
```

Sample

```
sp_helpdevice diskdump
```

Reports information about the dump device diskdump.

sp_helpgroup

Use to find information on what groups are available on the database and who belongs to those groups.

Syntax

```
sp_helpgroup [group_name]
```

Sample

```
sp_helpgroup developers
```

Displays information about the group developers.

Note: To get a report on the default group, public, enclose the name "public" in single or double quotes ("public" is a reserved word).

sp_helpindex

Use to report information about the indexes created on a table, including indexes created by defining unique or primary key constraints.

Syntax

```
sp_helpindex tabname
```

Sample

```
sp_helpindex sysobjects
```

Displays the types of indexes on the sysobjects table.

sp_helpjoins

Use to list the columns in two tables or views that are likely join candidates. First, it checks for foreign keys, then for common keys. If it doesn't find any, the procedure looks for keys that may be reasonably joined by checking for keys with the same user-defined datatypes, and if that fails, it checks for columns with the same name and datatype.

Syntax

```
sp_helpjoins lefttab, righttab
```

Sample

```
sp_helpjoins titles, authors
```

Displays a list of columns that are likely join candidates in the tables `titles` and `authors`.

sp_helpkey

Use to report information about a primary, foreign or common key of a particular table or view, or about all keys in the current database. It does not provide information about the unique/primary key integrity constraints defined by a create table statement. Instead, use `sp_helpconstraint` to determine what constraints are defined for a table.

Syntax

```
sp_helpkey [objname]
```

Sample

```
sp_helpkey
```

Displays information on the keys defined in the current database.

sp_helplanguage

Use to report information about a particular alternate language or about all languages.

Syntax

```
sp_helplanguage [language]
```

Sample

```
sp_helplanguage french
```

This example displays information about the alternate language french.

sp_helplog

Use to report the name of the device that contains the first page of the log.

Syntax

```
sp_helplog
```

Sample

```
sp_helplog
```

Displays the name of the device that contains the first page of the log in the current database.

sp_helpremotelogin

Use to report information about a particular remote server's logins or about all remote servers' logins.

Syntax

```
sp_helpremotelogin [remoteserver [, remotename]]
```

Sample

```
sp_helpremotelogin PRINCESS
```

Displays information about all the remote users of the remote server PRINCESS.

sp_helprotect

Use to determine what permissions are set for a particular user or database object. This procedure also treats groups as users and, as such, gives you any permissions that have been defined for a group. Use the object name plus the user name to determine what a specific user's permissions are for a specific database object.

Syntax

Version 4.x only:

```
sp_helprotect name [, name_in_db]
```

System 10 and System XI only.

```
sp_helprotect [name [, name_in_db [, "grant"]]]
```

Sample

```
sp_helprotect
```

Reports on all permissions in the database. (System 10 and System XI only. Version 4.x requires an object or user to be provided as a parameter.)

sp_helpsegment

Use to report information on a particular segment or on all of the segments in the current database.

Syntax

```
sp_helpsegment [segname]
```

Sample

```
sp_helpsegment logsegment
```

Reports information about the segment on which the transaction log is stored.

sp_helpserver

Use to report information about a particular remote server or about all remote servers.

Syntax

```
sp_helpserver [server]
```

Sample

```
sp_helpserver PRINCESS
```

Displays information about the remote server PRINCESS.

sp_helpsort

Use to display SQL Server's default sort order and character set. Binary sort order is the default.

Syntax

```
sp_helpsort
```

Sample

```
sp_helpsort
```

Displays the name of the server's default sort order, its character set, and a table of its primary sort values.

sp_helptext

Use to print the text of a system procedure, trigger, view, default, rule, or integrity check constraint. It must be in the current database. It prints out the number of rows in syscomments that the object occupies followed by the create text of the object.

Syntax

```
sp_helptext objname
```

Sample

```
sp_helptext pub_idrule
```

Displays the text of `pub_idrule` when issued in the database containing it.

sp_helpthreshold

System 10 and System XI only.

Use to report the segment, free-space value, status, and stored procedure associated with all thresholds in the current database or all thresholds for a particular segment.

Syntax

```
sp_helpthreshold [segment_name]
```

Sample

```
sp_helpthreshold logsegment
```

Shows all thresholds on the log segment. The status column is 1 for the last-chance threshold and 0 for all other thresholds.

sp_helpuser

Use to obtain information on a specified user of the current database or all users if no name is supplied.

Syntax

```
sp_helpuser [username]
```

Sample

```
sp_helpuser
```

Displays information about all users in the current database, including their users_name, id_in_db, group_name, login_name, default_db, and login_name of users aliased to user.

sp_indsuspect

Not in version 4.2.

Use to check user tables for indexes that have been marked as suspect during recovery following a sort order change.

Syntax

```
sp_indsuspect [table_name]
```

Sample

```
sp_indsuspect
```

With no parameter, a list is created of all tables in the current database with indexes that need to be rebuilt as a result of a sort order change. dbcc reindex can be used to check the integrity of the listed indexes and to rebuild them if necessary.

sp_lock

Use to report information about processes that currently hold locks.

Syntax

```
sp_lock [spid1 [, spid2]]
```

Sample

```
sp_lock
```

Displays information on all locks currently held in SQL Server, including spid, locktype, table_id, page, dbname and class. Use the `object_name()` function to derive a table's name from its id number.

sp_locklogin

System 10 and System XI only.

Use to lock a SQL Server account so that the user cannot log in, or displays a list of all locked accounts.

Syntax

```
sp_locklogin [login_name, "{lock | unlock}"]
```

Sample

```
sp_locklogin marie, "lock"
```

Locks the login account for the user `marie`. If `marie` is currently logged in, she will receive a warning that her account has been locked, but is not locked out of the account until she logs out. If locking a SSO's or SA's login account, `sp_locklogin` verifies that at least one other unlocked SSO/SA account exists.

sp_logdevice

Use to put the system table syslogs, which contains the transaction log, on a separate database device. It affects only future allocations of space for syslogs. The preferred method of placing a transaction log on a separate device is with the log on option to create database, which immediately places the entire transaction log on a separate device.

Syntax

```
sp_logdevice dbname, device_name
```

Sample

```
sp_logdevice titles, logs
```

Puts the table `titles.syslogs` on the database device `logs`.

sp_modifylogin

System 10 and System XI only.

Use to modify the default database, default language, or full name for a SQL Server login account.

Syntax

```
sp_modifylogin login_name, {defdb | deflanguage |
fullname}, "value"
```

Sample

```
sp_modifylogin marie, fullname, "Marie Worden"
```

Changes user `marie` full name to `Marie Worden`.

sp_modifythreshold

System 10 and System XI only.

Use to modify a threshold by associating it with a different threshold procedure, level of free space, or segment. You cannot use sp_modifythreshold to change the amount of free space or the segment name for the last-chance threshold. SQL Server uses the global variable @@thresh_hysteresis to determine how sensitive thresholds are to variations in free space. Once a threshold executes its procedure, it is deactivated until the amount of free space in the segment rises to @@thresh_hysteresis pages above the threshold.

Syntax

```
sp_modifythreshold database, segment, free_pages
[, new_procedure] [, new_free_pages]
[, new_segment]
```

Sample

```
sp_modifythreshold mydb, data_seg, 250, new_proc
```

Modifies a threshold on the data_seg segment of mydb so that it executes the new_proc procedure.

sp_monitor

Use to display statistics about SQL Server.

Syntax

```
sp_monitor
```

Sample

```
sp_monitor
```

Reports information about how busy the SQL Server has been by displaying the current values of a series of global variables and how much they have changed since the last time the procedure executed.

sp_password

Use to add or change a password for a SQL Server login account. In System 10 and XI, new passwords must be at least 6 bytes long. New passwords cannot be null.

Syntax

```
sp_password old, new [, login_name]
```

Sample

```
sp_password target, "2hot4me"
```

Changes your password from `target` to `2hot4me`. ("2hot4me" is enclosed in quotes because it begins with a numeral.)

```
sp_password lemming, changeme, marie
```

An SSO whose password is `lemming` has changed `marie`'s password to `changeme`.

sp_placeobject

Use to put future space allocations for a table or index on a particular segment. You cannot change the location of future space allocations for system tables.

Syntax

```
sp_placeobject segname, objname
```

Sample

```
sp_placeobject indexes, 'employee.employee_nc'
```

This command places all subsequent space allocation for the index named employee_nc on table employee on the segment named indexes.

sp_primarykey

Use to define a primary key on a table or view.

Syntax

```
sp_primarykey tabname, col1 [col2, col3, ..., col8]
```

Sample

```
sp_primarykey authors, au_id
```

The primary key of the table authors is the au_id field.

sp_procxmode

System 10 and System XI only.

Use to display or change the transaction modes associated with stored procedures. When used with no parameters, it reports the transaction modes of every stored procedure in the current database.

Syntax

```
sp_procxmode [procedure_name [, transaction_mode]]
```

Sample

```
sp_procxmode byroyalty, "anymode"
```

Changes the transaction mode for the stored procedure `byroyalty` in the current database to `anymode` so it can be executed in either chained or unchained sessions.

sp_recompile

Causes each stored procedure and trigger that uses the named table to be recompiled the next time it runs. By recompiling the stored procedures and triggers that act on a table, you can optimize the queries for greatest efficiency.

Syntax

```
sp_recompile tabname
```

Sample

```
sp_recompile titles
```

Recompiles each trigger and stored procedure that uses the table `titles` the next time the trigger or stored procedure runs.

sp_remap

System 10 and System XI only.

Use to remap a Release 4.8 or later stored procedure, trigger, rule, default, or view to be compatible with Release 10. Use on objects that the Release 10 upgrade procedure failed to remap. Before running sp_remap on an object, it is a good idea to copy its definition into an operating system file with the `defncopy` utility.

Syntax

```
sp_remap object_name
```

Sample

```
sp_remap myproc
```

Remaps a stored procedure called `myproc`.

sp_remoteoption

Use to display or change remote login options.

Syntax

```
sp_remoteoption [remoteserver, login_name,
remote_name, opt_name, {true|false}]
```

Sample

```
sp_remoteoption PRINCESS, john, jad, trusted, true
```

Defines the remote login from the remote server `PRINCESS` to be trusted (that is, the password is not checked). To display a list of the remote login options, execute `sp_remotelogin` with no parameters.

sp_rename

Use to change the name of a user-created object in the current database. Procedures, triggers, and views that depend on an object whose name has been changed work until they are recompiled. When SQL Server recompiles the procedure, trigger or view, it no longer works if the object name has been changed.

Syntax

```
sp_rename objname, newname
```

Sample

```
sp_rename titles, books
```

Renames the `titles` table to `books`.

sp_renamedb

Use to change the name of a database. You cannot rename system databases. Procedures, triggers, and views that depend on an object whose name has been changed work until they are recompiled. When SQL Server recompiles the procedure, trigger or view, it no longer works if the database name has been changed.

Syntax

```
sp_renamedb dbname, newname
```

Sample

```
sp_renamedb accounting, financial
```

Renames the accounting database to financial.

sp_reportstats

Not in version 4.2.

Use to report statistics on system usage.

Syntax

```
sp_reportstats [user_name]
```

Sample

```
sp_reportstats
```

Prints out the current accounting totals for all logins, as well as each login's individual statistics and percentage of the overall statistics. Statistics for any process with an suid of 1 (sa, checkpoint, network, and mirror handlers) are not recorded.

sp_role

System 10 and System XI only.

Use to grant or revoke roles to an SQL Server login account. You cannot revoke the SSO or SA role from the last remaining SSO/SA account.

Syntax

```
sp_role "{grant | revoke}", {sa_role | sso_role |
oper_role}, login_name
```

Sample

```
sp_role "grant", sa_role, alexander
```

Grants the System Administrator role to the login account named `alexander`.

sp_serveroption

Use to display or change remote server options.

Syntax

```
sp_serveroption [server, optname, {true | false}]
```

Options: timeouts, net password encryption (between SQL Servers of Release 10.0 and later)

Sample

```
sp_serveroption PRINCESS, "timeouts", false
```

Tells the server not to time out inactive physical connections with the remote server `PRINCESS`.

sp_setlangalias

Use to assign or change the alias for an alternate language.

Syntax

```
sp_setlangalias language, alias
```

Sample

```
sp_setlangalias french, francais
```

This command assigns the alias name `francais` for the official language name `french`.

sp_spaceused

Use to display the number of rows, the number of data pages, and the space used by one table or by all tables in the current database. The number of data pages and the space used by an object is computed. The number of rows, reported as rowtotal, is an estimate based on using the `rowcnt` built-in function. Use `select count(*)` if you need exact row counts.

Syntax

```
sp_spaceused [table_name]
```

Sample

```
sp_spaceused titles
```

Reports on the amount of space allocated (reserved) for the `titles` table, the amount used for data, the amount used for index(es), and the available (unused) space. Note that there is a known problem in version 4.2. After you drop an index, sp_spaceused does not report accurate information.

sp_syntax

System 10 and System XI only.

Use to display the syntax of Transact-SQL statements, system procedures, utilities, and other routines (depending on which

products and corresponding sp_syntax scripts exist on your
server). You can provide any fragment or portion of a command or
routine name, including the use of wildcards, to list all commands
or procedures with that fragment in its name.

Syntax

```
sp_syntax {command | fragment } [, module_name]
[, language]
```

Sample

```
sp_syntax "disk"
```

Lists all the commands containing the word or word fragment
disk. Since disk is a Transact-SQL reserved word, it must be
enclosed in quotes.

sp_thresholdaction

System 10 and System XI only.

Executes automatically when the number of free pages on the log
segment falls below the last-chance threshold (unless the threshold has been associated with a different procedure). Sybase does
not provide this procedure, you must create it. When the last-
chance threshold is crossed, SQL Server searches for the
sp_thresholdaction. If it does not find it, it sends an error message
to the error log.

Syntax

```
sp_thresholdaction @dbname,
```

```
@segment_name,
```

```
@space_left,

@status
```

Sample

```
create procedure sp_thresholdaction

@dbname varchar(30),

@segment_name varchar(30),

@space_left (int),

@status int

as

dump transaction @dbname to tapedump1
```

Creates a threshold procedure for the last-chance threshold that dumps the transaction log to a tape device.

sp_unbinddefault

Use to unbind a created default from a column or from a user-defined datatype.

Syntax

```
sp_unbindefault objname [, futureonly]
```

Sample

```
sp_unbindefault ssn, futureonly
```

Unbinds defaults from the user-defined datatype `ssn`, but does not affect existing columns of type `ssn`.

sp_unbindmsg

System 10 and System XI only.

Use to unbind a user-defined message from a constraint.

Syntax

```
sp_unbindmsg constraint_name
```

Sample

```
sp_unbindmsg positive_balance
```

Unbinds a user-defined message from the constraint `positive_balance`.

sp_unbindrule

Use to unbind a rule from a column or from a user-defined datatype.

Syntax

```
sp_unbindrule objname [, futureonly]
```

Sample

```
sp_unbindrule def_ssn
```

Unbinds the rule from the user-defined datatype named `def_ssn` and all columns of that type.

sp_volchanged

System 10 and System XI only.

Use to notify the Backup Server that the operator performed the requested volume handling during a dump or load.

Syntax

```
sp_volchanged session_id, device_name [, action
[, filename [, volume_name]]]
```

Sample

The Backup Server sends a message that a mounted tape's expiration date has not been reached. The operator changes the tape, then issues this command:

```
sp_volchanged 8, "/dev/nrmt4", RETRY
```

sp_who

Use this command to see your login name, the database you are using, and the status of any command you have issued, as well as any other logged-on users.

Syntax

```
sp_who
```

Sample

```
sp_who
```

Sample display:

spid	status	loginame	hostname	blk	dbname	cmd
======	==========	============	==========	===	========================
1	runnable	sa		0	master	SELECT
2	sleeping	sa		0	master	NETWORK HANDLER
3	sleeping	sa		0	master	NETWORK HANDLER
4	sleeping	sa		0	master	MIRROR HANDLER
5	sleeping	sa		0	master	CHECKPOINT
6	runnable	reader	PC Client	0	master	EXECUTE

In the preceding listing, you can see that you are logged on to the master database with the username `reader` and that you are executing a stored procedure. The spid is the Sybase process ID and is needed to kill processes without shutting down the entire SQL Server.

Summary

The preceeding list of system procs, complete with sample entry and output should give you a higher comfort level when you are running the more obscure procs in your own environment.

CHAPTER 7

Transact-SQL Syntax Reference

Sybase offers its own extensions to SQL, which is called Transact SQL or T-SQL.

In this chapter, you are exposed to the nature of the SQL extensions and what they allow a developer to do with the language.

Since T-SQL is used for dynamic SQL batches, stored procedures, triggers and in DB-Library applications, this section forms the basis for submitting SQL calls to the SQL Server.

SQL is not the only query language for relational database management systems. Others were developed such as QUEL from Ingres but the Structured Query Language has become a *de facto* industry standard and as such it is no relational database could be successfully marketed without it.

Officially, SQL is endorsed and approved by ANSI; however, to be truly useful, each vendor has had to implement its own extensions. There are a few key points about the Sybase implementation of SQL that you should keep in mind.

- Pre-Release 10.0 versions of T-SQL are written to the ANSI '86 Standard.
- SQL Server Release 10.0 T-SQL supports ANSI '89 compatibility Mode. This mode supports the Federal Information Processing Standard (FIPS).
- FIPS flagger Generates Warnings for All Non-ANSI '89 Commands.

Since System 10 you have been able to review T-SQL syntax to determine where extensions have been used with the FIPS flagger. However, most commercial production uses of SQL Server make extensive use of T-SQL extensions. This feature is also supported in System XI and will be especially useful for anyone looking to migrate their existing 4.x applications.

ALTER DATABASE

```
ALTER DATABASE database_name
[ON {DEFAULT | database_device } [=size]
[, database_device [=size]]...]
```

System 10 and System XI only.

```
[LOG ON {DEFAULT | database_device } [=size]
[,database_device [=size]]...]
[WITH OVERRIDE]
```

End System 10 and 11 only.

Secure server only:

```
[SET DBMAXHOLD [=] "label1"]
```

Not in version 4.2:

```
[FOR LOAD]
```

ALTER TABLE

```
ALTER TABLE [database.[owner].]table_name
{ADD column_name datatype
{[, next_column]}...
```

System 10 and System XI only.

```
ALTER TABLE [database.[owner].]table_name
{ADD column_name datatype
[DEFAULT {constant_expression | USER | NULL}]
{[{IDENTITY | NULL}]
|   [[CONSTRAINT constraint_name]
{{UNIQUE | PRIMARY KEY}
[CLUSTERED | NONCLUSTERED]
[WITH FILLFACTOR = x] [ON segment_name]
| references [[database.]owner.]ref_table
[(ref_column)]
| CHECK (search_condition)}]} ...
{[, next_column]}...
| ADD {[CONSTRAINT constraint_name]
{UNIQUE | PRIMARY KEY}
[CLUSTERED | NONCLUSTERED]
(column_name [{, column_name} ...])
| FOREIGN KEY (column_name [{, column_name}...])
```

```
REFERENCES [[database.]owner.]ref_table
[(ref_column [{, ref_column}...])]
| CHECK (search_condition)}
| DROP CONSTRAINT constraint_name
| REPLACE column_name
DEFAULT {constant_expression | USER | NULL}}
```

Secure Server only:

```
|SET {MAXHOLD [=] "label1", MINHOLD [=] "label2"}
```

BEGIN

```
BEGIN
statement block
END
BEGIN {TRANSACTION | TRAN } [transaction_name]
```

System 10 and System XI only.

```
BEGIN {TRANSACTION | TRAN | WORK }
[transaction_name]
```

CHECKPOINT

```
CHECKPOINT
```

CLOSE

System 10 and System XI only.

```
CLOSE cursor_name
```

COMMIT

```
COMMIT {TRANSACTION | TRAN } [transaction_name]
```

System 10 and System XI only.

```
COMMIT {TRANSACTION | TRAN | WORK }
[transaction_name]
```

CREATE DATABASE

```
CREATE DATABASE database_name
[ON {DEFAULT | database_device} [=size]
[, database_device [=size]]...]
[LOG ON database_device [=size]
[, database_device [=size]]...]
[WITH {OVERRIDE,}]
```

Not in version 4.2.:

```
[FOR LOAD]
```

Secure Server only:

```
CREATE DATABASE database_name
[ON {DEFAULT | database_device} [=size]
[, database_device [=size]]...]
[LOG ON database_device [=size]
[, database_device [=size]]...]
[WITH {OVERRIDE, DBMAXHOLD [=] "label1'}]
```

Not in version 4.2.:

```
[FOR LOAD]
```

CREATE DEFAULT

```
CREATE DEFAULT [owner.]default_name
AS constant_expression
```

CREATE INDEX

```
CREATE[UNIQUE]
[CLUSTERED | NONCLUSTERED]
INDEX index_name
ON [[database.]owner.]table_name
(column_name [, column_name]...)
[WITH {FILLFACTOR = x,
IGNORE_DUP_KEY, SORTED_DATA,
[IGNORE_DUP_ROW | ALLOW_DUP_ROW]}]
[ON segment_name]
```

CREATE PROCEDURE

```
CREATE PROCEDURE [owner.]procedure_name[;number]
[[(]@parameter_name datatype
[=default][OUTPUT]] [,@parameter_name datatype
[=default][OUTPUT]]...[)]]
[WITH RECOMPILE]
AS SQL_statements
```

System 10 and System XI only.

```
CREATE PROCEDURE [owner.]procedure_name[;number]
[[(]@parameter_name datatype
[(length) | (precision[, scale])
[=default][OUTPUT]] [,@parameter_name datatype
[(length) | (precision[, scale])
[=default][OUTPUT]]]...[)]]
[WITH RECOMPILE]
AS SQL_statements
```

CREATE RULE

```
CREATE RULE [owner.]rule_name
AS condition_expression
```

CREATE SCHEMA AUTHORIZATION

System 10 and System XI only.

```
CREATE SCHEMA AUTHORIZATION authorization_name
create_object_statement
[ create_object_statement... ]
[ permission_statement ... ]
```

CREATE TABLE

Version 4.x only:

```
CREATE TABLE [[database.]owner.]table_name}
```

```
({column_name datatype [NOT NULL | NULL]
[, column_name datatype [NOT NULL | NULL]]...)
[ON segment_name]
```

System 10 and System XI only.

```
CREATE TABLE [database.[owner].]table_name
({column_name datatype
[DEFAULT {constant_expression | USER | NULL}]
{[{IDENTITY | NULL | NOT NULL}]
| [[CONSTRAINT constraint_name]
{{UNIQUE | PRIMARY KEY}
[CLUSTERED | NONCLUSTERED]
[WITH FILLFACTOR = x][ON segment_name]
| REFERENCES [[database.]owner.]ref_table
[(ref_column)]
| CHECK (search_condition)}]}...
| [CONSTRAINT constraint_name]
{{UNIQUE | PRIMARY KEY}
[CLUSTERED | NONCLUSTERED]
(column_name [{, column_name}...])
[WITH FILLFACTOR = x][ON segment_name]
| FOREIGN KEY (column_name [{, column_name}...])
REFERENCES [[database.]owner.]ref_table
[(ref_column [{, ref_column}...])]
| CHECK (search_condition)}}
[{, {next_column | next_constraint}}...])
```

```
[ON segment_name]
```

CREATE TRIGGER

```
CREATE TRIGGER [owner.]trigger_name
ON [owner.]table_name
FOR {INSERT, UPDATE, DELETE}
AS SQL_statements
```

Or, using the IF UPDATE clause:

```
CREATE TRIGGER [owner.]trigger_name
ON [owner.]table_name
FOR {INSERT, UPDATE, DELETE}
AS
[IF UPDATE (column_name)
[{AND | OR} UPDATE (column_name)]...
[SQL_statements]...]
```

CREATE VIEW

```
CREATE VIEW [owner.]view_name
[(column_name [, column_name)]...
AS SELECT [DISTINCT] select_statement
```

System 10 and System XI only.

```
[WITH CHECK OPTION]
```

DBCC

```
DBCC
```

```
{CHECKALLOC [(database_name)] |
CHECKCATALOG [(database_name)] |
CHECKDB [(database_name)] |
CHECKTABLE ({table_name | object_id}) |
DBREPAIR (database_name, DROPDB)
```

Not in version 4.2:

```
FIX_TEXT ({table_name | table_id})
INDEXALLOC ({table_name | table_id},
```

End Not in version 4.2.

```
index_id[,{FULL | OPTIMIZED | FAST}
[,{FIX | NOFIX} ]] )
MEMUSAGE
PAGE ({database_name | dbid}, pagenum) |
```

Not in version 4.2:

```
REINDEX ({table_name | table_id})
TABLEALLOC ({table_name | table_id}
```

End Not in version 4.2.

```
[,{FULL | OPTIMIZED | FAST} [,{FIX | NOFIX}]])
TRACEOFF (number)
TRACEON (number)
number = 3605 - output to errorlog
number = 3605 - output to terminal
```

DECLARE CURSOR

System 10 and System XI only.

```
DECLARE cursor_name CURSOR
FOR select_statement
[FOR {read only | update [of column_name_list]}]
```

DECLARE VARIABLE

```
DECLARE @ variable_name datatype
[, @ variable_name datatype]...
```

DELETE

```
DELETE [FROM]
[[database.]owner.]{table_name | view_name}
[WHERE search_condition]
```

OR

```
DELETE
[[database.]owner.]{table_name | view_name}
[FROM
[[database.]owner.]{table_name | view_name}
[, [[database.]owner.]{table_name |
view_name}]...]
[WHERE search_condition]
```

OR

```
DELETE [FROM] [[database.]owner.]{table_name |
view_name}
WHERE CURRENT OF cursor_name
```

DISK INIT

```
DISK INIT
NAME = "device_name",
PHYSNAME = "physical_name",
VDEVNO = virtual_device_number,
SIZE = number_of_blocks
[, VSTART = virtual_address,
CNTRLTYPE = controller_number]
```

Open VMS only:

```
DISK INIT
NAME = "device_name",
PHYSNAME = "physical_name",
VDEVNO = virtual_device_number,
SIZE = number_of_blocks
[, VSTART = virtual_address,
CNTRLTYPE = controller_number]
[,CONTIGUOUS]
```

DISK MIRROR

```
DISK MIRROR
```

```
NAME = "device_name",
MIRROR = "physical_name",
[, WRITES = {SERIAL | NOSERIAL}]
```

Open VMS only:

```
DISK MIRROR
NAME = "device_name",
MIRROR = "physical_name",
[, WRITES = {SERIAL | NOSERIAL}]
[,CONTIGUOUS]
```

DISK REINIT

```
DISK REINIT
NAME = "device_name",
PHYSNAME = "physical_name",
VDEVNO = virtual_device_number,
SIZE = number_of_blocks
[, VSTART = virtual_address,
CNTRLTYPE = controller_number]
```

DISK REMIRROR

```
DISK REMIRROR
NAME = "device_name"
```

DISK UNMIRROR

```
DISK UNMIRROR
NAME = "device_name"
```

```
[, SIDE = {"PRIMARY" | SECONDARY}]
[, MODE = {RETAIN | REMOVE}]
```

DROP DATABASE

```
DROP DATABASE database_name [, database_name]...
```

DROP DEFAULT

```
DROP DEFAULT [owner.]default_name
[,[owner.]default_name]...
```

DROP INDEX

```
DROP INDEX table_name.index_name
[,table_name.index_name]...
```

DROP PROCEDURE

```
DROP PROCEDURE [owner.]procedure_name
[,[owner.]procedure_name]...
```

DROP RULE

```
DROP RULE
[owner.]rule_name [, [owner.]rule_name]...
```

DROP TABLE

```
DROP TABLE [[database.]owner.]table_name
[, [[database.]owner.]table_name]...
```

DROP TRIGGER

```
DROP TRIGGER [owner.]trigger_name
[,[owner.]trigger_name]...
```

DROP VIEW

```
DROP VIEW [owner.]view_name
[,[owner.]view_name]...
```

DUMP DATABASE

Version 4.x only:

```
DUMP DATABASE database_name
TO dump_device
```

System 10 and System XI only.

```
DUMP DATABASE database_name
TO stripe_device [AT backup_server]
[DENSITY = density_value,
BLOCKSIZE = number_bytes,
CAPACITY = number_kilobytes,
DUMP VOLUME = volume_name]
[STRIPE ON stripe_device [AT backup_server]
[DENSITY = density_value,
BLOCKSIZE = number_bytes,
CAPACITY = number_kilobytes,
DUMP VOLUME = volume_name]
[STRIPE ON stripe_device [AT backup_server]
```

```
[DENSITY = density_value,

BLOCKSIZE = number_bytes,

CAPACITY = number_kilobytes,

DUMP VOLUME = volume_name]]...]

[WITH {

[DISMOUNT | NODISMOUNT],

[NOUNLOAD |UNLOAD],

[NODEALLOC | DEALLOC],

RETAINDAYS = number_days,

[NOINIT | INIT],

FILE = filename

[NOTIFY = {CLIENT | OPERATOR_CONSOLE}]}]
```

DUMP TRANSACTION

Version 4.x only:

```
DUMP TRAN[SACTION] database_name

[TO dump_device]

[WITH TRUNCATE_ONLY

|WITH NO_LOG

|WITH NO_TRUNCATE]
```

System 10 and System XI only.

```
DUMP TRAN[SACTION] database_name

TO stripe_device [AT backup_server]

[DENSITY = density_value,
```

```
BLOCKSIZE = number_bytes,

CAPACITY = number_kilobytes,

DUMP VOLUME = volume_name]

[STRIPE ON stripe_device [AT backup_server]

[DENSITY = density_value,

BLOCKSIZE = number_bytes,

CAPACITY = number_kilobytes,

DUMP VOLUME = volume_name]

[stripe_device [AT backup_server]

[DENSITY = density_value,

BLOCKSIZE = number_bytes,

CAPACITY = number_kilobytes,

DUMP VOLUME = volume_name]]...]

[WITH {

[DISMOUNT | NODISMOUNT],

[NOUNLOAD | UNLOAD],

RETAINDAYS = number_days,

[NOINIT | INIT],

FILE = filename,

NO_TRUNCATE,

[NOTIFY = {CLIENT | OPERATOR_CONSOLE}]}]
```

EXECUTE

```
[EXEC]UTE]]

[@ return_status = ]

[[[server.]database.]owner.]procedure_name
```

```
[;number]
[[@parameter_name =] value |
[@parameter_name =] @variable [OUTPUT]
[,[@parameter_name =] value |
[@parameter_name =] @ variable[OUTPUT]...]]
[WITH RECOMPILE]
```

FETCH

System 10 and System XI only.

```
FETCH cursor_name [INTO fetch_target_list]
```

GOTO

```
GOTO label
```

GRANT

Object Permissions:
```
GRANT {ALL | permission_list}
ON {table_name [(column_list)]
| view_name [(column_list)]
| stored_procedure_name}
TO {PUBLIC | name_list}
```

System 10 and System XI only.

```
GRANT {ALL [PRIVILEGES] | permission_list}
ON {table_name [(column_list)]
```

```
| view_name [(column_list)]

| stored_procedure_name}

TO {PUBLIC | name_list | role_name}

[WITH GRANT OPTION]
```

Command Permissions:

```
GRANT {ALL | command_list}

TO {PUBLIC | name_list}
```

System 10 and System XI only.

```
GRANT {ALL [PRIVILEGES] | command_list}

TO {PUBLIC | name_list | role_name}
```

IF

```
IF logical_expression

statement

[ELSE

statement]
```

System 10 and System XI only.

```
IF logical_expression

statement

[ELSE [IF logical_expression]

statement]
```

INSERT

```
INSERT [INTO]
```

```
[database.[owner.]]{table_name | view_name}
[(column_list)]
{VALUES (expression [, expression]...]
|select_statement}
```

KILL

```
KILL spid
```

LOAD

Version 4.x only:

```
LOAD DATABASE database_name
FROM dump_device
LOAD TRAN[SACTION] database_name
FROM dump_device
```

System 10 and System XI only.

```
LOAD DATABASE database_name
FROM stripe_device [AT backup_server]
[DENSITY = density_value,
BLOCKSIZE = number_bytes,
DUMPVOLUME = volume_name]
[STRIPE ON stripe_device [AT backup_server]
[DENSITY = density_value,
BLOCKSIZE = number_bytes,
DUMPVOLUME = volume_name]
[STRIPE ON stripe_device [AT backup_server]
```

```
[DENSITY = density_value,
BLOCKSIZE = number_bytes,
DUMPVOLUME = volume_name]...
[WITH {
[DISMOUNT | NODISMOUNT],
[NOUNLOAD | UNLOAD],
FILE = file_name,
LISTONLY [=FULL],
HEADERONLY,
NOTIFY = {CLIENT | OPERATOR_CONSOLE}}]
LOAD TRAN[SACTION] database_name
FROM stripe_device [AT backup_server]
[DENSITY = density_value,
BLOCKSIZE = number_bytes,
DUMPVOLUME = volume_name]
[STRIPE ON stripe_device [AT backup_server]
[DENSITY = density_value,
BLOCKSIZE = number_bytes,
DUMPVOLUME = volume_name]
[STRIPE ON stripe_device [AT backup_server]
[DENSITY = density_value,
BLOCKSIZE = number_bytes,
DUMPVOLUME = volume_name]...]
[WITH {
[DISMOUNT | NODISMOUNT],
[NOUNLOAD | UNLOAD],
```

```
FILE = file_name,
LISTONLY [=FULL],
HEADERONLY,
NOTIFY = {CLIENT | OPERATOR_CONSOLE}}]
```

OPEN

System 10 and System XI only.

```
OPEN cursor_name
```

PREPARE

```
PREPARE TRAN[SACTION]
```

PRINT

```
PRINT {@ local_variable | @@global_variable
| string_const | format_string [,arg_list]}
```

Version 4.2 only:

```
PRINT {@ local_variable | @@global_variable
| string_const}
```

RAISERROR

Version 4.2:

```
RAISERROR error_number {@local_variable |
@@global_variable | string_const}
```

Version 4.9:

```
RAISERROR error_number {@local_variable |
@@global_variable | string_const |
format_string [, arg_list]}
```

System 10 and 11:

```
RAISERROR error_number {@local_variable |
format_string [, arg_list]}
[extended_value = extended_value [{,
extended_value
= extended_value}...]]
```

READTEXT

```
READTEXT [[database.]owner.]table_name.column_name
text_pointer offset size [HOLDLOCK]
[USING {BYTES | CHARS | CHARACTERS]]
```

Version 4.2 only:

```
READTEXT [[database.]owner.]table_name.column_name
text_pointer offset size [HOLDLOCK]
```

RECONFIGURE

```
RECONFIGURE [WITH OVERRIDE]
```

RETURN

```
RETURN [integer_expression]
```

REVOKE

Object Permissions:

```
REVOKE {ALL | permission_list}
ON {table_name [(column_list)]
| view_name [(column_list)]
| stored_procedure_name}
FROM {PUBLIC | name_list}
```

System 10 and System XI only.

```
REVOKE [GRANT OPTION FOR] {ALL [PRIVILEGES]
| permission_list}
ON {table_name [(column_list)]
| view_name [(column_list)]
| stored_procedure_name}
FROM {PUBLIC | name_list | role_name}
[CASCADE]
```

Command Permissions:

```
REVOKE {ALL | command_list}
FROM {PUBLIC | name_list}
```

System 10 and System XI only.

```
REVOKE {ALL [PRIVILEGES]| command_list}
FROM {PUBLIC | name_list | role_name}
```

ROLLBACK

Version 4.x only:

```
ROLLBACK TRAN[SACTION]
[transaction_name | savepoint_name]
```

System 10 and System XI only.

```
ROLLBACK {TRANSACTION | TRAN | WORK
[transaction_name | savepoint_name]
ROLLBACK TRIGGER [WITH raiserror_statement]
```

SAVE TRANSACTION

```
SAVE TRAN[SACTION] savepoint_name
```

SELECT

```
SELECT [ALL | DISTINCT] select_list
[INTO [[database.]owner.]table_name]
[FROM [[database.]owner.]{table_name|view_name}
[HOLDLOCK]
[,[[database.]owner.]{table_name|view_name}
[HOLDLOCK]]...]
[WHERE search_condition]
[GROUP BY [ALL] aggregate_free_expression
[, aggregate_free_expression]...]
[HAVING search_condition]
[ORDER BY
{[[[database.]owner.]{table_name.|view_name.}]
```

```
column_name | select_list_number | expression}
[ASC | DESC]
[,{[[[database.]owner.]{table_name.|view_name.}]
column_name | select_list_number | expression}
[ASC | DESC]]...]
[COMPUTE row_aggregate(column_name)
[, row_aggregate(column_name)]...
[BY column_name [, column_name]...]]
[FOR BROWSE]
```

System 10 and System XI only.

```
SELECT [ALL | DISTINCT] select_list
[INTO [[database.]owner.]table_name]
[FROM [[database.]owner.]{table_name | view_name}
[HOLDLOCK |NOHOLDLOCK] [SHARED]
[,[[database.]owner.]{table_name | view_name}
[HOLDLOCK |NOHOLDLOCK] [SHARED]]...]
[WHERE search_condition]
[GROUP BY [ALL] aggregate_free_expression
[, aggregate_free expression]...]
[HAVING search_condition]
[ORDER BY
{[[[database.]owner.]{table_name.|view_name.}]
column_name | select_list_number | expression}
[ASC | DESC]
[,{[[[database.]owner.]{table_name.|view_name.}]
```

```
column_name | select_list_number | expression}
[ASC | DESC]]...]
[COMPUTE row_aggregate(column_name)
[, row_aggregate(column_name)]...
[BY column_name [, column_name]...]]
[FOR {READ ONLY | UPDATE [OF column_name_list]}]
[FOR BROWSE]
```

Variable Assignment:

```
SELECT @variable =
{expression | select_statement}
[, @ variable =
{expression | select_statement} ...]
[FROM table_list]
[WHERE search_condition]
[GROUP BY group_by_list]
[HAVING search_condition]
[ORDER BY order_by_lists]
[COMPUTE function_list[BY bylist]]
```

See also UNION, WHERE [NOT]

SET

Version 4.x only:

```
SET {ARITHABORT | ARITHIGNORE | FORCEPLAN
| NO COUNT | NOEXEC | PARSEONLY | PROCID
| SHOWPLAN} {ON | OFF}
```

```
| OFFSETS {SELECT, FROM, ORDER, COMPUTE,
TABLE, PROCEDURE, STATEMENT,
PARAM, EXECUTE} {ON | OFF}
| ROWCOUNT number
| STATISTICS {IO, TIME} {ON | OFF}
| TEXTSIZE number
```

System 10 and System XI only.

```
SET ANSINULL {ON | OFF}
{ARITHABORT [ARITH_OVERFLOW
|NUMERIC_TRUNCATION]
  ARITHIGNORE [ARITH_OVERFLOW]
   {CHAINED, CLOSE ON ENDTRAN, NOCOUNT,
  NOEXEC, PARSEONLY, PROCID,
SELF_RECURSION, SHOWPLAN} {ON | OFF}
  CHAR_CONVERT {OFF | ON [WITH {ERROR
| NO_ERROR}]
  | charset [WITH {ERROR | NO_ERROR}]}
  | CURREAD label1 (Secure Server only)
  | CURSOR ROWS number FOR cursor_name
  | CURWRITE label2 (Secure Server only)
  | {DATEFIRST number, DATEFORMAT format,
  LANGUAGE language}
  | FIPSFLAGGER {ON | OFF}
  | IDENTITY_INSERT [database.[owner.]]
table_name {ON | OFF}
```

```
     | OFFSETS {SELECT, FROM, ORDER, COMPUTE,
TABLE, PROCEDURE, STATEMENT,
PARAM, EXECUTE} {ON | OFF}
     | QUOTED_IDENTIFIER {ON | OFF}
     | ROLE
{"sa_role"|"sso_role"|"oper_role"}{ON|OFF}
     | ROWCOUNT number
     | STATISTICS {IO, TIME} {ON | OFF}
     | TEXTSIZE number
     | TRANSACTION ISOLATION LEVEL {1 | 3}
```

SETUSER

```
SETUSER ["user_name"]
```

SHUTDOWN

```
SHUTDOWN

[WITH NOWAIT]
```

System 10 and System XI only.

```
SHUTDOWN [backup_server]

[WITH {WAIT | NOWAIT}]
```

TRUNCATE TABLE

```
TRUNCATE TABLE [[database.]owner.]table_name
```

UNION

```
SELECT select_list [INTO clause]
```

```
[FROM clause] [WHERE clause]

[GROUP BY clause] [HAVING clause]

[UNION [ALL]

SELECT select_list

[FROM clause] [WHERE clause]

[GROUP BY clause] [HAVING clause]]...

[ORDER BY clause]

[COMPUTE clause]
```

UPDATE

```
UPDATE [[database.]owner.]{table_name | view_name}

SET [[[database.]owner.]{table_name. |
view_name.}]

column_name1 =

{expression1 | NULL | (select_statement)}

[, column_name2 =

{expression2 | NULL | (select_statement)}]...

[FROM [[database.]owner.{table_name | view_name}

[, [[database.]owner.]{table_name |
view_name}]...]

[WHERE search_condition]
```

System 10 and System XI only.

```
update [[database.]owner.]{table_name | view_name}

SET [[[database.]owner.]{table_name.|view_name.}]

column_name1 =

{expression1 | NULL | select_statement)}
```

```
[, column_name2 =
{expression2 | NULL | (select_statement)}]...
WHERE CURRENT OF cursor_name
```

UPDATE STATISTICS

```
UPDATE STATISTICS table_name [index_name]
```

USE

```
USE database_name
```

WAITFOR

```
WAITFOR { DELAY time | TIME time |
ERROREXIT | PROCESSEXIT | MIRROREXIT }
```

WHERE [NOT]

```
WHERE [NOT] expression
comparison_operator expression
WHERE [NOT] expression [NOT] LIKE "match_string"
WHERE [NOT] expression IS[NOT]NULL
WHERE [NOT]
expression [NOT] BETWEEN expression
AND expression
WHERE [NOT]
expression [NOT] IN ({value_list | subquery})
WHERE [NOT] EXISTS (subquery)
WHERE [NOT]
expression comparison_operator {ANY | ALL}
```

```
(subquery)

WHERE [NOT] column_name join_operator

column_name

WHERE [NOT] boolean_expression

WHERE [NOT] expression {AND | OR}

[NOT] expression
```

System 10 and System XI only.

```
WHERE [NOT] expression

comparison_operator expression

WHERE [NOT] expression [NOT] LIKE "match_string"

[ESCAPE "escape_character"]

WHERE [NOT] expression IS[NOT]NULL

WHERE [NOT]

expression [NOT] BETWEEN expression

AND expression

WHERE [NOT]

expression [NOT] IN ({value_list | subquery})

WHERE [NOT] EXISTS (subquery)

WHERE [NOT]

expression comparison_operator {ANY | ALL}

(subquery)

WHERE [NOT] column_name join_operator

column_name

WHERE [NOT] boolean_expression

WHERE [NOT] expression {AND | OR}

[NOT] expression
```

WHILE

```
WHILE logical_expression

statement

BREAK

statement

CONTINUE
```

WRITETEXT

```
WRITETEXT
[[database.]owner.]table_name.column_name

text_pointer [WITH LOG] data
```

Comments

To incorporate comments into a batch, for improved readability and decreased maintenance effort, you must precede the comment with the /* symbols and end the line with the */ symbols.

For example:

```
/*   Comments are within these symbols        */
/*   You must have them on every line to be    */
/*   commented.                                */
/*   There must be closing comment symbols for */
/*   every open set. */
```

Summary

As you will no doubt pick up from other chapters, I believe strongly that T-SQL is a SQL dialect with a great deal of utility for developers.

More important, T-SQL has been used to develop highly sophisticated application logic through stored procedures. While some argue that it doesn't have as many constructs as Oracle's PL/SQL, I would point out that it also doesn't come with the inherited baggage of embedded SQL. T-SQL was designed from the beginning to allow client/server database programming in the real world under heavy transaction loads.

The real trick is to use its inherent functionality to meet your application requirements. But the raw material is all there for you.

CHAPTER 8

Structuring Your SQL Server Environment

The Installation Checklist

So it's finally arrived. There it sits on the corner of your desk. Hand the shiny box to a colleague or friend. Have them open it and remove the distribution CD before handing you back the "box o' books." Now they are not to return the CD to you until you have read fully and completely the entire installation manual. This brings us to step one.

- Locate and read the installation manual for your platform.

When I say read the installation manual I mean more than crack the cover open. Read through the description of the entire process and determine the high level installation or upgrade process. Decide on the high level installation path. Is this an upgrade or a new install? Identify the other people need to be involved. In short, address as many issues as possible in advance.

- Locate and read the "Release Bulletins" for your hardware and operating system platform.

Sybase maintains a list of known bugs and their fixes and workarounds for each certified platform. The very latest information on what you should be aware of when installing this product on your platform are reflected in these notes. This often contains critical information on required operating system patches among other things. These notes are frequently printed matter shipped with the distribution CD or tapes.

- Create a "sybase" userid and valid user account on your server.

This id will become the system owner. In that capacity it will be the account that you will use to perform the installation or upgrade. In addition, this will become the account used for all system maintenance and operations tasks. You may need to enlist the help of your operating system administrator to set up the appropriate ids and security. If you intend to run SQL Server on multiple machines you should ensure that the id is consistently named on all the intended target machines. If these are Unix machines, for instance, the sybase id should have the same uid number on all of them. This will prevent problems down the road. Don't try and get fancy with the user id string, "sybase" will be fine. Do enforce password checking on this id, and it's a good idea to enforce a 90-day password expiration on this account as well. Any person who gains access to this account can cause significant problems. This id should only be used by a single user who performs all of the installation and maintenance tasks. If this is impractical, disable direct logins on the account and monitor the access using the operating system event logging if available.

- Locate your customer authorization string (CAS). This is usually located somewhere on the distribution media. Adaptive Server installations have it in a file on the CD. Tapes generally have the string printed on the tape case.

This a long ugly looking gobbledy-gook string of characters that you will need to input as part of the installation. Sybase uses this string to verify your licensing. Do yourself a favor and write this

number down in a second safe location. Do Sybase a favor and
don't post it on the Internet.

- Create the installation directory where the actual distribution
  files will live.

This is not typically the home directory of the "sybase" id. This is
a system product and it should be installed in a location consistent with the other installed system products. Once again you
may require the services of your operating system administrator
to establish this location and read, write and create privileges on
this directory to the "sybase" id. Be prepared, your system administrator will ask "How much space ya need?" The answer varies
according to the actual products installed and the platform. As a
general rule, you should set aside 200 to 300 MB for the total
installation. This is in addition to any data storage space you may
require. For Unix systems if possible this directory should be allocated a disk slice on its own. This will make increasing the space
allocation later much easier. Obviously, if this is brand new space
it needs to be formatted for regular files before it can be used.

- Set the SYBASE environment variable for the "sybase" id to
  point to the created installation directory.

This variable is extremely important to the installation and ongoing use of the SQL Server system. You should ensure that all
users are pointing to the proper base directory. For immediate
concerns the "sybsetup" routine required to perform the installation will not run if this is not set properly.

- If this is an upgrade to an existing installation then determine
  the directory path where the upgrade will live.

Never install an upgrade or EBF patch over the existing installation directory. It's considered bad form to overwrite a working
SQL Server executable with a potentially corrupt, damaged, or
otherwise bad program. You should attempt to agree on a logical

naming structure for your directories. This will help in the future administration of the product.

- Perform a backup of the entire system before starting any of the actual installation tasks.

Back up early. Back up often. These are the watchwords of the efficient administrator. You can never have too many backups. You can, however, have too few backups. You will be making changes to things that can affect your operating system behavior. Occasionally sunspots or some other random effect (never the operator) can cause very strange things to happen. Practice safe computing. Make a backup before you head to the trapeze.

- If this is an upgrade ensure the previous release is up and running currently.

The upgrade process will not work properly if the previous release is not operational when the upgrade runs.

- Determine the exact products to be loaded from your distribution CD.

Your distribution CD certainly contains more than just the SQL Server executables. It can contain any and all of the SQL Server family of products including the Open Client, Open Server, SQL Server Monitor, Replication Server, or OMNIserver distributions. Determine exactly what products you intend to install. Certain combinations of products should be installed together to ensure compatibility. These should not be mixed between releases. You should verify these details in your installation manual.

- Confirm that your platform and operating system release will support the SQL Server version you are installing.

SQL Server version XI is supported on most mainstream Unix hardware including SUN, HP, IBM, DEC, SGI, and DataGeneral.

In these configurations you should verify the operating system release to ensure that it is current and compatible. If your O/S is backdated you will need to upgrade before the installation of SQL Server can proceed. System XI SQL Server is also supported on the Microsoft NT platform with both 3.51 and 4.0 versions. There are differences in the installation process and tools provided for the NT platform. The detailed installation package provided with the product should be carefully consulted before proceeding. New operating system releases in the primary platforms are routinely regression tested by Sybase for compatibility with current SQL Server releases. The results of this compatibility testing can be found on the Sybase web site at http://www.sybase.com. This information should be verified prior to performing an operating system upgrade on a system supporting SQL Server. The certification test reports are also available on Compuserve in the "GO SYBASE" forum libraries. If possible the web site should be consulted first. It contains more recent and accurate information as well as simply more resources.

- Install any required operating system patches.

Along with the certification notes or in the release notes provided for your platform, you may receive a list of required or recommended operating system patches that must be applied before installing SQL Server. Do not dismiss these as hints, guidelines, or vague rumors. These are all – every single one of them – required if your system is to remain stable. I recommend checking both the Sybase web site and your hardware manufacturers to determine the complete list of required patches. Be sure to hang onto these patches as well as the operating system distribution media in case you are called on to recover the entire environment or duplicate it another machine.

- Verify that your network configuration is working.

Even if this is the only machine on site and will serve as both the client and server, the network software must be properly configured and operational. It must also support the loopback interface. Generally speaking, any properly configured TCP/IP configuration will support this configuration. Other systems may also support IPX or named pipe connections. In all cases the network support must be operating before proceeding with the installation.

- If you are using a Unix system, then configure your DISPLAY variable to point to your workstation.

The installation utility for Unix will display and interact with information presented on the machine this value points to. If this is not set the utility will not start.

- For Unix systems, set the shared memory to at least the size of the memory to be required by SQL Server.

SQL Server allocates memory for its use from the operating system shared memory pool. If no shared memory is available your SQL Server installation is going to fizzle. The syntax for setting this variable varies from platform to platform so check your release notes carefully. Save yourself some headache and set this parameter to the highest value your platform supports from the beginning. This will save you having to remember to reset this with every SQL Server memory tweak. The SQL Server will only use what it needs and the operating system will always reserve enough for its requirements before assigning memory to the shared pool.

- Enable asynchronous I/O.

If your platform requires a special operating system parameter to enable asynchronous I/O then ensure that this is enabled. If you have any choice in the matter ensure that the maximum allowable values are configured. Although, not strictly required to run a SQL Server, this should be enabled to promote efficient and high performance operation. Once again the details are included in the platform specific release notes. At this point having modified these items your system should probably be rebooted to ensure that these settings have become effective.

- Ensure you have access to the device holding the distribution media.

If this is a local device then this activity may seem obvious, but if the device is remote or needs to be network mounted then this activity needs to be completed. Make sure you record the exact device name required.

- Allocate your database disk devices.

You will require a minimum of two distinct devices before your installation can proceed. These are required for the MASTER and SYSPROCSDEV devices. The MASTER device should be a minimum of 30 MB and the SYSPROCSDEV will require a minimum of 20 MB to get started. My personal advice would be to remember that hard disks are comparatively cheap. Fixing these allocations later can be a pain. I recommend using a minimum of 50 MB for both MASTER and SYSPROCSDEV. In some installations it can be difficult to get raw disk slices this small so have no fear if these get reasonably large. Worse things could happen. If you are planning to use the SQL Server auditing facility you will require an additional device to hold the SYBSECURITY database. The minimum size of the security device is 5 MB. The recommended minimum is 7 and even this is generally too small. The size required will vary depending on the number of users and the amount of audit information captured. These details are covered better in a latter chapter dedicated to security issues. For now you should understand that if the security database fills up, the SQL Server will stop working. Knowing this, most folks would choose to err on the side of making it too big rather than too small. For raw disks you will require the device name path to access the device. It is likely to appear in a format such as "/dev/rdsk/c0t0d0s4." If you are planning on using file system devices then you will need the directory name and path of the file that should be created. This will likely be in a format such as "/sybase/devices/production/datadev." For production Unix implementations, Sybase strongly recommends using raw file system devices and ignoring any use of the file system. Identify all disk names for the devices and the size that each should be.

- Determine the name of the SQL Server.

Each SQL Server has a name that must be unique within the hardware platform. For practical purposes the SQL Server name should be unique throughout your enterprise. If you do not already have a naming convention then make one up. Names should be chosen in a logical, consistent, and extensible manner. Naming your servers after U.S. presidents for instance probably wouldn't qualify.

- Determine the IP address of your server.

This will be used to locate and connect to the database server later.

- Determine the desired TCP port setting to be allocated to this SQL Server.

Record and allocate this value in your Unix system /etc/services file to ensure that no other service attempts to use this value. The combination of IP address and port is used by programs to connect to the server. In turn, the server will install a listener service on this port to respond to user requests. The port number reserved should be between 5000 and 65535.

- Determine the backup server configuration.

Once again the naming conventions come into play. The backup server will be loaded and started as part of the installation. This server also requires a unique name. If in doubt, leave it as the default name of "SYB_BACKUP." You will also need to determine the address and port number for this server. The port should be recorded in the /etc/services file on your Unix system. The backup server will also need to be setup with the appropriate localization information including the language and character set requirements. These should match the SQL Server settings so review the sections where these are determined before establishing the backup server configuration.

- Determine the name of the error log file.

SQL Server automatically logs all of its start-up information and error or status information to an operating system file that the administrator can review. Determine what name you will use for this file. The default is "errorlog," and that may be satisfactory if your hardware platform will only support one SQL Server instance. If you plan on using multiple SQL Servers on the same hardware then only one of them can use the default name and the rest must be more creative. You could save yourself some grief by determining a naming convention in advance. A popular solution is to add the server name to the end of the errorlog name. For example "errorlog_engineering."

- Determine language requirements.

The SQL Server can support international requirements including foreign language support. The required language support should be loaded as part of the installation. Of course, it can be added later, but why not deal with it early. Most locations should always install U.S. English support as the primary and default language and then the optional modules in addition. These include French, German, and Japanese.

- Determine the required character sets.

In addition to language support, the SQL server can support multiple character sets. These are typically associated with particular language requirements or other localization requirements. You should always install the ISO 8859-1 character set. This is required by many application programs particularly those that operate in 32-bit client environments. Save yourself some hair and install this character set as a minimum. You can add additional character sets as required for your installation. There is not a significant penalty for loading character sets or languages. These can also be loaded at any time as required.

- Determine the sort order.

SQL Server orders information in tables for indexing or queries based on the sort order specified for the server. Several different mechanisms are available. The most common one is the binary ordering associated with the ISO 8859 character set. There are also various case-sensitive or case-insensitive orderings available. This is set for the entire server so all data in the server will be affected by this setting. Some pre-packaged applications will require a specific sort order to be configured on the server and this will need to be respected. If possible, you should try to establish the sort order setting as a default common setting for all SQL Servers in your organization. You can encounter difficulties in migrating data between servers if they are using different sort orders. This is a configuration detail that should be checked when data are moved between servers.

- Sign on to your system as root or administrator.

This will allow you access to all the system devices and permission to load the SQL Server distribution from the media into the installation directory.

- Place the SQL Server distribution media in the installation device.

If you have a CD-ROM device, which is now Sybase's preferred method of distribution, then the CD device should be mounted as a file system. If you are using a tape drive ensure that the tape device is accessible. You can use the mt command to verify the drive operation. ensure that the user "sybase" has access to the device holding the media or to the file system that's been mounted.

- Sign into the system as user "sybase."

The rest of the installation should proceed as sybase. This ensures that all the files are created with the appropriate permissions and provides a separation of duties on your system between the operating system administration and the database administration.

- Unload the product files into your installation directory.

If your media is on CD-ROM then you will use the "sybload -D" command located in the file system where the CD drive was mounted. This is usually "/cdrom/sybload." If your media is on tape then you should unload your tape using the tar command. The tar command should be "tar xvf tape_device."

- Proceed to run the "sybsetup" utility to unload additional files or configure the SQL server.

This utility should be located in the installation directory. It can now be used to complete the installation. When invoked this utility will prompt the administrator for information that was collected as part of the planning exercise. When complete you should have your first SQL Server up and running. You can then remove the distribution media and save it in a safe location. The CD can be ejected using the "eject" or "umount" commands. The tape should be rewound and ejected using the "mt" command.

You might think at this point that everything is finished and that you can tuck your Thermos back into your lunch pail and go home. Not quite so fast. There are a few items that you may wish to do to polish off the fine details.

- Sign into the server using the ISQL utility.

This should have been provided as part of the overall installation process. It is normally located in a subdirectory of the installation directory labeled "bin." This should be added to your path if you intend to use SQL Server to any degree. In fact if you are a Unix user you should ensure that you define a shell variable SYBASE as pointing to your install directory and use that to extend your path.

```
setenv SYBASE /opt/product/system11
setenv PATH $SYBASE/bin;$PATH
```

Establishing a proper value for the SYBASE variable is important because it also ensures that you can access the "interfaces" file, which is used in all SQL Server client access requests. You can establish initial connectivity to the SQL Server using the following command.

```
Example
isql -Usa -Sservername
```

This attempts to establish a connection using "sa" system administrator account to your server. The command will prompt you requesting a password. We have not set a password yet so simply pressing the enter key should allow you access. This should place you in the command line entry mode with an "1>" prompt before your cursor.

- Establish a secure password for the sa account.

Having just signed on without a password our first priority is to establish a more secure environment. This includes setting the password with the sp_password stored procedure.

```
Example
sp_password null,"new_password"
```

Of course, your new password should be constructed in a manner that secures it as well as possible.

- Establish the server name.

At this point the server is running but may not know its own name. It needs an entry in the SYSSERVERS table referencing it as a local server. This is done using the sp_addserver procedure.

```
Example
sp_addserver servername, local
```

This ensures that the server is aware of its name and can respond to queries with the proper information.

- Dump the master database.

You've made some changes and you now have a functioning SQL Server. It would be a real shame if an accident were to happen and you had to start all over again. A more complete description of the SQL Server backup and recovery capabilities is given later in the book. This may be a good time to review that information, but you can expedite the process for this function using the following command within ISQL.

```
dump database master to "/filename/etc"
```

This will ensure that you have at least one complete master backup to use in restoring your system if required.

- Add any additional development or administration products.

If you are using Powerbuilder or many of the other front end development tools with your SQL Server you may need to install certain routines and data tables in order for these products to work properly. You may also be using management and administration products such as Platinum's Desktop DBA, or BMC products such as Patrol that require that specific set up procedures be followed for each SQL Server that will be managed. Review the installation guides for these products and ensure that all the required setup routines have been completed. This effort at the time the server is initially setup will prevent a lot of follow-up calls and issues that should have been addressed. Providing these services as part of the initial installation improves the professionalism of the process.

- Verify the ODBC connectivity.

If you are using ODBC services to connect to the SQL Server ensure that any required connectivity software is loaded. Sybase recommends using the Intersolv ODBC drivers for clients connecting to System XI Servers. The necessary procedures and tables should be added to the server as part of the initial installation. This ensures that not only is the SQL Server up and operating, but that a variety of clients can access and use the system as well.

Allocating physical resources

It seems that the system administrator's most important ongoing job is managing the available disk space. This involves insuring that adequate space is available for the intended application and data and insuring that the available disks are used in an efficient and effective manner. As a rule, I recommend that each System XI server have a single administrator responsible for all space allocations in that environment. This helps to ensure consistency and prevents problems from occurring when space is misallocated. Any of you who have seen the Word N Systems training video – *Who Killed SQL Server?* know the potentially dire circumstances of having your disk allocation pirated.

In Sybase System XI, like most database systems, making databases larger is easy. Making them smaller is much more difficult. Once a mistake in allocation is made, the problem can be awkward to correct. Knowing this it seems prudent to take all due steps to ensure that these activities are done properly the first time. A mistake can be made in seconds that can take days to correct. Consider the applicability of the old carpenter's saying: "Measure twice. Cut once."

The system administrator should also ensure that there is an adequate amount of unallocated space available to the server so that the inevitable requests for more do not catch the administrator short. This is usually at two levels. The first is within the SQL server insuring that the databases are not fully occupying all of the available Sybase devices. A rule of thumb is that application owners should be made aware of a potential problem when their allocated space drops below 15% of the total. This should be escalated to action when the available amount drops below 10%. These amounts should be adjusted depending on how quickly the application can use up any available space. These levels need to be established in such a manner that proactive efforts can occur to obtain more space. This can easily involve a protracted purchasing and delivery cycle that needs to be accounted for.

The overall operating system administrator needs to ensure that an adequate reserve capacity exists to provide the database system with additional resources on demand. Roughly the same threshold values of a 15% warning and a 10% action level are appropriate. In some cases acquiring new hardware resources including the decision and approval cycles can present a significant time period and the system administrator needs to stay ahead of these constraints when planning. The most effective organizations include these activities as part of the ongoing trending, capacity planning, and budgeting cycle. These activities and the overall space planning should be carefully coordinated with the system development workplans. This will enable the administrator to predict beyond what simple trend analysis might indicate.

Sybase generally recommends that all database devices be allocated to "raw" disk devices. In Unix parlance, this refers to disks that have not been formatted for file system use. In effect this means that once Sybase is allocated these devices the operating system has little or no interaction with them. Sybase maintains that using the disk resources in this direct manner ensures that they can maintain the integrity of the database system. Problems with system integrity can occur when the operating system transparently caches file activity in an attempt to improve performance. SQL server assumes that once a record is written to a device that the information is permanently recorded. It then erases its own capability to recreate that activity. If SQL Server is mistaken in this assumption because the operating system determined it was better to delay that activity for a more convenient time then there is the potential for a serious problem to develop. If the system is interrupted prior to the operating system physically completing the updates the SQL Server is unaware that any recovery is required. This will leave the entire system in an inconsistent state. It's best not to use filesystem devices at all if it can be avoided. If you must use file systems for SQL Server devices caching should be disabled particularly for write operations.

In pre-System XI servers Sybase had on some occasions recommended that the tempdb database be placed on operating system files rather than raw device. Under most conditions the additional operating system caching available in this configuration provided a significant performance improvement and did not compromise system integrity. This was true providing that sufficient operating system buffers were available to cover the tempdb activity. With the move to System XI it appears as if this advice is largely out of date. The most appropriate configuration is probably to allocate tempdb its own cache (see next section). This allows the entire System XI configuration to reside completely on raw disk partitions.

One of the side effects of using raw disk resources is that the operating system is no longer aware of what resources are allocated. It becomes possible for the same physical disk resource to be allocated to two different Sybase servers on the same physical machine. This, as you may have guessed, would be a bad thing. This would cause a serious system crash and force the administrator to perform a significant recovery. So you probably want to keep careful records of all the disk resources on the system and which space has been allocated to which applications. This documentation needs to be maintained in a strict fashion and updated as space is allocated. Many system administrators use spreadsheet applications to track this information. Most Unix systems are constrained in the number of separately addressed disk partitions that can be provided for each physical disk. The typical number of available chunks for each physical disk is seven. One of these sections is usually reserved for operating system use. If you are using raw partitions as recommended, then the first cylinder of each physical disk should be reserved in its own slice for operating system labeling. This usually means that you only have five available chunks to work with for each physical disk. As disk sizes have increased over the years this makes it difficult to allocate small disk chunks. Once upon a time hard disks were no larger than 2 GB. Dividing this up into 5 sections yields and average size of 400 MB. As disk sizes have increased to, let's say, 9 GB recently. This means that average has jumped to 1.8 GB. This can sometimes lead to wasted space if the administrator is being forced to allocate more space than is required to a device. The larger disk drives can also be slower. The use of more, smaller disks is typically better for database performance than fewer large disks. This provides more opportunity to spread out the physical device access to a larger number of devices and disk controllers. This can dramatically improve overall system throughput.

If your operating system requires that you allocate file system devices then this improves the flexibility in space allocations but it can extract a penalty in operating system overhead. You can still pay careful attention to the underlying physical hardware and optimize the device activity across multiple physical devices and disk controllers where possible.

Let's look at the SQL Server device creation command.

```
disk init
name = "device_name",
physname = "physicalname",
vdevno = virtual_device_number,
size = number_of_blocks
[, vstart = virtual_address,
cntrltype = controller_number]
[, contiguous] (OpenVMS only)
```

The "device name" parameter supplies the name that the SQL Server will use to access and describe this device. It has no real meaning beyond the confines of the SQL Server. The "physical-name" is the operating system name for the physical resource. If this is a file system device then this is the fully qualified path of the file name for this device. The SQL Server will create this file for you so it should not already exist. If this is a raw device in a Unix system then this will be the device file associated with that device. Each SQL Server device is assigned a unique number to identify it to the system. This is used by the SQL Server to determine the page addresses that are located on the device. This is assigned by the administrator as the device is created. The administrator should obtain an available device number by using the "sp_helpdevice" procedure to determine what numbers are already used and use the next available number. Devices can be dropped using the "sp_dropdevice" command. Unfortunately, the assigned vdevno for that device is not available for reuse until after the system has been restarted. After the vdevno is determined the administrator assigns a size for the device. The units

for this command are in 2k pages. If you know the number of MB
you wish to assign then the number of pages required can be
determined using the formula.

$$2k \text{ pages} = (\text{number of MB} * 512) \qquad \textbf{(EQ 1)}$$

The other command parameters should only be used in special
circumstances and should be avoided at other times. This
includes the "vstart," "cntrltype," and "contiguous" options.

```
Example:
```

To create a small 50 MB raw device called TESTDEV_DATA on a
Unix system.

```
DISK INIT
NAME = "TESTDEV_DATA",
PHYSNAME = "/dev/rdsk/c0t0d0s3",
VDEVNO = 5,
SIZE = 25600
```

To create a larger 100 MB file system device called
TESTDEV_LOG on an NT System.

```
DISK INIT
NAME = "TESTDEV_LOG",
PHYSNAME = "D:\SYSTEM11\DEVICES\TESTDEV1",
VDEVNO = 6,
SIZE = 51200
```

It is important to ensure that the SYBASE user id on the systems
where the devices are being created has appropriate read, write,

create, and modify permissions on the physical devices and directories being created. If this is not done correctly the commands will fail. For Unix systems the raw device files should be changed to have an ownership of SYBASE and all access except this id disabled.

I strongly recommend that administrators and organizations sit down and determine a device naming convention prior to embarking on their first SQL Server implementation. My personal preference is to use device names that imply or indicate the underlying device configuration. This allows the administrator to quickly determine the operating characteristics of the device from the name.

In creating databases, Sybase promotes the practice of separating the database data from the log. This helps ensure recoverability in the event of a disk failure and improves performance. In order to support and promote this most administrators create at least two data devices. One dedicated to storing data and the other devoted to logging.

Most administrators indicate the intended purpose of the device in the name, e.g., "DISK1_DATA" or "DISK2_LOG." These cues help the administrator more quickly and effectively assign device space. This can remove another frustration and potential cause of mistakes when emergencies occur.

Beyond creating the required data and log devices, the next step is to create application databases that use these devices. As a matter of principal and common sense you will require at least two separate devices for each database created. The user account attempting this action must have been granted the "create database" privilege and be a valid user in the MASTER database or they will not be successful in creating a new database. Assuming that all of these prerequisites are met, the user can then issue the "create database" command. The resulting database will assume the ownership of the id that originally created it. This can be changed later if required.

In practice the most common situation is for the System Administrator on the system to create all of the databases and maintain control over the space allocations to ensure efficient use. Only in rare circumstances is the administrator required to transfer database ownership to another user. In all SQL Server implementations the System Administrator account is always able to access the database as the virtual owner. This allows the administrator to correct mistakes and keep the system operating smoothly.

The database owner is considered a special user and is identified as the "dbo" or database owner when physically operating within the created database. This ownership role provides a high level of privilege to create, remove or manipulate any object within the database. This level of privilege should be carefully controlled to ensure the integrity of the system.

When the "create database" command is issued the SQL Server performs several operations.

- Verifies that the database name specified is unique.
- Ensures that the device names are valid.
- Obtains the next available unique database identification number.
- Assigns space for the database on the specified devices and updates the "sysusages" table.
- Adds a row to the "sysdatabases" table.
- Copies the MODEL database into the new space.
- Clears all the remaining pages in the databases and prepares them for use.

The MODEL database is used as a template for creating all new databases on the system. Every object and feature of MODEL is faithfully reproduced in the new database including users, permissions, system tables, user tables, views, procedures, options, defaults, and rules. Most installations have certain default settings and configurations that are common. Time can be saved by the administrator by establishing the standard features in the MODEL database. These will then be automatically propagated to each new database as they are created. As a minimum, most administrators make sure that the MODEL database is established with the appropriate default database options. If there is insufficient space on the target device for the MODEL template then the "create database" command will fail. If space exists for the MODEL template but not enough for the requested allocation a warning message will be displayed and as much space as possible is allocated for the database. This is a change from pre-System XI servers that would fail if the requested space was not available.

The syntax of the "create database" command is:

```
create database database_name
[on {default | database_device } [= size]
    [, database_device [= size ]]...]
[log on database_device [=  size]
    [, database_device [= size ]]...]
[with override]
[for load]
```

The specified database_name must be unique for each database on the system. This is the only required parameter. If no device information is provided then the database is created on the "default" device. This is typically the master device and it should never be used for regular user databases. If this is done you will inevitably create a problem for yourself.

In a similar fashion, if no log device is specified, the data and log for the database will be created on the same device. As already indicated, this is not considered good form. In short, always specify your database devices in your create statement. The "size" parameter is optional as well and will default to the value specified in the server configuration setting, typically 3 MB.

In practice, this value should always be specified. The database size is specified in MB. This is unlike other commands which specify sizes in 2k pages. This inconsistency is manifested in every Sybase SQL Server release. If this database is being created as part of a recovery operation then the "for load" option can be specified to skip the initialization of the database pages which will be overwritten during the recovery anyway. This can save a considerable amount of time if the database is of any reasonable size. The last option is the "with override" option which allows the administrator to explicitly set the data and log devices to the same value and should only be used in rare circumstances when no other space is available or workable.

Example

```
create database test1
on disk1_data = 5
log on disk2_log = 3

create database test2
on disk1_data = 3, disk3_data = 4
log on disk2_log = 3

create database test3
on disk1_data = 5
log on disk2_log = 2
for load
```

Experienced system administrators always keep the current database create statements in external scripts which they can execute as required to recreate the database. This becomes very important during recovery operations where the database must be recreated prior to loading the data. Once a database has been created for the first time it can be expanded using the "alter database" command. This is similar in syntax to the create database command.

```
alter database database_name
   [on {default |  database_device} [= size]
       [, database_device [=  size]]...]
   [log on  {default |  database_device} [=
size]
       [, database_device [=  size]]...]
   [with override]
   [for load]
```

The same parameters and guidelines that apply to the create database command also apply to the alter database command. Again, good administrators either update the create database scripts or add the alter database command to their recovery scripts.

One of the most common questions that new administrators ask is, "How big should the transaction log be?" As a starting point the guideline I recommend using is 10% to 15% of the data size. The transaction log needs to be large enough to allow the transactions to accumulate between the regular transaction log dumps or truncations. This will very depending on the number of concurrent users and the size of submitted transactions. Once the transaction log fills to capacity the SQL Server clients will experience various problems. Depending on the thresholds established the administrator should receive ample warning of impending log space problems. There are established procedures in place to estimate the data sizes required based on the table specifications. There is even an included SQL Server procedure "sp_estspace" available to assist administrators in predicting the required database size. The Sybase documentation provides excellent documentation on estimating the space for various objects. In all of these exercises you must be intimately familiar with your data model and application requirements to be successful.

Once the database is created the administrator can transfer ownership if required using the sp_changedbowner procedure. In practice this is only rarely used. A more common requirement is to establish proper database options for the intended use. This is accomplished using the sp_dboption stored procedure.

```
sp_dboption [dbname, optname, {true | false}]
```

This is issued by the database owner while within the MASTER database. This process is used to enable or disable certain database options. The available options are:

- `abort tran on log full` – The default behavior for transactions in progress when a database log becomes full is to suspend until sufficient log space becomes available. When this option is enabled transactions abort and roll back instead. If your transactions can potentially hold locks or work synchronously with a client workstation then it may be advantageous to have the transactions abort rather than be delayed an indefinite period.
- `allow nulls by default` – The default SQL Server behavior for columns in newly created tables is to disallow nulls. This is the exact opposite of the current ANSI SQL language standard. If your site is concerned with standards then this option should be enabled for all created databases. The ideal place to make this change is in the MODEL database.
- `auto identity` – When enabled the SQL Server will automatically and invisibly add an "identity" column to each table created. The precision of the generated identity value is determined by a server configuration variable but defaults to 10 digits. This column can be explicitly viewed in queries only by using the column name "SYB_IDENTITY_COL."
- `dbo use only` – When enabled only the database owner can perform operations in the target database.

- `ddl in tran` – The default SQL Server behavior is to disallow object modification statements when running within a defined transaction. These statements acquire locks on system tables which may not be released in a timely fashion if the transaction becomes suspended. When set to true certain DDL statements are allowed to be used in this manner, but should be used with caution. The SQL Server documentation includes a comprehensive listing of these commands.

- `identity in nonunique index` – When enabled the SQL Server ensures that all indexes created on tables are unique by including an "identity" column when they are created. The IDENTITY column must previously exist in order for this to be successful.

- `no chkpt on recovery` – This option is normally disabled, allowing the database to recover and checkpoint as part of the system start-up. This modifies an internal value associated with each database. If you are using primary and secondary databases with the same information and using the dump and load process to maintain synchronization then internal renumbering can cause problems so this option should be enabled. For all other circumstances this option should remain false.

- `no free space acctg` – Normally the SQL Server keeps internal track of the amount of data contained on each allocated database page. This tracking can cause some performance degradation particularly on system start-up. When this option is set to true this accounting for the data pages is disabled, potentially improving performance. The drawback is that some commands such as sp_spaceused can report inaccurate results when this is set. For most installations this option should remain disabled.

- `read only` – When this is enabled users can retrieve and query the database data, but may not manipulate it.

- `select into/bulkcopy` – There are certain SQL Server commands and utilities which for performance reasons do not completely log their actions. This includes "select into" and "fast BCP." If you wish to use these commands on your database then this option should be turned on.

- `single user` - When this option is enabled only one user is allowed to access the database at a time. This is typically used by the administrator as part of performing some maintenance activities.
- `trunc log on chkpt` - When this option is enabled the database transaction log is automatically truncated with each system generated checkpoint command. This defeats the purpose of having transaction logs because the information is tossed away with no management of recovery ability included. If your data is static and user modification is minimal or the system is used only in system development then this option can be enabled.

Once the ownership and database options are set the database is ready for use. The only other consideration is whether to subdivide the database space with additional user-created segments.

Segments are the SQL Server mechanism for subdividing the available database and device space into areas for particular purposes. Each database created automatically comes with three already created segments. These are the "logsegment", "default", and "system" segments. The default and system segments automatically encompass all of the device space used for data. The logsegment extends over all of the devices and space allocated for transaction logging. Most SQL Server administrators will be satisfied with the system-created segments and never venture into user-defined segments.

There are circumstances in which using this SQL Server feature affords the administrator new performance and integrity options. When new objects are created in a database, unless otherwise specified, they are created on the "default" segment. The exception is if the object creator deliberately places objects on a named segment. Using segments the administrator can carefully control the placement of database objects on specific SQL Server and underlying hardware devices. In this manner the administrator can improve system performance by efficiently using his devices.

Tables and their corresponding indexes can be placed on different devices reducing contention and speeding up access. High use tables, views, and procedures can be placed on dedicated or special purpose devices.

An administrator can place certain tables out of the way of the general or user-created objects and dedicate storage space to these objects which cannot be accidentally eaten up by an ill-behaved application or user. Removing the "default" and "system" segment from the devices where the named segments exist effectively walls these areas off from the casual sight seers. This can save many a late night application support call to add space after some innocent client creates a temporary table to hold the results of his Q.F.H. (Query from Hell).

The mechanics of using segments revolves around three system stored procedures; sp_addsegment, sp_extendsegment, and sp_dropsegment. Segments are initially created using the sp_addsegment procedure.

```
sp_addsegment segname, dbname, devname
```

Segments must be created by the database owner. Each segment in a database requires a unique name. Once again, don't underestimate the benefits of consistent and informative naming conventions. The named segment is then assigned to a specific SQL Server device that has already allocated space for this database. This command must be executed from within the target database but the database name must still be supplied in the command. Obviously, creating named segments makes the most sense in situations where multiple SQL Server devices are available and used to partition database allocations.

```
Example
sp_addsegment big_table, userdb1, DISK2_DATA
```

Once added, if additional space is allocated for this database on the named device, then this segment automatically includes all of the additional space. The segment can be extended across multiple devices using the sp_extendsegment procedure.

```
sp_extendsegment segname, dbname, devname
```

The parameters are the same as the create database command and when used all of the space on both devices is available for this segment. It confuses the issue somewhat to realize that a device can potentially have many database segments living within it. Any object in those segments could potentially use any of the available free space. Most administrators try to avoid this situation by removing any unwanted segments from certain database devices. If the administrator did not want users accidently creating objects on a certain device then it is a simple matter of removing the "default" segment from that device. The mechanism for doing this is the sp_dropsegment procedure.

```
sp_dropsegment segname, dbname, device
```

This removes unwanted segments from the named device. When the last device is removed from a named segment the segment ceases to exist any further. The default, system, and logsegments cannot be completely removed and must exist on at least one device. It is considered bad form to have a device assigned to a database, but have no segments allocated to that slice. This effectively makes that space unusable and wasted.

There are many ways to use these features, and you should carefully consider how these can help you improve your installation.

Memory and storage options

An old adage among the collectors of 1960s era muscle cars is that "There is no substitute for cubic inches." And for you Godzilla fans, of course we know that "Size Does Matter!" Bigger is better when it comes to SQL Server memory configurations as well. One of the most significant features affecting overall system performance is the use of cache memory. The SQL Server implementation tries to minimize the number of real disk read requests it makes by storing as much information in memory as possible. If the server is able to do this then your SQL Server installation will be highly effective. Unfortunately, the SQL Server is only able to allocate memory for cache use after all of its other requirements are satisfied. For most implementations the minimum workable memory configuration is 12 MB. In reality, even a 16 megabyte implementation is unlikely to provide acceptable performance even for small sites. As a general rule, on all platforms, you should try to ensure that the SQL Server software has a minimum of 32 MB of memory available and configured for its use. This will start to allow the server to allocate data cache to avoid performing physical disk reads.

For large systems it is not uncommon for the systems to be configured for a GB or more of memory. You really cannot go wrong by providing your SQL Server with too much memory.

By providing lots of memory you will open up many opportunities to optimize your System XI Server installation for your application mix. System XI allows your memory allocations to be used more flexibly and creatively allowing very specific performance tuning activity to occur. With System XI memory can be removed from the general data cache space and set aside for specific uses. The mechanism to do this in Sybase parlance is "named cache spaces." Once created, these named cache spaces can then have specific objects or databases associated with them. This ensures that those objects will have access to an appropriate amount of memory. This is ideal for objects that are frequently in regular application use. This ensures that these are always available without the fear that some other activity taking place on the server will displace these objects from the general cache space. This process of having large reads displace other more essential information from cache is referred to as "bumping." Through allocation of a separate place for objects you don't want to have bumped, you can be assured that the pages you want are in memory. If your object is reasonably sized and you allocate enough memory for the cache space you can ensure that the entire object is stored in memory. If this is the only object in that cache space then you have effectively pinned that object in memory and ensured that no physical disk activity is required. This technique is often combined with special start-up procedures that perform priming read operations on the objects to be pinned in memory to ensure that these objects are placed in memory from the start.

In addition to providing specific cache spaces, System XI allows each of these areas to be allocated an optimum I/O size. In pre-System XI servers the only available I/O size was in 2 kilobyte pages. Under System XI this can be configured up to 16 kilobytes. This can reduce the number of read or write requests to the cache pool and can optimize access to large objects.

To use these facilities effectively, you will need to be familiar with three System XI stored procedures.

- sp_cacheconfig
- sp_poolconfig
- sp_bindcache

The sp_cacheconfig procedure provides the mechanism to view the existing data caches and their particulars or to create or remove data caches. Changes made to the cache configurations will require that the system be shut down and restarted in order to make those changes effective.

sp_cacheconfig [cachename [," cache_size[P|K|M|G]"
] [,logonly | mixed]]

Each cache name must be unique in the system. If the command is given without any parameters, information is provided on all of the available caches in the system. If provided with only a cache name, then the specifics of that cache are provided. When included with the other parameters, then changes to the cache are invoked. This includes specifying the size of the cache in pages, kilobytes, MB, or GB depending on the P, K, M, or G parameter. This cache can specifically be allocated for log use only, but the default behavior is for mixed data and log use. Allocating a memory size of 0 for an existing cache will cause that cache space to be removed at the next restart.

Having created a named cache space with some specific configuration then it may be appropriate to modify the I/O behavior using the sp_poolconfig procedure.

sp_poolconfig cache_name [, " mem_size[P|K|M|G]", " config_poolK" [, " affected_poolK"]]

Using this procedure, an administrator can modify the default 2k page manipulation of the SQL server to a larger and more optimum size. If only the cache name is provided, then this procedure provides information on the current configured memory pools in that cache. A single cache space can have many different I/O pools configured each with a different size. These are specified using the "mem_size" parameter to indicate the amount of cache memory available in the various sizes of i/o pools. The specific pools are specified in kilobytes from 2k to 16k. The pool amount is allocated from one of the existing pools. When a cache is created all of its memory is by default configured into the 2k pool. If the affected pool parameter is not specified then the pool is allocated from the 2k pool.

Finally, having created an appropriate cache and i/o behavior specific objects and databases can be associated or bound to that cache using the sp_bindcache procedure.

```
sp_bindcache cachename, dbname[,
[ownername.]tablename[, indexname | "text only"]]
```

In this case the cache and dbname are required parameters and additional specifications can be provided to identify specific objects. In some early releases of System XI you can encounter problems with binding whole databases to a named cache space. If you are using Release 11.02 or better you should not encounter these problems.

The final piece of advice concerning System XI named caches is that although Sybase has provided advanced tools for dealing with memory these need to be used with care and caution. You should ensure that you have an excellent knowledge of your data structures and application usage before using these tuning options. All proposed changes should, where at all possible, be tested first in a non-production environment. A full system backup needs to be taken prior to changing these configurations and a copy of the pre-change configuration file needs to be made to allow for a rapid rollback of the changes if things don't proceed as planned. These changes have the capability of dramatically affecting the performance and stability of your environment. All affected clients and application developers need to be informed of planned changes and appropriate change control procedures followed.

There are some performance junkies lurking in the application jungles. These are individuals unlikely to be impressed with the speed or options provided by the System XI facilities alone. For these folks the next step is to step into the realm of hardware hot rodding including the use of solid state disk devices. These units are essentially large external memory units that look to the hardware in general and the System XI server in particular like regular disk resources.

Essentially, these devices are identical to regular disk except for the significant fact that these units perform a hundred times faster. Many Sybase systems suffer from a common malady of being tempdb constrained. This means that almost all activity even if nominally using another database requires the use of tempdb to perform intermediate operations and this resource very quickly becomes i/o bound and unable to respond to the workload. This occurs even if all the other system resources are underutilized. High performance installations would resort to placing the tempdb database on these high-speed devices to alleviate this I/O bottleneck. The nature of tempdb was that information contained here does not have the same integrity concerns that the other databases do so this seemed sensible. Some concerns even started using battery-backed solid-state disk devices for some logs to again speed performance.

For most installations, the additional options in System XI make the use of solid state disk devices less common. Normally, these would be considered a last resort and used only under extreme conditions.

The primary concern is ensuring the system integrity if the system should be interrupted in mid-stream; how is the information on the solid state device is recovered? For installations considering investing in one of these units a couple of words to the wise. Ensure that the unit you are evaluating is battery backed and capable of operating in the event of a power failure and capable of writing its contents fully to real disk before shutting down. These units should contain an option to turn off the caching features for writes allowing these to proceed straight to disk. This will help ensure your system integrity.

As a final thought, make sure that you are in fact constrained at the physical disk level. If your disk controller or operating system is the real bottleneck then these devices will not dramatically improve your performance. Try before you buy. For most organizations I recommend using the System XI named cache spaces and the existing system memory resources in conjunction with

RAID 5 disk resources including disk controller caching for high throughput systems.

System Configuration Options

One of the most important elements in configuring a new Sybase SQL server is establishing appropriate settings for the server configuration variables. Each server should have these reviewed and set in a manner that's appropriate to the intended application usage. For example, applications leaning heavily toward OLTP functions will be optimized in a different manner than a data warehousing application.

Even administrators experienced in pre-System XI SQL server systems will find it worthwhile reviewing the new features and options very carefully. With System XI Sybase has done an admirable job of improving the configuration process. The most welcome change is the addition of "configuration files." In pre-System XI implementations, configuration information was stored in the sysconfigures and syscurconfigs tables within the MASTER database. Many administrators have had the unfortunate experience of modifying one of the configuration parameters in such a manner that the system will no longer start. Without the system being able to start there is no way to correct the problem you created for yourself. In most cases this now required the administrator to perform a MASTER database recovery to correct the problem. Savvy administrators always dumped the master database prior to modifying any configuration variables.

With System XI configuration files the values for these parameters are also stored in external files. The server reads the configuration file as part of the system start-up and initialization process. The configuration files are stored in ASCII readable text form. An administrator who 'craters' his systems accidently can manually edit the configuration file or recover the backup of only that file and restart the server. Then wiping beads of sweat from their forehead they can reconsider the implications of the planned change.

The system administrator can choose to apply all modifications directly to the configuration files by manually editing them. For the most part I recommend this method only be used in emergencies. Regular updates or modifications should be implemented using the "sp_configure" stored procedure.

In pre-System XI SQL servers only the most commonly manipulated parameters were included within the set of parameters accessible through the sp_configure procedure. Other parameters were modified using trace flags or running the "buildmaster" command off-line. System XI allows the entire set of modifiable parameters to be accessed through the sp_configure process. That's not to say that just because you can modify them does that you should. Even knowing that recovering from incorrect configurations is less painful than in past versions does not relieve you from the obligation to proceed with caution when modifying your environment.

By consolidating all of the tunable settings into a single place, the total number of variables that can be tweaked becomes quite large. Sybase again has done a good job of combining variables into different groupings for manipulation. Each parameter is designated as either "dynamic" or "static." When a dynamic parameter is modified it takes effect immediately. Static parameters will become effective the next time the system is restarted. This is because these parameters require a change in the system memory allocation. In previous Sybase releases the configuration parameters were made effective by issuing the "reconfigure" command. This command has been discontinued with System XI. The reserved word "reconfigure" is still active with the current release of System XI. It will not cause a syntax error if issued, but it is not required and is only available to ensure compatibility with previous releases. Sybase has not committed to insuring that they will continue to provide this bridge. Administrators are advised to discontinue use of this keyword.

Besides the static and dynamic groupings, parameters are associated based on the area of server behavior they affect. Sybase refers to these groupings as the "parameter hierarchy." The parameter hierarchy includes:

- Backup/recovery
- Cache manager
- Disk I/O
- General information
- Languages
- Lock manager
- Memory use
- Network communications
- Operating system resources
- Physical memory
- Processors
- SQL Server administration
- User environment

Each parameter is assigned to a primary group and in some instances they may also have a secondary group affinity. These groupings of parameters are also assigned a management or "display" level. There are currently three assigned display levels.

- Basic
- Intermediate
- Comprehensive

Only those parameters assigned to a level currently at or below your set display level will be visible. This is another mechanism introduced with System XI to manage the complexity introduced with all the available settings that can be modified.

In the SQL Server environment by default all valid users can view the configuration parameter settings. Modification of these parameters is restricted to those users who have "SA_ROLE" or "SSO_ROLE" assigned. There are also certain parameters that can only be modified by the "system security officers."

Sybase's default settings are based on certain assumptions. They assume that your server has at least 15 MB of RAM dedicated to the SQL Server and that the system will be used heavily for update activity. They also assume that you have a small set of stored procedures that are accessed frequently. Although I have no issues with basing the default settings on these assumptions. I also believe that most sites will find that some of the default settings are suboptimal for their intended use.

The primary command for manipulating the configuration parameters is sp_configure. This command can be issued in a number of different configurations and that have different effects.

- sp_configure – Issued by itself the command returns a list by parameter hierarchy of all the configurable parameters and their current and default settings. This list will vary depending on the setting of your "display level."
- sp_configure "parameter" – Issued with a parameter name the command returns the current and default settings for that option alone.
- sp_configure "group_name" – When the command is issued with a specific group only the parameters that exist within that group are returned along with their current and default settings.

- sp_configure "parameter," value – This resets the named parameter to whatever value is provided. This is the mechanism used to adjust or tune the system parameters as required.
- sp_configure "parameter," 0, "default" – When used in this manner the named parameter is returned to its default setting. This is often useful when recovering from incorrect settings.
- sp_configure "configuration file," 0, "sub_command," "file_name" – when used in this fashion the settings are established based on a specific configuration files settings.

When the parameters are named within the sp_configure command, the names provided are valid providing they are enough to uniquely identify a specific parameter. If more than one parameter could contain the string provided, then the list of potentially valid matches is returned by the command. The sp_configure command can also be used with a specific configuration file. In some instances, the administrator may wish to create a different configuration file rather than modify the existing settings or file. The administrator may wish to test the proposed settings before modifying the production configuration. In some circumstances, the administrator may create and maintain multiple configuration files suitable for different application tasks and rotate between them depending on the function. The system may have a different configuration profile for both the on-line work during the day and the batch work load at night with a scheduled restart daily to clean the system and prepare for the nightly batch run.

Each time a configuration parameter is modified a new file is created with a file name of "server_name.001" or "server_name.002," etc. This ensures that a backout path for the process exists.

By default the server reads the "$SYBASE/server_name.config" file on start-up. An administrator can change this behavior by modifying the "dataserver" command in the run file to include the "-c" option and the configuration file to be used. The configuration files need to be maintained with security that allows the starting process to read it and manipulate it. For most sites this means that the file should contain all permissions for the user "SYBASE," but all other users should be restricted to read-only access.

A final warning before I describe the individual configuration parameters. You should always make a copy of the configuration file before changing any parameters. In addition, I generally recommend that a MASTER database backup be made prior to modifying any parameters. This may be overkill, but better safe than sorry.

print deadlock information

In previous releases this parameter was set using the trace(1204) command. By default this setting is turned off with a value of "0." When enabled by setting the value to "1" additional deadlock debugging information is printed to the system errorlog. This is a dynamic parameter viewable from the intermediate level. Enabling this level of tracking can degrade overall system performance and should only be enabled as required to assist in debugging application problems. This is not a general use setting. I usually only turn this on within test environments.

allow sql server async I/O

In previous releases this setting was enabled using the trace(1604) flag. The default is a setting of "1" allowing the server to access the disk resources using asynchronous I/O. This is only true if the operating system provides such a service and it is enabled at that level. If your operating system does not support this asynchronous I/O then this setting should be changed to "0." Under almost all other conditions this setting should remain with the default. By allowing the server to use asynchronous I/O your allowing the server to continue performing useful work instead of waiting for each request for data to return. The default setting is the best performance setting for all types of workloads. This is a static parameter so the server will require a restart to make any changes effective. It's viewable as an "intermediate" display level parameter.

tcp no delay

This used to be enabled using the trace(1610) flag but now its a configurable server parameter. The default value is "0" allowing the server to be a good network citizens by bundling up communication packets into larger chunks and sending less material over the network. This usually involves a very slight delay in sending data over the network allowing packets to accumulate into worthwhile units. As this parameter is static a server restart will be required to make any changes effective. This is viewable if your display level is set to comprehensive. Modifying this parameter effectively requires a detailed knowledge of your networking environment. The first potential pitfall to avoid is to ensure that your host server operating system and hardware are not doing the same thing.

If the host server is dedicated to the database function then the operating system and hardware should be configured for no delay. Otherwise your network packets can potentially be delayed at both the SQL Server and operating system level. You should be aware of and set this parameter in conjunction with the "default network packet size" and "max network packet size" parameters.

These all need to be set in a manner that efficiently uses the underlying network of your specific installation. If you do not use TCP communication or your network does not involve collisions then this parameter should be set to "1" allowing packets to be sent as soon as possible. If you have no idea what I'm talking about then leave it at the default setting.

lock shared memory

This parameter's default setting is "0" disabling the feature.
When enabled this allows the operating system to set aside a portion of its shared memory segment which SQL Servers uses as
permanently allocated. That means that the memory that SQL
Server is using will never be paged to disk by the operating system. Although this is a desirable feature not all operating systems support this behavior. Even those that do support the
function may not respond to the SQL Server request. Check with
your hardware vendor and Sybase technical support before setting this parameter to "1."

If you do decide to enable this feature you will need to reboot your
SQL Server to make it effective. In previous releases of SQL
Server this was set using the trace(1611) flag. As a more general
piece of advice, if you suspect that your experiencing performance
problems due to memory paging then its time to put more memory in your server, don't mess around with configuration parameters. You may also wish to review the overall workloads on your
server and increase capacity or move some of the work to another
unit.

additional network memory

If your configuration allows applications to request larger network packet sizes than the default then you correspondingly need
to allocate additional internal memory to this function. The
default setting for this parameter is "0" specifying that no additional memory is allocated. This reflects the assumption that
default "max network packet size" parameter matches the default
size. Because this parameter affects the memory allocation is will
require a server restart to become effective. As a rule the default
settings for the network parameters are sufficient for OLTP
applications oriented toward short insert, update, and delete
activity or single row lookups. If your application menu runs more

toward Data Warehousing, Data Mining, or other decision support activities that may return large query sets to the requesting workstation then these parameters should be reviewed.

The following calculation should be made to determine the value of this parameter:

- Determine the number of clients that will simultaneously be requesting large packet sizes under peak loads.
- Multiply this number by three to represent the number of buffers each client connection requires.
- Multiply this number by the max packet size configured on the server.
- Add 2% to this figure for overhead.
- Round this number to the nearest 2048. This parameter is set in bytes, but SQL server wants to allocate the space in 2k pages.

Once this value is determined, it can be entered into the configuration parameter. The memory requested for additional network use is in addition to the regular allocation your SQL Server obtains from the O/S. You also need to ensure that your site has enough real physical memory to support this request. SQL Server ensures that every configured client request can obtain a connection using the default packet size. As clients request larger packet sizes, then they are allocated space if possible from the pool of additional network memory. If no space exists, then the SQL Server rejects the client request for a larger packet size.

allow updates to system tables

This is a dynamic parameter that when configured to true using a value of "1" will allow the SA to directly insert, delete, or update information contained in the SQL Servers system tables. This is not an activity that is encouraged. The default setting is "0" disallowing this access. This parameter is displayed at the comprehensive level only. This parameter should only be set to "1" for the duration of a specific procedure as directed by the Sybase trouble-shooting guide or under the guidance of Sybase technical support. Manual modification of your system tables can very easily cause your system to crash in very spectacular ways.

audit queue size

The default value is 100 and can be configured up to a value of 65535. This parameter determines how frequently audit records are written to the sybsecurity database. The lower the number, the more frequently this information is written and the more intrusive the auditing activity is to the overall system performance. A higher number means that audit records are queued longer resulting in less performance impact but a greater risk that the auditing information could be lost if the system crashed. This affects the amount of memory that is allocated to this activity and the server must be restarted to make any setting changes effective. This is an intermediate-level process. If you are not using auditing then this parameter can be configured for the minimum value of '1.' If your application requires auditing but is more concerned with performance, then the default value should be increased accordingly.

memory alignment boundary

This parameter in previous SQL Server releases was only accessible as a buildmaster parameter. It is currently a comprehensive-level parameter that under most circumstances should not be modified. In fact, you should only modify this parameter if advised to do so by Sybase technical support. If this parameter is changed, the selected value must be a multiple of 2048.

sql server clock tick length

Once again, this setting in previous releases was only accessible by modifying the cclkrate parameter using the buildmaster program. This somewhat mysterious parameter tells the SQL Server how long in microseconds the actual hardware CPU clock tick lasts. This determines along with the "time slice" parameter how the SQL Server process scheduler will operate. The SQL Server process determines its scheduling based on counting CPU clock ticks. Obviously, this is very hardware dependent and for most applications the default setting should remain the preferred choice. The lower the setting the more frequently SQL Server will relinquish the CPU that may help I/O bound applications. If your application is CPU intensive then larger numbers will allow them better CPU access and therefore better application throughput.

This will also affect how frequently SQL Server runs its maintenance activities. This parameter should only be changed under the direction of Sybase technical support. Changes should be made very carefully to this parameter as your SQL Server performance could be dramatically lowered if set incorrectly. Changes to this static parameter are only effective after a system restart.

permission cache entries

SQL Server caches permission entries from the sysprotects tables. This improves performance for determining access and prevents repeated reads of the sysprotects tables. The default value is 15, establishing a number of cache entries available per task. All of the cache entries are flushed when permissions are changed. This parameter was accessible previously using build-master as the "cfgcprot" variable. Increasing this value may improve performance if an unusually high number of protection checks is required. The larger value may be inefficient if frequent grants and revokes are run. This is a comprehensive level parameter and should probably remain at the default value.

stack guard size

For each user connection to the SQL Server there is an allocated stack area that is used for storing processing results etc. as the execution continues. At the end of each stack area the SQL Server places a marker referred to as a "guard word." Beyond the guard word SQL Server leaves a configurable amount of buffer space to the next task. This is intended to ensure that a misbehaving Sybase process that overruns its stack area does not corrupt its neighbor and can be terminated easily. The default guard area is set at 4096 and should not be modified under any reasonable circumstance. If your errorlog frequently shows processes being terminated for stack violations then you may wish to increase the overall stack size per connection. This has memory implementations to the overall environment so this should be carefully considered prior to implementation. This is a comprehensive parameter previously accessed as "cguardsz" using the buildmaster program.

number of index trips

As index pages are placed in memory they are swapped out on a "least recently used" basis. This dynamic parameter determines the number of times that an index page in cache can be bypassed in the page chain before it becomes a candidate to swap out. The default value is "0." Leaving index pages in cache by configuring for higher values may result in processes being unable to acquire cache resources. If you're a professional benchmarker then you should consider adjusting this comprehensive parameter. All other mere mortals should just leave it alone.

max number network listeners

Changes to this comprehensive parameter will require a server restart. The default value of this parameter is 15. This will be overkill for most implementations but does not significantly affect performance. If your implementation communicates over multiple network methods then this parameter may need to be increased. Each master port will require one network listener. Most application communication is via the TCP socket interface and therefore a value of one is acceptable to most installations.

i/o polling process count

In previous lives this parameter was the buildmaster "cmax-scheds" variable. This comprehensive parameter determines how frequently the SQL Server schedular checks for I/0 or network completions. The default value is 10 allowing this check to occur every 10 times a SQL Server process runs. This is a dynamic parameter where changes made are immediately in effect. As a rule of thumb lowering this value will improve response time but decrease throughput. Increasing the value will improve throughput but decrease response time. This is also affected by the clock tick and time slice parameters. Changes to this parameter should be made with caution. Values greater than 30 are not advised.

number of alarms

If your application uses a large number of "waitfor" statements and you consistently get errorlog messages indicating that alarms are unavailable then this parameter should be increased from the default 40. Each alarm structure will require a small memory allocation so resetting this parameter will require restarting the server. This is a comprehensive level parameter previously accessed as the cnalarm buildmaster parameter.

disk i/o structures

Each user process requires access to a disk i/o structure in order to initiate i/o requests. The number of available structures is determined at system start-up. Each structure requires a pre-determined amount of memory to operate. If insufficient structures are available then processes will be delayed waiting for structures to become available. Configuring too many will result in wasting memory. The default value is 256. This number should be set in a manner consistent with your operating system capabilities. In previous SQL Server releases this corresponds to the cnblkio buildmaster parameter.

number of languages in cache

SQL Server maintains a separate cache space for language information. This parameter determines the number of languages that can be simultaneously accessed. The default value is 3, but it can be set as high as 100. For most applications the default value is fine and should not be adjusted. This is viewable as an intermediate level parameter.

max async i/os per engine

This parameter was previously the cnmaxaio_engine variable which could be configured from the buildmaster command. This determines the number of issued asynchronous disk I/O requests that a single SQL server engine can have outstanding before it waits for one to return. The default value is also the maximum of 2147483647. In reality this needs to be set in conjunction with your operating system limits. This number should always be set lower than the corresponding operating system limitation. This ensures that the SQL Server will not be refused or blocked a request by the operating system. If this occurs frequently it can cause quite a performance degradation. Entries in your errorlog will be helpful in determining if this parameter needs adjustment. The physical server has more than a single SQL Server operating on it then each SQL Server needs to be tuned in a manner that ensures that the combination of outstanding requests does not exceed any O/S limitations. This needs to be set in coordination with the "max async i/os per server" parameter. This parameter should never be set less than 50 and for most installations a setting of 500 should be sufficient. For heavy decision support activity a setting of 1024 may be more appropriate.

max async i/os per server

This was previously known as the cnmaxaio_server variable in the buildmaster configuration. This works in a coordinated manner with the underlying operating system to ensure that the SQL server limits its requests for asynchronous disk access to a level that can be accommodated by the operating system and the hardware. It turns out that it's easier for the SQL Server to put on the brakes then it is to deal with O/S refusals. The default value is the maximum of 21474863647. This should never be set less than 50 and a starting value of 500 seems pretty reasonable. For heavy decision support then this can be set up to 1024 with no unreasonable memory demands. Changing the async variables will require a server restart to invoke the new values. These are comprehensive level parameters. If these values are insufficient then you will obtain errorlog messages indicating that certain I/O requests are being repeated.

number of mailboxes

Mailboxes are one of the mysterious kernel structures that SQL server uses internally to keep track of all the things it has juggled into the air. In this particular case mailboxes are used in the internal interprocess communication functions required to keep all the threads and processes working together. This is a static parameter and should only be modified under the direction on Sybase technical support staff. The default value is 30 and it can be viewed at the comprehensive level. This was previously the buildmaster cnmbox variable.

number of messages

This is an internal parameter reserving a number of kernel structures to be used in coordinating the various SQL Server processes and threads. The default value is 64 and it should only be changed under the direction of Sybase Technical Support. This is a static and comprehensive parameter.

number of oam trips

Sybase uses "Object Allocation Map" pages to determine how it has allocated space for various objects. Not surprisingly it needs to access this information frequently. It stores a certain number of OAM pages in cache and refreshes that list of pages based on a most recently used schema. This parameter determines how many time the SQL Server can traverse past an OAM page before it becomes a candidate for replacement with a more active page. For most practical applications this should remain at the default setting of 0. If your application appears to be thrashing its OAM cache and obtaining most OAM pages from disk then this parameter needs to be increased to allow the pages to remain in cache for a longer time. If your application tends toward more infrequent manipulation of large tables or objects then increasing this parameter will be helpful.

number of pre-allocated extents

This parameter is used exclusively by the Sybase "BCP" utility to allow the BCP program to allocated space in larger chunks than single 8 page extents. This reduces the number of calls to the SQL Server page manager, but can be potentially wasteful by overallocating space to objects. The default value is 2 for this static, and comprehensive parameter. If you perform frequent BCP activities on large tables then increasing this value will allow this activity to proceed faster. This was known previously as the cpreallocext buildmaster variable.

cpu accounting flush interval

This was previously the "cpu flush" variable. This determines how frequently CPU usage accounting information is copied from sysprocesses to syslogins. This is done to accommodate CPU resource tracking by login id. These values are manipulated using the "sp_clearstats" and "sp_reportstats" procedures. Setting this value to a low value ensures that whenever this information is queried it contains reasonably up to date information. Setting this to a higher value reduces system overhead.

You should be warned that the SQL server uses this information to choose deadlock victims. Purging this information to quickly can cause this process to choose candidates unwisely. If you are not using the accounting information then set this parameter to the highest possible value of 2147483647. This is a dynamic parameter and is viewable at the comprehensive level.

runnable process search count

This used to known as the infamous cschedspins variable accessible from the buildmaster command. This command determines how long a SQL Server engine will remain on the physical machine CPU cycling looking for database processes to execute. When set to low numbers the engine process will more frequently relinquish the CPU and allow other processes to cycle through. When set to higher number the engine will continue to wait and look for SQL Server tasks to execute. The default value is 2000 for this comprehensive level tuning parameter.

This is one of the key parameters that should be adjusted depending on the environment and relative workloads. For most uniprocessor systems this value should be set to a relatively low value. A setting of 1 may even be appropriate. This ensures that the single SQL Server engine process does not hog all the CPU cycles. If the corresponding application is CPU intensive then a slightly higher value such as 5 may be more appropriate.

The base setting for multiprocessor environments is 500. This should be increased for CPU intensive application with values up to 1500 being appropriate. This may be reduced for I/O bound applications to allow the I/O operations to complete without undo no-op CPU cycling. This behavior may also be affected by the "server clock tick parameter."

number of sort buffers

This parameter determines the number of available buffers to hold pages read from input tables. When tuning in conjunction with the "extent I/O buffers" this should be set for starters at 8 times the number of extent buffers. This is a dynamic parameter and can most effectively be set under controlled benchmarking conditions. The default value is 0 for this particular variable.

sort page count

When SQL Server is performing sort operations it borrows data pages from the default data cache. Setting this parameter determines the maximum amount of memory that a sort operation can use. A good starting value can be determined by calculating (number of sort buffers x rows per data page)/50. This value can be changed dynamically and is viewable only from the comprehensive level. The default value is 0. This used to be known as the csortpage variable in the buildmaster configuration.

cpu grace time

The grace time parameter determines at which point a SQL Server task running on an engine is declared a runaway and is terminated with a timeslice error. SQL Server processes are expected to voluntarily release the CPU periodically to ensure proper operation. Programs that do not do this frequently enough will encounter this problem. The default value is 500 and this can be increased if you are encountering a specific problem. This is intended more as a debugging tool than a production fix. Changing this value will require a server restart to make it effective. This is viewable at the comprehensive level only. This was previously known as the ctimemax variable.

default database size

When the SQL Server creates a new database it determines the size in MB from this parameter. Under most circumstances this should be set to the same size as the model database. If you consistently create large databases then this value can be increased to reflect that. It should never be smaller than the size of the master database. The default value is 2 and changing it will require a server restart. This is viewable at the intermediate level.

default character set id

Do not change this parameter manually. This is set during the sybinit installation process and should only be changed with the sybinit program. Changes to this parameter will require a server restart to make it effective. This is viewable at the intermediate level.

default language id

This parameter is another of the ones that should not be manually changed. This is changed as part of setting up the language information with sybinit. The default id of 0 identifies us_english as the language of choice. The SQL Server process uses this information in displaying all system messages.

default network packet size

This configuration defines the basic unit size for network traffic. The default setting is 512 bytes and all settings up to 524288 must be a multiple of 512. Settings other than that are rounded down to the nearest multiple. The default is adequate for most implementations. I would only recommend changing this to a larger value for dedicated reporting or batch activity with very controlled client access. If you change this parameter then the system will need to be rebooted to make the change effective. This does affect the amount of memory available to the SQL Server so it should be changed with caution. You need to ensure that memory is available by calculating (number of clients * 3) * default number of bytes. This number is subtracted from the total available memory to ensure that a positive number results. The memory remaining is all that is available for caching, etc. Changing this parameter will require a system restart.

default sortorder id

This value is set during the sybinit installation and should not be manually modified. It indicates the id of the sort order currently installed on the server. The default value is 50 with valid values begin between 0 and 255. This is only changed with the sybinit program.

number of devices

This parameter sets how many total devices or device numbers that the SQL Server can allocate. This is a static parameter and will require a system restart in order to make any changes effective. This value can be set to any number up to 255. I generally opt to configure the server for the maximum number of devices even if I don't currently have them available. There is very little overhead associated with increasing this number. By setting it to the maximum figure it potentially allows you to add devices and increase space on the fly without having to bring the system down.

number of extent i/o buffers

The number of extent i/o buffers determines how many buffer pages are available for use when creating indexes. The default value is 0 making each page read or write an independent operation. By setting the extent i/o buffers value to a higher amount then more pages are available for buffering resulting in lower system overhead and faster index creation. This value should never be set higher than 100. If two create index commands are executed simultaneously all of the buffers are assigned to the first process identified. This is a static and comprehensive variable.

default fill factor percent

This parameter determines how full to make the index pages when creating a new index. After the initial creation the available free space may be used as data rows are inserted and deleted. A value of 100 leaves no room for additional entries. This can cause a large performance degradation due to page splitting behavior. This may be the most efficient setting for read only data. Using a setting of 0 causes the leaf page data to be stored as fully compressed, but the other levels are stored with an appropriate fill factor. This is the default setting.

If your application is heavily involved with data manipulation such as on-line activities then you should choose a reasonable percentage that reflects the amount of activity. Normally values of 10 to 15 percent are accessible. This is a static comprehensive parameter.

identity burning set factor

SQL Server allows table columns to have a datatype value of "identity" meaning the SQL server will take responsibility for setting the column value to a unique integer value. This variable determines the size of the block of contiguous number that are available. This is normally expressed as a percentage of the total address space available. The default value is 5000 making a block of 5000 unique ky values available for use in satisfying a table request for an identify. Setting this to a lower number increases the overhead required to assign identity keys. If the server is stopped before all the numbers are used these numbers remain unavailable leaving a slight hole in the contiguous values. This is typically a small loss. There is no particular reason to change this static and comprehensive parameter.

i/o accounting flush interval

This is part of the accounting system configuration specifying the amount of time clock ticks the SQL Server allows i/o counts to accumulate in the sysprocesses table before writing the information into the syslogins table by user id. Leaving this value to a high number minimizes the amount of system overhead associated with this activity, but may allow out of date information to be reported. If you are not using the accounting information set this parameter to the maximum value of 2147483647. The default value is 5000. This parameter is dynamic and can be changed on the fly without restarting the SQL Server. This is viewable as an intermediate level parameter.

number of languages in cache

This determines the number of simultaneous languages that can be held in cache. The default value is also the minimum value of 3. The maximum is 100, but for most applications this parameter should never be adjusted. If an adjustment is required then the server will need to be restarted to make the change effective. The display level for this parameter is intermediate.

number of locks

This is a static parameter that affects the amount of memory allocated to the SQL Server. This determines the total number of locks available to the entire server. The default value is 5000. If this proves insufficient because of the amount of concurrent activity or the type of processing that is occurring then this should be increased. Sybase recommends creeping upwards in increments of 1000 until the problem no longer occurs. Your application vendor may be more helpful in determining an appropriate lock level. I've certainly some application using 40,000 or more locks. This does have memory implications so some caution is advised. This is a basic level parameter.

max online engines

Sybase SQL Server is a multi-threaded kernel capable of efficiently operating in multiple processor configurations. In order to perform this effectively the max online engines parameter should be set to the number of simultaneous physical CPUs you wish to use. For most applications this will match the total number of available CPUs.

In Sybase parlance an engine is a Sybase process capable of performing work. Each configured engine appears to the operating system as a separate process and is assigned to an available physical processor based on the regular operating system scheduling algorithm. This is probably the long way around of saying your not helping yourself by configuring this to a value greater than the number of available physical CPUs. You will just end up competing for resources with yourself and increasing the system overhead.

In some implementations the value should be set to one less than the total number of CPUs to ensure that the system overhead tasks have sufficient capacity to operate effectively. System XI is considerably more CPU friendly than previous releases and most of these restrictions have disappeared. In previous releases there as no significant value in setting this configuration value to a number greater than 6. These limitations have been conquered in

System XI and larger multi-processing configurations can now be effectively implemented. Sybase claims that System XI will scale linearly past 32 engines.

max network packet size

This is a static parameter requiring a system restart in order to implement any changes. This is viewable with a display level of intermediate. The default value is 512. Values must be set in multiples of 512 up to a maximum of 524288. This must be set in coordination with "additional network memory" parameter. Actual use of this parameter is dependent on client applications requesting larger packet sizes from the SQL Server. If the client application fails to do this then they are assigned the default size. The BCP program can be configured to use large packet sizes. This can provide a significant performance improvement for large copies. If the application manipulates image or text types a great deal then they can benefit from increasing the packet size.

total memory

This parameter indicates the total memory that the SQL Server allocates from the operating system for its use. Changing this parameter will require a system restart. The operating system must be configured to allow this amount of shared memory to be allocated or the system start will fail. Following the platform specific installation procedures will ensure that adequate resources are available. The values entered for this variable are in 2k pages. To determine the minimum amount of memory that your installation requires use the following formula

- Executable code size +
- Static overhead (1MB) +
- (Number of user connections * stack size) +
- (Number of user connections * stack guard size) +
- ((default network packet size *3) * number of user connections) +
- (number of open databases * 644 bytes) +
- (number of locks * 32 bytes) +
- (number of devices * 45,056 bytes) +
- size of procedure cache +
- total data cache size +
- (number of extent i/o buffers * 16k)

Remember if your result is in bytes to divide by 2096 to determine the number of 2k pages. If you know how many MB to allocate then multiply that number by 512 to determine how many corresponding 2k pages.

More memory is better. Remember to leave enough for the operating system to function efficiently. Allocate as much as you can for SQL Server. Using memory effectively is a key technique for performance tuning so having more gives you more options. With System XI you really can't give the server too much memory.

min online engines

This determines the minimum number of engines in an SMP environment should be started. This is an intermediate static parameter. The answer is always 1. There is no value in changing this from the default.

shared memory starting address

This static comprehensive parameter was previously the mrstart variable. It should be set to a platform specific value and should never be modified except as directed by Sybase Technical Support.

allow nested triggers

The default is 1 which allows triggers to fire other triggers if they modify other data. There are settings available to set whether a trigger can fire itself in the course of modifying data. To disable this behavior set the value to 0 and restart to server. This is an intermediate level parameter.

number of open databases

Changing this parameter will require a system restart to make the changes effective. This is a basic parameter that determines how many simultaneous databases can be open at a time. The default value is 12 which includes all of the system databases. Each open database requires 17k of memory so increasing this parameter has memory implications. Applications will fail and errorlog information will be recorded if there are more requests for open databases then can be accommodated.

number of open objects

The default value for this parameter is 500. Making changes to this basic parameter will require a system restart. This determines the total number of objects that the SQL Server will allow to be manipulated simultaneously. There are no significant implications to making this number large. As we like to say "Go big or go home."

systemwide password expiration

This is a dynamic password configurable by the System Security Officer and has an intermediate display level. The default value is 0 implying that passwords will never expire. Setting this parameter to another value sets the number of days until passwords will become invalid unless changed. SQL Server will issue a warning when less than 25% of the interval remains or 7 days. Applications that might encounter this warning need to be modified to respond appropriately and not terminate abruptly. For most sites an expiry interval of 90 days should be appropriate. Set this value to 120 if your application is not well behaved with the warning message so that an effective 90 day expiry is maintained.

remote server pre-read packets

The default value is 3 and changes will require a system restart. This is an intermediate level tuning parameter. This determines the number of packets a SQL Server site handler will read ahead of a requesting process. There is seldom any need to change the default.

procedure cache percent

Of the available cache memory after the system overhead is removed a portion of this can be reserved to save and compile stored procedures. The default is 20% allocated for this purpose. If your application makes extensive use of stored procedures then increasing this basic variable may improve system performance.

print recovery information

During system start up the system displays either summary or detailed information on the recovery status of each database. The default value of 0 indicates that summary information is displayed. A setting of 1 therefore indicates that transaction level recovery information is requested. This is static parameter viewable at the intermediate setting.

recovery interval in minutes

The default for this parameter is 5 and it can be changed on the fly. This is a basic level parameter and it determines the maximum number of minutes that a recovery process should take. The recovery process applies or reverses transactions and the amount of effort involved for each database is determined by this parameter.

allow remote access

This parameter determines whether the SQL Server will communicate with other external processes. This can be set by the System Security Officer. The default value is 1 and this should not be modified. The SQL Server does require connections to external services such as the Backup Server so disabling this can have unexpected results.

number of remote connections

This determines the number of simultaneous connections that a single SQL Server can support. Once reached the SQL Server will refuse to accept new connection requests. The default value is 20 and changes will require restarting the SQL Server. This is an intermediate level parameter.

number of remote logins

This should be set to the same value as the "number of remote connections." This determines then number of distinct login ids that will be allowed to simultaneously participate in remote communications with this machine. Changes will again require a system reboot to make effective.

number of remote sites

The default value of 10 indicates that 10 distinct sites or servers will be allowed to initiate communications with this server simultaneously. Each configured site will require an independent site handler to process requests. Changing this value will require restarting the SQL Server.

executable code size

This value is platform dependent and is system calculated. You cannot modify this value and you wouldn't want to if you could. This is viewable at the basic level.

stack size

This parameter should always be established in multiples of 2k pages. The minimum and default values are platform dependent. Increase this value if the errorlog information indicates that user processes are encountering numerous stack overflow errors. This is a static parameter viewable from the basic display level.

tape retention in days

This is important if you are dumping your data or transaction data directly to tape. This determines the number of days that must pass before the tape can be reused. This is to prevent accidently clobbering a good backup tape. The default value is 0, allowing tapes to be immediately reused. This is a static parameter viewable at the intermediate level. This can be explicitly overridden when executing the dump command if required.

time slice

This is a comprehensive parameter and changes will require restarting the system. This sets the number of milliseconds that a user process can run on the SQL Server scheduler. If this is set too low unnecessary context switching can occur. If set to high then CPU intensive processes can monopolize the CPU. The default value is 100. This can be increased for CPU heavy applications. This can also be decreased for I/O intensive applications. This should be modified with great care.

upgrade version

This value is set by the Sybase installation and upgrade programs. This value should never be changed in any other manner by the administrator. This value may be requested when contacting Sybase technical support.

number of user connections

The default for this entry is 25 connections. This determines the maximum number of simultaneous user connections that can be made to a SQL Server. This must always be set lower then the operating system file descriptor limit. Each connection requires approximately 52k of memory. Enough connections must exist to support all data devices, backup server, mirror devices, and site handlers in addition to any regular requests. Changing this value will require a server restart to make them effective on the system.

address lock spinlock ratio

The SQL Server process uses an internal table to coordinate access to memory addresses between multiple engines. Access to these resources is enforced by spinlocks. In essence, in order to access a memory address the process must first acquire a lock on the appropriate memory resource. When another process attempts to use that memory address it is blocked and must spin waiting for the lock to be released. The internal address protection table is always 1031 entries long and is filled in using a hashing algorithm as memory addresses are acquired. Each of these hash table entries may be protected by one or more spinlocks. In single engine configurations this is irrelevant as there can be no contention for these resources. In multi-CPU environments then the optimum ratio in almost all instances is 11 locks protecting the 1031 entries. The total number of spinlocks protecting a table can be expressed as:

```
(1031/address lock spinlock ratio) +1
```

Although it is possible to lower spinlock contention by setting this to the lowest value of 1. In reality this provides minimal performance advantage and is wasteful of other memory resources. This is a comprehensive parameter and should never be adjusted by mere mortals.

configuration file

This parameter indicates the name of the configuration file currently in use. This should not be manually adjusted. This is a comprehensive parameter.

deadlock checking period

Deadlocking is a situation where two processes put themselves in position where neither can proceed because of locks that they hold and can't release until some other resource is freed up. These processes would sit in this uncomfortable position forever except that they occasionally look around to see if this is the case and initiate a resolution process if this is detected. The process of detecting deadlocks is pure overhead and can be quite intensive depending on the number of locks in use. The frequency of this check is determined by this parameter, and the default is 500 milliseconds. Setting this to a larger value may provide some benefits in systems that encounter few deadlocks in the normal course of events. Setting this for more frequent checks will enable resources to be freed up faster and allow processes better throughput in applications with a higher frequency of deadlocks. For most applications this parameter should not be adjusted. A server restart will be required to make any changes effective.

deadlock retries

Once a deadlock condition exists and has been detected, the newest transaction is chosen as the deadlock victim. The remaining transaction will try several times to reacquire the lock that it was waiting for. The number of times that this is attempted before the transaction is terminated is determined by this parameter. The default value is 5. This is an intermediate level parameter.

event buffers per engine

The SQL Server engine records event information that can be reported to the Sybase SQL Server Monitor product. The default value is 100. If this parameter is set to low, event information may be overridden before the SQL Server Monitor can record it. If you are using the SQL Server Monitor product, then setting this to a higher value will increase performance and system efficiency. The correct value will change depending on the number of engines in the system and the amount of activity. Each event buffer will require 100 bytes of memory. It would be common to set this value to 2000 or more for general monitoring and even as high as 20000 depending on system activity. If you are not doing event monitoring, then set this parameter to a value of 1. Changing this parameter will require a system restart. This is a comprehensive level parameter.

freelock transfer block size

SQL Server uses 2 sets of internal structures to determine whether a lock is available. There is a set of freelock structures associated with each engine and a set of structures used globally by the server. Each engine accumulates lock structures from the global pool until it reaches its maximum level. As locks are released they are returned to the global list in blocks. The value of this parameter determines how many locks are returned to the global pool with each such transfer. The default value is 30. This value is dynamic and can be changed on the fly. Making this value larger reduces the amount of overhead associated with this process. It also increases the risk that the server will run out of global locks. Smaller values increase the overhead and can increase contention for the global freelock table.

housekeeper free write percent

This parameter sets the percentage amount that the housekeeper task is allowed to increase the normal database write activity. Under System XI the housekeeper task can write additional cached pages to disk when there is CPU idle time available. This, in turn, reduces the amount of buffer washing that's associated with the regular cache write and checkpoint cycle. The default is set to 1, which improves CPU performance in most systems and reduces recovery activity. Setting this value to 0 disables the housekeeper process. A setting of 100 forces the housekeeper to work continuously. Lightly loaded systems may benefit from slight increases in this parameter. This is a dynamic intermediate parameter.

identity grab size

This is a dynamic and intermediate level parameter that determines the number of contiguous numbers that can be inserted into a table with IDENTITY data types. The default value is 1. If your application likes you to have contiguous numbers, this should be set to a high value.

lock promotion HWM

This is a dynamic and intermediate level parameter that allows the system administrator, in combination with the "lock promotion LWM," to affect page lock to table lock permutation behavior. This value is server wide requiring some compromise. The default is 200, requiring a user to obtain 200 page locks on a server before becoming eligible to obtain a table lock. The HWM abbreviation stands for "High Water Mark."

lock promotion LWM

This is the low water mark for page locks to be escalated to table locks. Below this value the SQL Server will never attempt to escalate to a table lock. This is still a server wide parameter, and it is dynamic in nature so it can be changed on the fly. This parameter is viewable on the fly. The default setting of 200 is probably fine for almost all applications. It is probably more appropriate to spend time tuning the lock behavior for specific tables using the sp_setpglockpromote and sp_pglockremote procedures rather than changing the default for the entire server.

lock promotion PCT

This setting is used in conjunction with the "lock promotion HWM" and "lock promotion LWM" to determine table locking behavior. This sets the overall number of pages locked as a percentage of the total number of pages that will trigger an escalation from page locks to a table lock. That is, providing the number of pages locked is above the LWM and below the HWM. This is a dynamic parameter that defaults to 100. It is probably more appropriate to configure different settings on a per object basis rather than modifying the default behavior. This is viewable at an intermediate level.

max engine freelocks

This dynamic parameter sets the largest number of freelocks that each engine in a multi-engine configuration can acquire from the global freelist. This is specified as a percentage of the total number of locks. This determines the total number of locks available for the engine freelock lists. This is divided by the number of engines to determine how many are available per engine. Once this number is reached the engine will start returning freelocks to the global freelock list. The default value is 10. Setting this number to high can cause a depletion of the global freelist and cause application to fail because freelocks were unavailable. Setting your display level to comprehensive will allow you to view this parameter.

o/s async i/o enabled

This is a read-only parameter viewable at the comprehensive level. This indicates a value of 1 if the operating system has been configured to support asynchronous i/o.

o/s file descriptors

This is a read-only parameter that indicates the operating system setting for maximum file descriptors per process. If this parameter is configurable at the O/S level then it should be set to its maximum value. Do not try to set this SQL Server parameter manually.

page lock spinlock ratio

This is a static parameter viewable at the comprehensive level. It indicates the number of spinlocks allocated to protect the page locking hash table. These resources are only used in multi-engine configurations. The number of spinlocks available is determined by the formula.

```
(1031/page lock spinlock ratio value) +1
```

Unless you're a SQL Server god involved in benchmarking applications for the NSA, you should not adjust this parameter from the default value of 100.

page utilization percent

Setting values for this parameter determines the mechanism the SQL Server will use to allocate new pages. If set to a value of 100 during the page allocation request, the SQL Server will search through all of the objects OAM pages to find unused pages. If that search is unsuccessful, then a new extent is allocated. If this is set to any other value the SQL Server will compare the number of unused pages to the number of total pages and only search the OAM pages if this ratio is below the value of this threshold.

This can speed up allocation by allocating a new extent faster rather than searching the OAM pages. This can also be wasteful of disk space allowing unused pages to exist within objects. This is a dynamic parameter so it can be changed temporarily for some operations and later changed back. The BCP utility ignores this parameter and always allocates space with new extents.

partition groups

This is a static parameter with a default value of 1024. This determines how many partition groups to allocate. These objects are internal structures that control access to individual partition tables. Each partition group has 16 partition caches. Tables with fewer than 16 partitions waste some of the available cache space. Tables with more require multiple groups. These structures are allocated when the table partitions are created or the first time the table is accessed after a restart.

partition spinlock ratio

The default is 10 for this static parameter. This is only viewable at the comprehensive level. The partition spinlocks help coordinate access to table partition caches in a multi-engine configuration. This ratio determines how many cache spaces are protected by each spinlock. Do not change the default value of this parameter unless you're pretty sure you know more about computers than all the software engineers at Sybase put together. (Or they tell you to!)

size of auto identity column

This sets the precision of the IDENTITY column created in tables that are created when the "auto identity" database option is enabled. The default value is 10, and this should be sufficient more most applications. This is an intermediate parameter that can be modified on the fly.

table lock spinlock ratio

This is a static parameter viewable at the comprehensive level. It indicates the number of spinlocks allocated to protect the table locking hash table. These resources are only used in multi-engine configurations. The number of spinlocks available is determined by the formula.

```
(101/page lock spinlock ratio value) +1
```

Unless you're a SQL Server guru involved in benchmarking applications for NASA, you should not adjust this parameter from the default value of 20.

total data cache size

This parameter is viewable at the basic level and is calculated for display purposes only. You should not attempt to set this value manually. The amount of total memory and internal structures you assign will affect this parameter.

user log cache size

The SQL Server assigns a cache buffer to each user process to hold log records prior to updating the database cache. This reduces log contention and makes more efficient use of the resource. When the user log cache is full, it is flushed to the database log. This should be set no larger than the size of the smallest log allocation in the system, and ideally would be just large enough to hold the largest transaction. Setting this value to high can cause contention for the protective spinlocks. The default value is 2048 and is acceptable for most applications.

user log cache spinlock ratio

In a multi-engine configuration, this parameter determines the total number of spinlocks that are available to control access to the user log cache buffers. The default value is 20, and you should not try to change this at home.

Users, groups, and permissions

Okay, what's worse than having your Mother-in-law come stay with you for a week while her house is fumigated? Give up? How about a whole day interrogation by the site security officer and the I.T. auditor? It just gives me the willies thinking about it. If you're like most healthy, normal human beings, you could skip this experience and not feel that your life lacked in richness. The individuals who take up these roles in organizations are sometimes the kids that the schoolyard bullies picked on, and they are now out for revenge on society. Not that I harbor any resentment or have any personal knowledge. I'm just speculating, you understand.

As with any information technology, security is not something that can be carelessly added as an afterthought to a SQL Server installation. Security starts with careful planning, consistent implementation, and careful review. The SQL Server incorporates a range of security features that can be implemented within an application.

The most basic security starts with establishing individual access to the SQL Server and the underlying data that it contains. With any implementation there are trade-offs to be made between the level of security that is maintained and the administration effort required to provide the ongoing support. The more rigorous and finely tailored the security scheme the more administration it will require. The challenge is to find the right balance for each organization. Once this challenge is met, it's appropriate to ensure that the security program is administered in a consistent fashion. The system will only be as secure as the weakest link in the chain. This is particularly true in networked client server environments. These systems often require clusters of servers and workstations to function as a cohesive unit. There are explicit and implicit trust relationships between these units. A security hole or inconsistency in one leaves the entire group vulnerable.

The first decision the administrator must make is how SQL Server users will be identified to the system. It would be possible for all the clients to sign on to the system as the "sa" account. Possible, but definitely not recommended. The "sa" account is one of the user ids that exists automatically when the server is created and has god-like privileges in the SQL Server environment. Allowing all users access at this level is courting disaster. Even worse, when the disaster occurs (and it will) you won't know which "sa" did the deed. Most administrators create user logins that do not contain these powers for the mere mortals and reserve the "sa" account for themselves. Once again, you can create a single SQL Server login account that every user uses when accessing data in the SQL Server. While this will definitely cut down on administration and clutter, it probably does not allow for adequate protection and auditing of the database system. As a rule most organizations insist that each SQL Server user have a specific individually identifiable user login name to the SQL Server. In other words, no two people will use the same name when they use the SQL Server. This ensures that appropriate permissions can be granted for each person based on their need for access, and it allows changes and activities to be traced back to the specific individual. It's a good idea again to determine a naming convention for user ids prior to implementation to ensure that the system is administered consistently. For instance, it's an invitation for frustration to have one administrator creating ids as last name followed by first initial and another doing the opposite. There are informal groups out there who seem to think "Bob" makes a perfectly good login name. You'd be surprised at the near fist fights that erupt when a new "Bob" joins the group and asserts his rights to the definitive user id. Make your user names simple, but sufficient to guarantee that each user can be unique.

Once you've determined that you're going to create a login id for each user, and you've determined an appropriate naming standard, you can proceed through the mechanics of adding the user to the SQL Server.

There are really three levels of user security in the SQL Server environment. The first is the ability to login to the server itself. While a user may be able to login to a server, this in itself does not allow access to the information contained within. The second level of security is the database level. Each user must be granted specific access to each database that they require. Having been added to a database, the user may still have no specific access to any of the data contained within the database environment. Each user must then be granted access to the specific objects such as tables, views, and stored procedures contained within the database.

In order to satisfy the first security hurdle the user is added as a SQL Server login using the sp_addlogin procedure.

```
sp_addlogin loginame, passwd [,  defdb]
[, deflanguage [, fullname]]]
```

This procedure can only be executed by a user who's been designated as a "System Security Officer." I'll cover this in more detail later. For now, suffice it to say that the "sa" account has this privilege by default. The first parameter is required and is used to specify the name that the user will use to sign in to the SQL Server. This is the short identifier that uniquely identifies the user. This is followed by the initial user password. This is also a mandatory field requiring each account be setup with a password. It may be tempting to use the same password for each user account created. Resist. Of course the users are able to and should change their passwords later. This policy can be enforced by setting the automatic expiry interval. Passwords can consist of any sequence of letters, numbers, or symbols in the SQL Server character set. The only requirement is that is must be at least 6 characters long. Each user created can be assigned to a database where they will be automatically placed after signing into the system. This is identified as the "defdb" parameter. If this is not specified, then the default location will be the MASTER database. Whichever database it is, the user must also be added as a user in this database before the login can be successful.

The "deflanguage" identifies the language module to be used for this account. This language must have previously been set up within the SQL Server to be effective. The last parameter is more or less a comment field, but has in most installations been used to hold the string containing the users complete name. If some parameters are omitted then the word "null" can be substituted in the command to allow the SQL Server to default the value if possible.

```
Example
sp_addlogin jsmith, "french1"
sp_addlogin jsmith2, "monday", null, null,
"Jim Smith"
```

Presuming the user has now been successfully added as a login id to the server the next step is for the system administrator or database owner to add the user to a specific database. This is accomplished using the sp_adduser procedure.

```
sp_adduser loginame [, name_in_db [,
grpname]]
```

This is issued from within the database that the user is being added to. The only required parameter is the "loginame" which, of course, is the unique name that was used as the first parameter to the sp_addlogin procedure. The user can be identified as another name within the database if desired. Of course, that's if your desire is to confuse yourself and your users. It is generally best if the "name_in_db" parameter is allowed to default to the login name. The user can also be added to a group that may simplify some aspects of security implementation. In fact, each user added will automatically be included in the group "PUBLIC." The database owner can establish other group names and a user can be assigned to one of these groups. Once again, if you choose not to specify a parameter, you can fill in a value of "null" to indicate this.

```
Example
sp_adduser jsmith1
sp_adduser jssmith2, null, engineers
```

Each database that is created automatically has a special user added to it. This is identified as the moniker "dbo" which of course stands for "Database Owner." This user within the database has special access to all of the objects within the database. They have the ability to create or remove database objects and control security among other things.

The system administrator is automatically the dbo within any database. Other users can be set up with this privilege through other mechanisms. There is another special user that can be established by the administrator or dbo. This is the "guest" id. If this user is added to a database any user with a valid SQL Server login can obtain access to the database information as this guest user.

Most administrators limit this access to allow only read access. The SQL Server can still track individual actions through the audit facility but it does become more cumbersome. The guest user, when added, is automatically a member of the "public" group, so it may be desirable to set the guest id permissions specifically to ensure that no unexpected access is obtained.

Within a database, the dbo or administrator can create any number of named groups. These serve as security containers that database users are assigned to simplify the security administration. Security can be granted or revoked from these groups and users assigned to the appropriate group. This saves having to grant and revoke privileges to each individual and helps ensure consistency. The only significant issue to be aware of is that a user in a database can only be assigned to one group. This is in addition to the fact that each user will always be in the group "public" as well. Groups are added to a database using the sp_addgroup routine.

```
sp_addgroup groupname
```

The groupname parameter must be unique in each database and the command must be issued within the targeted database. The group must previously have been created before a user can be added to it. If users are assigned individual permissions using the grant and revoke commands these permissions will override any permissions obtained by virtue of group membership.

Another way to extend user permissions and access within the SQL Server is using aliases. Using this feature, a user within a database can assume the identity of another already valid user, and by extension, their privileges. This is commonly used to allow many users within a SQL Server to function as the dbo user within a database. The individual user is not added to the database, but their id is aliased to an existing user. In this case, dbo. When the user attempts to access the database, their permissions are validated and for all practical purposes they become the aliased user. Each login id can only be aliased to one user in each system database. There is no limit to the number of logins that can be aliased to each database user. As permissions are granted to the database user, these are automatically assumed by all logins that are aliased to that id. Aliases are established using the sp_addalias procedure.

```
sp_addalias loginame, name_in_db
```

Once a user is properly defined with a unique SQL Server login id and added to the relevant databases and groups, the next step is object security. Access to specific objects is controlled by granting or revoking access to them. The types of access that a user might have are determined by the type of object involved. (See table 8.1)

TABLE 8.1 **Access rights by object type**

Object	Access
Table	Select, insert, delete, update, references
View	Select, insert, delete, update, references
Column	Select, update, references
Stored Procedure	Execute

Each of these object permissions can be specified for each object and for each individual user. This provides a high level of granularity to the security system. When mixed with other techniques such as object views and stored procedures the SQL Server security system can be quite powerful.

In addition to the object access permissions, the database owner can delegate permission to create new objects in the database. The create object permissions can be granted separately for each object type including databases, defaults, procedures, rules, tables, and views. Again, each permission for each object type for each user. Once a user has created an object, s/he can in turn grant object access rights to it to other users.

The statement for allowing access to objects is the "grant" command.

```
grant {all [privileges]|  permission_list}
on { table_name [(column_list )]
    | view_name[(column_list)]
    | stored_procedure_name}
to {public | name_list |  role_name}
[with grant option]
```

With this command, the grant statement is followed by the list of specific access privileges that are being authorized and then followed by the specific object or object portion affected by this statement. The types of permissions named must match the object type. For instance it makes no sense to grant "execute" permission on a view. This will generate an error.

If the owner wishes to delegate all access permissions, this can be done in short form by using the keyword "all" as the permission list. Once the permissions and objects are identified the command continues to specify which users or groups are obtaining this permission. If the keyword public is used, these permissions are granted to all users in the database. When used with the "grant" option, the command allows the named users to propagate their permissions to other users using the grant syntax.

The other form of the grant command is used to assign the create object permissions.

```
grant {all [privileges] |  command_list}
to {public | name_list |  role_name}
```

This version is similar and simpler than the object access syntax. Again, the grant command is followed by the list of privileges being granted and then the list of users this applies to. The keywords "all" and "public" are valid to simplify granting broad permissions to the whole user community.

```
Examples
grant insert, delete on titles to mary, sales

grant execute on add_data to engineering

grant select, update, delete on authors to
aubrey with grant option

grant create table, create database to mary,
john

grant create table, create view to public
```

For what the advice is worth, I recommend avoiding granting permissions at the individual user level. This becomes tedious to maintain, and it becomes much easier for errors and holes to creep into the security architecture. The first level I recommend establishing is a base level of access that applies to all valid users in the database.

Let's say, for example, you determine that all valid users in your database will be granted select only to the views within the database. The grant select statement is run for every view in the database to public. This then provides a level of read-only access to support decision support applications with query tools such as Microsoft Access. Data changes are enabled via an application front end.

Each of the application users is assigned to a security group depending on their job function. Each of these groups is granted additional insert, delete, and update access to the required views and stored procedures. No access is granted to the underlying tables and all application data updates are done via stored procedures. As application users are setup in the system the security officer only needs to assign the user to the appropriate group and rest assured that the appropriate security rules are in place.

As you may have guessed there is a mechanism to remove access. This is accomplished using the "revoke" command. This command looks and functions much like the grant command. The revoke keyword is followed by the list of object access or create permissions being retracted and the users to which this applies.

```
revoke [grant option for]
{all [privileges] |  permission_list}
on { table_name [(column_list )]
    | view_name [(column_list )]
    | stored_procedure_name}
from {public | name_list |  role_name}
[cascade]
```

The revoke command can also cancel out any permissions that were obtained through the extended use of the "with grant option." When permissions are revoked with "cascade," those permissions are also revoked from all users who were subsequently granted access by the original target. The grant option itself can be selectively removed without harming any of the existing other privileges by revoking only the "grant option" privileges.

```
revoke {all [privileges] |  command_list}
from {public | name_list |  role_names}
```

Object create permissions are removed in a similar manner by revoking the named commands from the provided list of users.

Again, as a hint, I recommend that administrators and developers keep grant and revoke permission scripts in external files that can quickly be reapplied or audited as required.

Having covered the basic issues and techniques around SQL Server logins, database users, and object permissions, you now have a pretty solid grounding in the fundamentals of SQL Server security. The keeners in the crowd may have noticed that I skipped over any explanation around the "role names" parameter in the grant and revoke statements. The role capability is the final piece of securing your SQL Server environment. Within the SQL Server there is one additional layer of optional security checking that can be used. This involves the use of "roles" within the SQL Server. The System administrator account (sa) has a high level of access to the SQL Server and its data and operations.

In the past, almost all of the maintenance functions required to keep the SQL Server high and dry required the use of the "sa" account. When multiple individuals are responsible for various services or aspects of the system, the administrator account no longer provides accountability to a specific individual.

In addition, all of the folks providing these services were granted complete unrestricted access to rape and pillage the entire landscape. It would be more prudent to only allow them access to the specific functions required to do their jobs.

The role capability of the Sybase SQL Server provides a mechanism to provide both accountability and granularity of access. In some scenarios this lends itself naturally to promoting separation of duties and improving the overall control environment in the SQL Server. This is a key requirement for large commercial systems.

SQL Server provides three distinct roles that encompass various job functions.

- System Administrator
- System Security Officer
- Operator

The System Administrator is expected to be responsible for:

- installing the SQL Server
- managing disk storage
- granting permissions to SQL Server users
- Maintaining the SQL Server logins
- Monitoring the SQL Server automatic recovery procedure
- Diagnosing system problems
- Tuning the system for optimum performance
- Creating and granting ownership of user databases
- Granting and revoking the System Administrator role
- Setting up groups to assist in administering security

The System administrator is automatically the database owner in all the SQL Server databases and has full access to every object in the system.

The System Security Officer is responsible for the general health and maintenance of the security features in the system. This includes:

- Creating server login accounts
- Granting and revoking the system security and operator roles
- Resetting user passwords
- Establishing the system wide password expiry interval
- Maintaining the audit system and reviewing the records

The security officer has access to all databases but the access is restricted to regular user level.

The Operator has access to the system to perform required backup and recovery operations on the data, but not necessarily any access to look at or modify any information.

As these are job functions that provide access to certain capabilities they can be assigned to potentially any existing user in the system. These users can then function with a high level of access, but still be accountable to their own identities. The roles are not exclusive, and an individual account may be assigned multiple duties.

In some circumstances all three roles are assigned to a single individual who provides roughly the same service level that logging in as "sa" could provide. The assignment and maintenance of roles to individual users is administered with the sp_role procedure.

```
sp_role {"grant" | "revoke"},
{sa_role | sso_role | oper_role}, loginame
```

The first parameter to the command is whether this role is being granted or revoked. Note that this description must be provided inside of quotes. Then the type of role being applied is described, and finally the login id that this applies to. Each role must be assigned with a separate command. If a user is being granted all the roles then three invocations of the sp_role procedure will be required.

Once the security and permission structure for your SQL Server is established you will sometimes wish to inquire what permissions and users privileges have been established. The most useful command for inquiring about users is the sp_displaylogin command.

```
sp_displaylogin [loginame]
```

When used without the optional loginame parameter the command will display information regarding your own id. If the issuing id is a security officer or system administrator then information regarding other users can be displayed by specifying them. Permissions that have been granted to a specific objects or users can be identified by using the sp_helprotect procedure.

```
sp_helprotect [name [, username [, "grant"]]]
```

The name provided can be any database object or user. Without any parameters the procedure returns all permissions in the database. The use of the name and username parameters narrows the criteria down to a specific user, item, or combination of these. The "grant" option identifies permissions that were enabled as a result of the "with grant" option on an original grant command.

Defining and using dump devices

Okay, so you've carefully constructed a really nice and reliable SQL Server. You've defined devices, added databases, established and implemented a security policy, and you're ready for real data. Right? Well, not quite. Before you can safely allow users and application developers to use your system, you need to make sure that you can cover their assets with a robust backup and recovery plan.

I think an engineer once made the comment, "If architects built buildings the same way programmers built systems, civilization would have been wiped out by the first woodpecker." The comment is a strong indictment of the "plan for the best" attitude of many computer types.

Of course, you're much smarter and more experienced than that, not to mention strongly motivated to plan in advance for the day when the wheels come off. It turns out that SQL Server is well equipped to assist you in protecting your company's information. The larger issue is how to plan and use these SQL Server features appropriately.

In order to properly understand the backup and recovery capabilities of the SQL Server, you will need to understand more of the inner workings of the SQL Server. The first insight to grasp is that SQL Server always, always, always updates information in two locations. Of course, the data itself gets updated when a user or application provides the proper instructions. In addition, the SQL Server writes a record of the changes it is making to the database log.

If for some reason a temporary problem develops in the database, the SQL Server can automatically update the database data using the information stored in the database log. So each database update command changes both the data and the log information.

In fact, SQL Server uses "write ahead" logging mechanism that updates the log before the information is reflected in the data. Performing the operations in this order ensures that the log has the most current information and can be used in all situations to bring the actual data values up to date.

Understanding that the database log is used to ensure database integrity and is used concurrently with the database information, explains why Sybase recommends that the data and log devices be located on physically separate devices. It becomes important from an integrity perspective to prevent the event that damages the data from affecting the log.

SQL Server cannot complete a transaction until both the data and log operations are completed. If these must be processed in a serial fashion, waiting for the physical device to respond, this is less efficient than allowing the operations to proceed in parallel to separate devices.

The log also performs a critical role in ensuring transaction integrity where multiple database operations must be treated as a single complete entity. If any individual operation fails, all of the already completed ones must be reversed to "rollback" the entire transaction. The information stored in the database logs is used to reverse the database entries that have been completed. SQL Server is designed specifically to operate efficiently and effectively in online processing applications such as financial, stock broker, or credit approval applications. Entries made by individual users need to be guaranteed to complete properly and high levels of system availability are required.

The SQL Server backup and recovery mechanisms are designed to operate in this environment. As a result, they operate on both the data and log in complementary fashions. In addition, they operate concurrently with the other regular system functions. This means that the system does not need to be shut down or taken off-line to perform a backup. The system administrator does need to plan carefully and use the SQL Server features properly to maintain the overall system integrity.

In order to safely preserve the information in a database, the administrator or operator must issue a dump command to export the information.

```
dump database database_name
to stripe_device [ at backup_server_name ]
     [density = density_value,
      blocksize = number_bytes,
      capacity = number_kilobytes,
      dumpvolume = volume_name,
      file = file_name]
[with {
      density = density_value,
      blocksize = number_bytes,
      capacity = number_kilobytes,
      dumpvolume = volume_name,
      file = file_name,
      [dismount | nodismount],
      [nounload | unload],
      retaindays = number_days,
      [noinit | init],
      notify = {client | operator_console}
      }]]
```

Although the command appears daunting in practice, its operation is usually quite simple. The essence of the command is the instruction to dump the contents of a specific database to the device named in the command.

```
dump database pubs to "/dev/rmt0"
```

Once complete, the entire contents of this database are safely exported to the external device in a format that facilitates the reloading of the entire structure. Additional parameters to the command allow the device specifications to be further refined including blocksize and other relevant parameters.

In fact, multiple devices can be specified using the "stripe on" specification and accept database data streamed to them in parallel. This allows the backup to complete much faster. For large databases, this is critical to being able to perform the backup in a reasonable amount of time. The SQL Server works reliably with most common tape units. Overriding the default SQL Server information obtained from the operating system for capacity, density, or blocksize is not recommended.

I'm sorry to be judgmental here, but if the only way you can make your tape device work is to override the SQL Server parameters, then I suggest it's time to change tape drives. You can specify the volume name recorded in the tape label with the volume parameter. SQL Server checks this label before loading data from a backup to ensure that the correct tape is at the ready.

The dump file created has a default name that consists of the last 7 characters of the database name, a 2-digit year number, a 3-digit julian date, and the number of seconds since midnight. By all means use the default name. You can override the default naming using the file = option, but for all realistic purposes this is likely to become confusing.

SQL Server allows considerable flexibility in naming the dump device. In previous incarnations the dump device had to be pre-defined to the system as a specific dump device. This proved to be inconvenient on many occasions. By allowing the direct specification of the device name in the dump command, additional areas of flexibility were opened up.

The device name can be provided as a parameter to a stored procedure that performs the actual dump operation as part of an overall process. Besides specifying a physical device, such as a tape drive to store the data, the operator can specify an operating system file name.

Most installations also expend considerable systems management effort to backup and recover operating system files. One of my favorite techniques for improving overall backup performance is to coordinate these backup activities between the database and the operating system. This involves creating a two-tier backup and recovery system. The technique for this involves performing all of the immediate SQL Server database dumps to an operating system file. Then, trust the operating system file backup to make a copy of this information to tape later. This requires keeping enough iterations on disk to ensure that the tape system has had sufficient time to make good copies on tape. It can also require a significant buffer of available operating system disk space to use.

If for some reason the tape system is unavailable, you need to have sufficient room available to continue until these can be safely stored away on tape. Once a dump file is written to disk, it can be compressed for more compact storage as long as you remember to uncompress prior to recovering the file. After all, disk is cheap.

By saving the database backups to disk first, you can gain some significant performance advantages. Avoiding the mechanical overhead of working with the tape device provides a many times speed improvement. In addition, besides the fact that writing to disk is fundamentally faster than writing to tape, the file system caching allows a significant benefit as well.

By speeding up the backup process, more room is provided in the operation for real application work. Still, that's not the most important benefit. The real payback occurs when it is time to do a recovery. The same speed advantages work in reverse, dramatically decreasing the time required to put a system back into operation. I recommend keeping at least two generations of backup immediately available on disk. As a general rule, if a recovery is required, the most recent backup is used. If an older version is required, it is first loaded from tape to disk and then recovered into the database.

The SQL Server mechanism for performing backups is the Sybase backup server. This is included with the distribution of the SQL Server itself, but it is a separate executable and in fact a whole extra server that must be started and stopped as part of the enterprise. This is in reality a Sybase Open Server product that exchanges data with the SQL Server. Once the dump is initiated by the SQL Server, the backup server product handles the physical interaction between the SQL Server and the operating system.

A single backup server can expedite backup requests from a number of SQL Servers simultaneously. It can interact with up to 32 separate operating system devices per dump command. This server product is optimized to perform this process and in practice, it performs these tasks extremely well. This also provides a standardized way for third party backup products to interact with the SQL Server. The only visible reminder of this interaction within the SQL Server itself is the site handler task that is invoked as if it were any other remote SQL Server.

The backup server itself can be a remote server. A single backup server instance could handle all of the backup tasks for an entire SQL Server enterprise. This has some administrative and architectural benefits, but it is likely to play havoc with the network so it's generally been avoided. For most installations a single backup server per physical machine works best.

The default name for the backup server is "SYB_BACKUP." This name can be changed to anything an administrator likes providing an appropriate entry is made in the INTERFACES file. The correct server name will also need to be added as a remote server in each SQL Server using the sp_addserver procedure.

As a caution, the backup server version and type should match the SQL Server. If the SQL Server is upgraded, certainly the backup server should be upgraded as well. If your site is running multiple versions of SQL Server, you will also require multiple active backup servers to ensure proper dump and load operation.

The same general process and description apply equally to dumping transaction logs as well as entire databases. Dumping the transaction log is an incremental backup of the database changes that have occurred since the last transaction dump. The dump transaction command places a marker in the database log indicating to what point it has already saved information. The dump command syntax is modified to reflect that the actual command issued is "dump transaction" as opposed to "dump database," but all the other device options are the same.

In addition, certain dump operations on transaction logs do not require specifying a dump device. This is because they do not actually export any information.

```
dump transaction pubs with truncate_only
```

This removes the inactive portion of the log just like a regular dump does, but the information is not saved for later recovery. This, like a regular dump transaction command, writes a log record indicating the log pages dumped. As this activity is a logged operation, it will not be allowed to proceed if the database log is already filled to capacity. If this occurs, another dump transaction option may be useful.

```
Example
dump transaction pubs2 with no_log
```

This command removes the inactive log records but makes no record in the log of what information has been successfully completed. This effectively renders this database log useless for any recovery purposes. The administrator now needs to complete a full database dump before he or she can sleep well.

The more normal course of events is to dump the database transaction logs on a regular schedule. This ensures that no information is misplaced and that these logs can be used to bring the database system up to almost current levels.

```
dump transaction pubs2 to tapedump1
```

The combination of transaction and database dumps is organized in a manner that fully protects the information. An administrator may choose to perform full database dumps at 6 AM and 6 PM with incremental transaction dumps every 2 hours during the day. This ensures that, as a worst case scenario, the database can be returned to a status no older than 2 hours.

The need for data integrity and protection is weighed against the performance requirements and the overhead associated with the dump activity. The dump process itself works on a page-by-page basis. Only the page being currently dumped is locked from use. This allows the dump transaction and dump database commands to process while other operations are in progress.

If the data segment for a database becomes corrupt, it may still be possible to obtain a complete copy of the transaction log that can be applied as part of the recovery. This allows the administrator to recover the system to the point just prior to the failure. The option to obtain a copy to the transaction log in this situation is the "no_truncate" option.

```
dump transaction pubs2 to "/dev/rmt0"
with no_truncate
```

In order for this feature to work, the logsegment of the database must reside on a separate device than the data. Using this mechanism allows full recovery to within whatever time period is specified for the "checkpoint interval" or recovery time. For most systems the default value is 5 minutes. So it should be possible in most circumstances to recover user data to within 5 minutes of the failure.

I will return to the dump and recovery process in a moment.

First, it will be beneficial to more fully understand the database checkpointing process. In the process description to this point, the implicit assumption is that all the relevant information is properly and securely written to disk. Although that generalization is true for the most part, the SQL Server mechanism is more complex than that.

In order to provide the maximum performance possible, the SQL Server works very hard to avoid actually having to perform physical read or write operations to disk. These activities rely on the speed of the mechanical hardware which is many times slower than could be achieved by the system itself. In order to avoid physical disk activity, the SQL Server performs operations in memory as much as possible and only occasionally performs physical disk operations.

This process of using system memory is called caching. Database and log pages are retrieved to memory when they are first encountered or required. The changes are then written to these copies in memory. The SQL Server will, on a periodic basis, examine its memory for pages that have been modified and update the same information on the physical disks. This process of writing dirty cache pages to disk is called a checkpoint. The checkpoint interval is a significant factor in determining how long it will take to recover and reconcile each database when the system is started.

During the SQL Server start-up, each database and log are examined. If there are completed transactions in the log that need to be reflected in the data, these transactions are applied. If there are entries in the data for transactions that have not completed, the logged transactions are rolled back. The checkpoint interval determines how current the data and log is kept, and therefore, how long the recovery process will take for each database. The checkpoint process wakes up every minute or so and determines for each database if sufficient work exists to run the checkpoint process.

This automatic system checkpoint behavior can be extended by manually entering the "checkpoint" command in a database. This forces a manual checkpoint and physical update of all data and log pages. This is a required operation when the database options are changed. This is rarely required at any other time.

The system will automatically attempt to checkpoint all databases prior to performing a system shutdown. When the "shutdown with nowait" option is requested, the system does not perform this checkpoint process prior to quitting. This may result in a longer start-up time while the data and log records are reconciled.

New with SQL Server System XI is the "housekeeper" process. This process augments the automatic checkpoint process by stealing unused SQL Server processing cycles to write dirty pages to disk. If the SQL Server has idle cycles the housekeeper wakes up and uses these cycles to review the cache buffers for dirty pages.

If a dirty page is found, it is physically updated. If all the cache buffers are processed, the housekeeper will notify the checkpoint process and an extra checkpoint is run. As the dirty pages are already written to disk, this is a quick process. This ensures that the actual recovery interval is as short as possible. If the system is heavily loaded, the housekeeper is less active and the actual checkpoint process becomes more noticeable in regular system operations.

If the application does not make use of the transaction log information, the database will often be flagged to include the "trunc log on chkpt" option. The transaction log is automatically truncated after every automatic checkpoint. This log information is therefore thrown away on a regular basis. This option is commonly used in development environments, but rarely enabled in production operation. The exception to this is on data warehouse systems. The data access in these systems is typically read-only so no data updates are expected. In these situations, there is no rigorous requirement for transaction logging. The data is, in most cases, refreshed in a batch fashion from the source systems. Properly planning full database dumps can provide appropriate coverage for these applications.

The transaction log for a database needs to be large enough to not completely fill up between transaction dumps. This size will vary depending on the frequency that transaction dumps are taken and the number of users in the system. This will also vary depending on the type of application and the amount of logging it generates. One of the potential problem areas to watch out for is the phenomenon of "long running transactions." All of the actions associated with cleaning up the transaction logs, including transaction dumps and even no_log operations, presume that all of the operations are completed. In the description of the dump transaction process, you may have noticed that only the "inactive" portion of the log is removed. This inactive portion only covers those transactions that are fully committed to the system. If the possibility remains that the transaction will be rolled back, it would be impractical to remove the information required to perform this from the log. If, for instance, the application tried to load a million rows into a table as a single transaction the database log could easily fill up suspending or terminating this process even though the administrator was diligently dumping the log.

The SQL Server wraps all operations inside transactions. There are, in fact, implicit begin and end transactions around all application and user activity. If large operations are performed, this implicit transaction behavior may create "long running transactions." Wherever possible, the application developers should take care to explicitly define appropriate transaction boundaries and sizes to ensure that log space is properly maintained.

If an administrator encounters a situation in which the log space is filled to capacity, and all attempts to dump the transaction log fail to resolve the problem, you have a transaction problem.

The recovery process for this problem is to identify the guilty process and force it to rollback and free up the log space it occupied. Identifying these problem transactions is easier in System XI than in previous SQL Server releases. The administrator can query the "syslogshold" table and determine the oldest active transaction in a database.

```
Example
use master
go
select * from syslogshold
where dbid = Database_ID
go
```

Having identified the oldest transaction, or the most likely candidate, the process can be aborted using the "kill" command by the administrator. It can take a considerable amount of time for these transactions to rollback and clear the log after being killed. In general, allow at least 15 to 20 minutes for this activity to process before embarking on an anxiety attack.

The SQL administrator may wish to examine how full the database log has become and the before and after dump status. There are several ways to determine log information, but for accurate information to be returned the database log needs to reside on a separate device than the data segments. The administrator can use the following commands to obtain log information.

```
sp_spaceused syslogs
sp_helpsegment logsegment
dbcc tablealloc(syslogs)
```

Try these options out and examine the information returned. These commands are very useful in determining the status of the database log.

The concept of having the database log fill up is a generalization of the actual SQL Server process. The SQL Server never allows the database log to fill completely. It maintains a threshold that ensures that action is taken prior to the log filling completely. This is intended to ensure that there is enough free space in the log so that the administrator can still have a dump transaction command registered in the log. In most circumstances this should allow the log free space to return to normal levels.

The level at which the SQL Server will take action to prevent the free space from falling to low is referred to as the "last chance threshold." This level is maintained automatically by the SQL Server as space is added to the transaction log. By default the SQL Server suspends all user transactions in a database once the free space drops below the "last chance threshold" level. At this point, only unlogged commands and dump commands can execute. When sufficient free space becomes available the transactions will become active again. The administrator can override the last chance level and allow user processes to continue with the lct_admin function.

```
select lct_admin("unsuspend", dbid)
```

This command should be used with extreme caution. By simply overriding the threshold, the transaction log can fill completely and only a server shutdown will be able to clear the problem. This is normally used in circumstances where the administrator identifies a long running transaction and issues a kill command on the guilty process. Then by using the lct_admin function the process is allowed to wake-up and receive the kill command. The process then performs a rollback and frees up the hostage log space.

By default, the SQL Server maintains the "last chance threshold" on all database log segments. This same facility can be used by the administrator to establish additional thresholds and corresponding actions that should occur. These thresholds can be set on any database segment, not just the log, and used to manage the amount of available free space. Multiple thresholds can be established on a database segment to implement appropriate escalation procedures. It may be appropriate to take different actions as free space falls from 50 percent to 25 percent of available space. The administrator can report on existing thresholds using the sp_helpthreshold procedure.

```
sp_helpthreshold [segname]
```

This returns information on all thresholds defined on a segment including the level at which the threshold is established and the procedure to execute when this level is crossed.

New threshold levels can be established using the sp_addthreshold procedure.

```
sp_addthreshold dbname, segname, free_space,
procname
```

This procedure identifies the database and segment to which this threshold corresponds. Then the free_space is specified in pages. The final parameter is the procedure to execute when the free space in the segment falls below the specified number of pages.

Let's say the default segment of a user database "pubs2" is 50 MB and you wish to establish a 50% threshold.

```
50 MB = 256000 pages
50% = 128000 pages

sp_addthreshold pubs2, "default", 128000,
sp_defaultproc
```

This technique can be used to add additional thresholds to the logsegment and take action before the last chance level is passed. This would hopefully allow transactions to continue without ever becoming suspended. Common types of actions might include printing messages in the errorlog and performing dump transaction commands. The SQL Server passes information to all threshold procedures including:

- database name
- segment name
- space remaining
- last chance flag

The threshold procedure can determine what action is appropriate based on the information received. Organizations would be well served by establishing default levels for thresholds and applying these universally on all database segments. There is no restriction preventing all the thresholds from calling the same procedure. Expending some effort to create a flexible threshold procedure that determines what action to take based on the supplied parameters can help standardize the SQL Server operation and improve availability. The threshold information can be modified using the sp_modifythreshold procedure.

```
sp_modifythreshold dbname, segname,
free_space
[, new_proc_name] [, new_free_space] [,
new_segname]
```

Providing the database name, segment, and existing free space level uniquely identifies the threshold being changed. Then the user can specify a different procedure to execute or a different level to move the threshold to. This threshold can be relocated to another segment if desired. Parameters that are not specified are not changed. Using the keyword "null" allows a parameter to be skipped.

```
Example
sp_modifythreshold pubs2, "default", 128000,
NULL, 100000
```

This moves the threshold in default to a higher level allowing the free space to fall below 100,000 pages before triggering. The procedure executed is not changed however.

Presuming that the administrator has taken the appropriate steps to dump the database and transaction log contents you would be in a position to implement a system recovery. The standard procedure for recovering a corrupted or damaged database is straight forward.

- Drop corrupt or damaged database.
- Recreate database using the "for load" option.
- Load the most recent database dump contents.
- Load the transaction log dumps starting with the first one after the database dump and proceed incrementally forward to the most recent file.

Damaged database can be removed using the "drop database" command or the "dbcc dbrepair" command. The create database command is the same set of statements originally used to create and alter the database. The load database command is issued for the most recent database dump command.

```
load database pubs2 from "/dev/rmt0"

load database user_data from "/data/backups/
user_data.960712"
```

This will load the database contents from the dump and proceed to initialize any unused pages in the database. You should be aware that this is a physical process that restores page images to the database. In other words, if the created database does not match in size and configuration to the database that the dump was taken from the load will fail.

Conversely, any created database that matches in size and shape to the original can be loaded from this file. The database name and even the server do not have to be the same as the original. This provides you with a mechanism to migrate or copy data from one server to another. This capability should be used with care. There may be information stored in other server databases that will be corrupted or invalid if it has specific relationships with objects in the migrated database.

After the database is loaded, the administrator or operator can restore the transaction logs to bring the server up to the closest time period. These logs must be applied in order starting with the oldest and proceeding towards the most recent.

```
load transaction user_data from "/data/
backups/user_data960712.6am"
load transaction user_data from "/data/
backups/user_data960712.10am"
load transaction user_data from "/data/
backups/user_data960712.noon"
```

Once this action is complete, presumably all of the available data is recovered. SQL Server automatically places the database in "off-line" status after a load operation. This ensures that all of the recovery operations can proceed without user interactions causing an inconsistency. After the completed loads, the database is now in a consistent state to the point that the last transaction log dump was taken. The final operation is to place the database back into service.

```
online database user_data
```

The time to complete the recovery will vary depending on the size of the database and the speed of the dump hardware. Generally speaking, the load times will take slightly longer than the dump times.

It's important that these recovery processes be implemented and tested on a regular basis. The dump files themselves need to be tested to ensure that they are sufficient to recover the system and data. Besides implementing regular dump procedures, the administrator needs to regularly verify the integrity of the database data to ensure that the database dumps are not corrupt.

The Sybase dump and load commands provide an effective system recovery mechanism. They do not, however, cover the entire spectrum of features that might be desirable in this type of facility. At least one company has introduced additional utility products to assist in managing the backup and recovery process. Datatools produces a product called "SQL Backtrack" that works with the SQL Server backup server to provide both standard backup and recovery capability, but also some additional features.

The Sybase provided utilities function at the physical level only. The administrator is required to recover the entire database and the target location must be a physical match for the recovery to work. The SQL Backtrack product provides a "logical" recovery capability that allow an administrator to recover specific objects such as tables into a database without disrupting the other information. This also allows database information to be recovered to a target location that is not a size and shape match for the original. These capabilities are in addition to providing robust physical database backup and recovery functions. Using the logical functions can depending on the objects require a substantial amount of time. Still, it's a product worth investigating.

Implementing a robust backup and recovery process for your system requires a knowledge of the underlying product features along with a knowledge of your business and application requirements. Just because you can do something does not mean you should. Choose the features that work best for your organization and implement them in standard and consistent ways. Finally, remember that these processes need to be tested before you can let your business rely on them.

Summary

This chapter has taken on the significant task of walking through the installation, structure, and administration of a Sybase Adaptive Server Enterprise environment.

If you are a developer, or only have occasional opportunity to work as sa, you might find much of this to be esoteric. But in our experience, providing Sybase dba support to large and small organizations alike, these are the key issues you are likely to encounter.

From this chapter, even an experienced administrator should have a good idea of what's new as part of the System XI architecture and a quick reference for some important, though hopefully underused commands.

CHAPTER 9

System XI Query & Data Management

In this chapter we take a down and in look at exactly how your Sybase server manages the logging of any changes to its data by a transaction. As a developer, no doubt you're most interested in how a user of your application can screw up and make your program look bad. We cover this, along with how systems administrators can change configuration variables in either SQL Server or on the box that affect transaction behavior.

Arguably, relational databases are inherently useful because of the way they allow data to be stored and queried without redundancy. What we've found is that in terms of value from the tool, this is pretty much taken for granted. Third normal form in a relational database is pretty much as inherent as using a mouse is with a GUI. You'd have to have a pretty good reason to avoid it.

The real value of a relational database engine, specifically System XI, is that it supports on-line, real-time multi-user access to data from a variety of applications. And for this, the transaction log is absolutely vital. This chapter is when we get down and in on that very topic. By the time we're done you may never be able to look at your SQL Server in the same way again.

Transactions Defined

A query is not a transaction. It's a process, yes, but for our purposes a transaction is a specific block of work which either adds, deletes, or changes objects within the database.

Notice that we referred to objects. Specifically this means tables, views, rules, devices, and so on, not just data. In a number of Sybase classes, I have run into conflicts with folks who had philosophical differences with the inclusion of Views in this context. Yes, you can under some circumstances modify a table by writing a change to a view. No, that's not a normal (nor terribly useful) thing to do. However, the creation or dropping of a view is handled through T-SQL and that SQL is part of a transaction. The same applies to rules, and so on.

Part of the reason for this is that changing meta data in the SQL Server at some level involves changing the value in a column and row of a table. No doubt you remember that an inherent feature of the relational model is that data about the server and its contents is maintained in tables exactly like user data.

To define transactions then, it's about the process rather than what is affected by the process. A transaction is a change to an object and this change is managed by SQL Server.

Rules of Engagement

By now everyone should be pretty comfortable with the concepts behind dirty reads and writes; you know, the idea that a database should not present data which is about to change to another process who is about to change it.

Of course, there are real-world applications where this is just fine from a business standpoint. People talk about how you shouldn't be able to see an airplane seat marked available while another travel agent is looking at the same seat and preparing to allocate it to some other competitive soul who had the foresight to dig out their Visa number before talking to the agent.

In that particular example the database has no requirement to tell you what data "may" be changed. The requirement is to be the first person to confirm that a seat has been bought, not be the first person to reserve the right to consider whether or not you want it, since after all, your call was answered first and you're special... .

The point is that the database has to be able to manage multiple accesses of the same data, as we all know. This is handled by locks and now is just as good a time as any to discuss that process.

Locks: What, Why & How

In Sybase there have always been four kinds of locks:

- Exclusive locks – for transactions about to write data
- Shared locks – for transactions that read data
- Intent locks – to reserve a place in the queue for an exclusive lock
- Hold locks – to block granting other shared locks in case the transaction wants to come back and change data after reading it.

Deadlocks refer to a hairstyle adopted primarily by Rastafarians...wait, those are dreadlocks. A deadlock, or deadly embrace, is not actually a kind of lock but a condition that occurs when two transactions mutually block each other from completion. More on the dreaded deadlocks later in this chapter.

Exclusive Locks

To ensure that no one takes your seat on the airplane while you're thinking about it (the ideal world again), the booking application would have to search for an available seat on the route, dates, and fare parameters. Once these are identified, the transaction is granted an exclusive lock on the data until the application decides to pass or play.

Shared Locks

While leisurely looking for available flights, the application is granted a shared lock so a bunch of folks can peruse the options. Queries are granted shared locks, though you can explicitly override this with a hold lock. Shared locks are granted to whomever comes along asking for the right to review data, which means shared locks can accumulate as new queries access the same data. Exclusive locks must wait for shared locks to complete prior to being enforced.

Intent Lock

Obviously, you don't want a transaction that changes data to be held hostage by a query that is simply looking at the data which is about to be changed. At the same time, it would hardly do to have every query bumped just because someone was about to change some data. Fairness in the workforce and all that. To arbitrate access to data, a transaction which looks to change data first tries to get an exclusive lock on the data pages. If a running select has already accessed the required page, a shared lock is already granted. At that point, the write transaction gets instead an intent lock not an exclusive lock. This says basically, fine, up to four more shared locks can be granted from this moment on, but after those complete, that's it, I get my exclusive lock. SQL Server manages this within the kernel, and you can't change it.

Hold Lock

However, what you can do is code your query so that if you can read the data, you can write the data. This means of course that absolutely everyone has to wait for your transaction to complete before they can do anything. But we'll assume that's what you want.

Page versus Row Locks

After reading some of the hoopla generated by Oracle, and to a lesser extent Microsoft, over the row locking issue, we woke up with cold and hot flashes in the middle of the night. What if we'd bought the wrong technology? How could we have been so stupid, locking an entire page? Oh no!

Let's get this thing in perspective. First, a page is basically 2k in System XI and other versions of Sybase (on all platforms except Sequent where its 4k, but there's the exception to prove the rule). A 200-byte row would allow approximately 10 rows per page (it's actually less due to internal overhead, but whatever).

When the database engines first came out, Sybase was by far the superior performer in OLTP benchmarks over Oracle. You should take from this that there is nothing intrinsically inferior or superior to row versus page locking. The engineers at Sybase decided that the time spent in calculating the exact offset for a specific row would take more time that locking the page, making the change, and releasing it.

Designing Your Transactions

Of course, the page lock does have an effect on the way you design your transactions. Naturally, the worst thing you can do is write an application that goes up against a busy database, issues a begin tran at the beginning of the day, puts hold locks on all of its queries, and then commits its work at the end of the day.

That wasn't you asking why that would be so bad was it? Just in case, the short answer is that you just made everything your application touches a single-user dataset – guaranteed to make you unpopular. And it's even worse if someone else does it to you!

The point here is that you need to write your code so that it commits its work as soon as it can. The application must be broken down into the most discrete blocks of complete work and those changes must be made as quickly as possible.

Sample Transactions

By default, each insert, update, and delete statement issued against tables in a SQL Server database is treated as a transaction. SQL Server has four main transaction control statements:

```
BEGIN TRANSACTION [name]
```

This initiates a transaction and optionally names it.

```
SAVE TRANSACTION other_name
```

This specifies a point in the transaction for partial rollback.

```
ROLLBACK TRANSACTION [name or savepoint name]
```

This reverses the changes to the savepoint named or to the beginning of the transaction if no name is provided.

```
COMMIT TRANSACTION
```

This writes the changes made within the transaction to disk, making the changes permanent.

You don't need to enter the word transaction as part of the transaction syntax; you can use tran as the short form with begin, save, rollback, and commit.

The main characteristic of a transaction is that until it has completed successfully, the database changes specified in the transaction can be rolled back. These changes are written first to the transaction log and second to the database. The process of making the changes to the affected tables themselves is known as the commit. This process is most useful when making a series of changes to multiple tables in a database. For example, here is how you would write a transaction that adds a new book and author to the pubs database:

```
use pubs

go

begin tran new_book

insert titles
     values ("PC8088","Sybase Developers Guide",
"business","null",null,null, null, null, "null",
"May 1, 1994")

insert titleauthor
     values ("416-597-9257", "PC8088")
```

```
insert authors
     values ("416-597-9257","Worden", "Daniel",
"416-597-9258","null","null","null","null",1)

commit tran
```

In this example, all the insert statements must be executed successfully or the entire set is rolled back. However, if you wanted to ensure that the first two statements executed even if the last one failed (which it would if the author already existed in pubs), you could structure the transactions like this:

```
use pubs
go

begin tran new_book

insert titles
     values ("PC8088","Sybase Developers
Guide","business","null",null,null, null, null,
"null","May 1, 1994")

insert titleauthor
     values ("1-800-387-8722", "PC8088")

save tran newbooktran

if not exists (select * from authors where au_id =
"416-597-9257")

insert authors
     values ("416-927-7887","Worden", "Daniel",
"416-555-1212","null","null","null","null",1)

else
```

```
rollback newbooktran

commit tran
```

With this modification, the title and titleauthor values are still inserted, even if the insert authors statement fails. You would generally incorporate condition testing to determine whether to roll back your changes. In this example, you are looking for the existence of an author in the table already. If not found, the values are inserted; if a row with that value for author ID already exists, the insert statement is rolled back to the savepoint. Without the save tran tran_name statement, the entire transaction would have been rolled back.

Summary

The behavior of any transaction is governed primarily by the locking mechanism of the relational database. This chapter should have helped provide a brief primer on the types and natures of locks in System XI.

Remember, when it comes to transactions – commit early and commit often!

CHAPTER 10

Tuning & Optimizing System XI

Monitoring Resource Usage

In this chapter, we take a look at the different perspectives involved in identifying and troubleshooting performance problems. In a typical development shop, there are several different technical disciplines involved in configuring and operating the database server. Frequently, a combination of these forces is needed to arrive at an appropriate balance of the workload.

One Administrators Perspective...

We know that most developers suspect their administrators of exactly this attitude...

Can't you just hear those voices? "The server's slow. The server's slow." They act like it's somehow my fault. Like I personally "niced"* their process into a peaceful afternoon slumber. They also seem to think, for some reason, that because the sign on the door is labeled "System Administrator" that I'll be delighted to stop playing Minesweeper and leap to their rescue.

I tell you, some people just have no consideration. Unfortunately, it turns out that today's occupant of the office labeled "Operations Manager" is equally as obsessed about these things. So rather than squander a perfectly good chance at a pension, I try to at least humor them. If I can respond with reasonable dispatch I can get back to Minesweeper.

The good news for me is that the cause of the problem almost always has nothing to do with any hardware or database system problem, but more likely an application problem. All I have to do is demonstrate that fact, and I can safely reassign the problem back to System Development. This leaves me free to return to my previously scheduled activities.

(*For those not used to Unix terminology, 'niced' is past tense for demoting the priority of a job relative to other server jobs.)

Problem? What Problem

Of course, the trick comes down to being able to demonstrate that the overall system is running tickety-boo. The first insight gained from studying the operations logs of ancient Peruvian administrators is that performance problems are caused because of a lack of system resources. You should meditate on this insight for a few moments. In other words, if every request to the system were able to immediately gain access to whatever it wanted there would be no waiting and therefore no performance problems – at least none that appear to occur intermittently.

So in order to demonstrate that the system is not to blame for any perceived performance problems, you must demonstrate that the system is not resource constrained and is providing access to all the system resources promptly. At the highest level, we want to ensure that sufficient CPU, memory, and disk hardware resources are available. These resources are normally measured at the Operating System level.

OS Level Checks

For Unix systems you will want to use the administrator commands such as "sar," "vmstat," "iostat," or "mpstat" to obtain overall system and operating system utilization information. In the NT world you can use the "Performance Manager" utility available under the overall Administration utilities. These allow the administrator to track and identify the utilization levels of the various hardware and operating system resources used in the system.

CPU Checks

You first want to identify any CPU conflicts or utilization problems. The key to this is determining the overall CPU utilization and utilization by individual CPU's in multi-CPU machines. If your system is running with an overall CPU utilization of less than 100% then in theory some CPU cycles should still available to be had for any application that wants them. On machines using multiple CPUs you will want to make sure that the overall load is balanced roughly equally between all of the CPUs. It does no good to have an overall utilization of, let's say, 75% with one CPU running at 50% and the second one at 100%.

In situations like this the operating system is not using the processors in a symmetric configuration. Even though the average utilization is low enough you still have a constrained CPU situation. A more telling statistic – if it's available to you – is the average length of the "run queue" parameter for each CPU. This indicates how many processes are in line waiting to get some CPU cycles. Systems that are operating efficiently will never have any processes sitting in their queues. Processes will be dispatched directly to an available processor.

You may occasionally catch a process in transition from the queue to the CPU. If the number on average or per CPU becomes higher than 3 then you potentially have a CPU issue. The more efficient the operating system and database system are, the more effective the hardware resources will become.

Memory

You also need to pay careful attention to the overall memory usage on your system. The most telling indication of memory problems is page-swapping behavior. This indicates how often the operating system is forced to save pages from memory temporarily to disk. If the system is forced to do this then some processes are being delayed waiting for their memory information to be recovered from disk. Each process running on the system is assigned the amount of memory requested from the operating system. If this total requirement is larger than the physical amount of memory on the system then page swapping will occur. The goal for most database systems should be to ensure that the system only page swaps in very rare circumstances. If your system is swapping then you need to obtain more memory for your system. This advice applies equally to Unix and NT systems.

Disk Drive Performance

The final hardware information you wish to locate is the individual disk drive usage. Even with everything else running well on the system, significant performance problems can occur if congestion occurs getting service from a particular disk. If an individual disk drive starts becoming more than 20% busy or the numbers of blocks read or written approaches the disk drive limit then you may be encountering I/O slowdowns.

It's probably a good idea to know what resource utilization is normal for your systems. This is a concept known as baselining. It's difficult to spot resource utilization problems if the only time you review the information is when a problem is reported. It's much more efficient to have a record of what normal behavior is and identify variances in that. This also helps when doing predictive analysis to forecast capacity requirements.

The same tools you use to look for problems when performance problems are reported can be used at least periodically to obtain a snapshot of normal performance information. By obtaining a suitable snapshot every week and reviewing these month by month you can start to establish a performance trend.

By being knowledgeable about the normal utilization information you can more quickly identify anomalies in the performance data when problems are reported. Correction for these types of problems typically requires a hardware response. The good news is that these tend to be very painless ways to improve performance. The bad news is that you probably will have to wait for the part delivery before the problem can be resolved.

Beyond the hardware resources there are other operating system resources that you may wish to review. The number of available asynchronous disk devices available or number of allowable outstanding i/o requests are examples of some of these. The number of open files per process is another configuration setting that can cause problems.

SQL Server Performance Factors

Moving beyond the hardware and operating system environmental issues we can then become more focused on the internal behavior of the SQL Server system. Although there are good third-party performance analysis tools available a good starting place is the built-in utilities provided with the default SQL Server system. The first performance command to become familiar with is the sp_monitor stored procedure.

sp_monitor

Once issued this procedure responds by providing the amount of database system activity that has occurred since the last time this command was executed. This usually makes the first invocation of the command useless, because you don't know the last time this command was issued. Proceed by running the command the first time and then repeat it every minute. This provides a minute-by-minute snapshot of system activity. This command reports CPU busy and CPU idle statistics. Then it continues to provide the overall I/Obusy information for the SQL Server. This is followed by the overall network statistics including packets sent and received.

Sample Output:

```
last_run                        current_run
seconds


--------------------------- ---------------------------
-----------

Apr 3 1996 3:40AM           May 31 1997 2:49PM
36587356

cpu_busy                io_busy                 idle


------------------------ ------------------------ ---
--------------------

88(75)-0%                   56(53)-0%
80894(80636)-0%
```

```
packets_received          packets_sent
packet_errors

----------------------- ----------------------- ---
---------------------

2869(1973)               2860(2399)              0(0)

total_read               total_write             total_errors
connections

------------------ ------------------- ---------------
---- -----------------

332(-404)                195(-3495)              0(0)
7(-2)
```

This command can be run several times when a performance problem is reported to identify at a high level the overall SQL Server performance. Obviously if problems are indicated with high CPU or I/O use the problem is probably an overall capacity issue over the total system. If network or packet errors are occurring then you may be encountering some network problems that are affecting performance.

The sp_monitor procedure has been a SQL Server feature starting with System 10. It represents a first generation attempt by Sybase to include some basic tuning commands. With the release of System XI Sybase provided a much more robust tool with the "solipsism" procedure. This again reports overall system performance information, but at a much more detailed level. This tool can be used reasonably effectively to measure and analyze the overall SQL Server performance. The one caveat to be aware of using this procedure is that is uses and resets internal system counters which are also used by the SQL Monitor product. This means that these tools should not be used together. If they are they can report inaccurate information.

The basic invocation for the sp_sysmon procedure is:

```
sp_sysmon interval
```

This is where interval is the measurement time in minutes from 1 to 10. When started the procedure clears all the internal counters and then waits for the specified interval to complete. At the end of that time the procedure wakes up and reads the counters to produce a query report. Once again, these snapshots can be accumulated and used to determine trends or the outcome of changing system parameters or workload. The command itself will contribute an additional 5% to system workload as a minimum. The more CPUs in the system, the more this overhead becomes. This is not minimal overhead and this command should be used somewhat sparingly so that the measurement process does not by itself become a performance problem.

The report produced by the sp_sysmon procedure needs to be reviewed as a whole. The various parameters reported with the query can be unexpectedly related. A change that affects one element to your advantage may affect another negatively. The various trade-offs need to be understood before final decisions are made. The information presented in the report is broken down into sections. Within each section different information is reported.

Often information is available in both per unit of time and per transaction. The per transaction data is very useful and accurate when you know the exact transaction mix that the unit is handling. This occurs most easily under benchmarking conditions where the workload on the server is controlled b the test environment. Having a test load available for your machine that matches your production loading is very useful when used to determine the ideal tuning configuration for your site. The ability to duplicate the exact same run each time with various settings and measure the results is ideal for producing high performing systems.

SQL Server use of CPU Resources

The first section of the report is the kernel section. This starts by identifying the specific CPU loading per SQL Server engine. If the CPU busy parameter remains higher that 90% for extended periods of time then you may wish to add an additional engine or CPU to your system. The CPU utilization reported in this utility will often vary from the same value reported at the operating system level. This reflects that they are actually reporting on slightly different values.

The sp_sysmon procedure is measuring the behavior of the SQL Server engines and not the physical CPUs. This is the opposite of the O/S description which reports physical utilization even if the SQL Server engine is merely spinning hoping for a new task to become available. The next portion of the report indicates CPU yields per Engine. This determines whether a low overall CPU utilization is an indication of the SQL Server really having enough horsepower or whether some other task at the operating system is hogging all the ponies.

If the SQL Server is voluntarily yielding the CPU back to the operating system and the overall utilization is low then your looking good. If utilization is low and there is no yielding activity your little SQL Server is being starved externally. This is followed by a section on network checking. This determines how frequently the engine performed various types of checks with the network to see if any information was available to process. The two types of checking are blocked and non-blocked. If the SQL Server is mostly idle and only occasionally receiving network data then it may be beneficial to increase the frequency of network I/O checking that is done. This may allow for faster response to queries.

If this checking is done too frequently in busy systems then this may detract from overall performance. The last section of the Kernel section is the Disk I/O section which determines how the engines behave in determining if any requested disk activity has completed. If a SQL Server process requests data from disk the request is made but the process is left sleeping until the disk data is returned. The SQL Server engine itself continues on with other activities and occasionally checks to see if any disk I/O request has completed. If it has, the sleeping process is placed back in the run queue for operation with the returned data. How frequently the system checks for returned I/O and how often it obtains something can affect the overall system throughput in multi-user situations. Tuning parameters are available to have the engines check more or less frequently depending on the actual requirements.

Task Connection and Context Switching

The next section of the report indicates the task connection and context switching behavior. The first section indicates the total number of connections established during the test interval. This may be application connections or remote connections. Unusual activity in this area may indicate poorly behaved applications that are unnecessarily requesting excess connections. The context switching behavior indicates how often and for what reason the various SQL Server engines switch between processes. Are too may physical I/Os being requested? Are the CPU intensive tasks reaching their timeslice and forced off before they can complete?

You probably want to pay close attention to the "Cache Miss" portion to determine if you may benefit from better cache management. If processes are being switched due to inability to obtain an object lock then the application behavior and locking parameters may need to be adjusted. Reviewing this data may highlight areas that are suboptimal for your particular work load. You want to review the activity in each section and ensure that you understand the implications of each section. Look for unusual patterns of activity in these numbers. Identify the highest causes of context switches and make sure that this is reasonable.

The Sybase Performance Tuning guide is a wealth of information on these topics. This will frequently result in modifications to the sp_configure system variables. to assist with disk or network behavior. It can frequently indicate aspects of poorly written application software. Tasks which voluntarily yield the CPU for context switching are able to complete all of their required work prior to reaching the time when the SQL Server will require the process to yield. This is typically a condition to a very CPU intensive workload with minimal contention. If this is the case then the administrator could consider increasing the system time slice parameter in the configuration.

The next section identifies tasks that were forced off the SQL Server engine because the requested page was not in cache and the system needs to issue a physical I/O request before this task can proceed. If the percentage of context switches identified in the "Cache Search Miss" section is large then presumably better cache tuning would yield dramatic improvements. This information should only be reviewed after the system has been running continuously for a reasonable period of time to avoid reporting inaccurate start-up information where the cache is being initially loaded.

The following section identifies tasks that were switched because they requested a disk write or a page that was being written to by another process. The SQL Server normally issues regular page write requests as asynchronous requests which do not require context switching. There are certain types of page writes that must be completed before a task will be allowed to continue. These are writes for page splits, recovery or OAM page updates. If an unusually large percentage of tasks are being switched because of page splitting then you have an excellent opportunity to optimize the index and data page layout to reduce this problem.

The SQL Server process tries to be considerate of the environment that it runs in. One of the features of this is that it avoids flooding the system I/O system during operations that request large amounts of I/O. It does this by performing the operations in batches. Where the requesting process is asked to wait until all of the outstanding batch requests can be completed. If your system is forcing processUnixes to yield the CPU as part of its "I/O pacing" algorithm and your system is not currently I/O bound you can increase the number of writes per batch and increase the overall system throughput. This is accomplished using the "dbcc tune" command. The default value is 10 but values up to 50 can be configured.

```
dbcc tune(maxwritedes,30)
```

The section on "Logical Lock Contention" identifies the number of processes that were switched out due to contention for database locks. If this is affecting system throughput the administrator needs to follow-up and review the application behavior and determine the type and identity of the resources being used and the type of locking behavior encountered. Most of these corrections need to be made within the applications or the workload mix on the system.

Address Lock Contention

Our previous discussion leads neatly into the next section on "Address Lock Contention." The SQL Server system provides internal locking on memory addresses during certain operations such as allocation page updates. If tasks are forced to yield the CPU for this type of activity then this is not a feature of the application deployment but the internal SQL server behavior. Fortunately, this is only likely to occur in extremely high-throughput environments.

Tasks that yield the SQL Server due to "Log Semaphore Contention" are being bitten by another form of internal SQL Server resource logging. Log semaphores are used to coordinate log updates between multiple SQL Server engines. As a result this only occurs in SMP environments. If this occurring then the administrator should check the "Transaction Management" section of the sp_sysmon output to determine if the "user log cache" is being effectively used. For some conditions, performance improvements can be made by reducing the number of SQL Server engines being used. If your system has a low engine utilization and the system seems to encounter a large amount of log semaphore locking then reducing the number of engines may actually yield better performance.

Tasks can be switched off the system waiting for log pages to be written to disk after committing a transaction. This information needs to be correlated with the information in the "Committed Transaction" section to obtain an accurate picture of the system behavior. Tasks will wait until the log page is full before it gets written to disk. Depending on the number of active transactions and the size of the log I/O page size the percentage of tasks in this state at any moment will change. Changing I/O size for log pages and the transaction mix in the environment will affect this type of behavior. In adjusting these values remember that the goal is overall system throughput and that certain trade-offs need to be made to accomplish this goal.

Sleeping Tasks

The next section is related to by identifying the number of tasks that were put to sleep waiting on the "Last Log Page" to be written. In this case the log page is full but the task cannot continue until this information is fully committed. This is again affected by the configured I/O size for the log. The administrator should review the "Avg # Writes per Log Page" variable to determine if the SQL Server is performing appropriately.

Modify conflicts are situations in which the SQL Server switches a task to wait for an internal lock to be released. The particular type of lock in this case is used in special circumstances to avoid high overhead types of activities. Processes require exclusive access to certain pages even though they do not modify the contents.

The I/O contention information is another example of behavior associated with internal locks used to coordinate activity between multiple engines. In this case if two engines request physical I/O from the same device then one must wait until the first one completes. This will force the task on the waiting engine to yield. Adding devices and better table distribution may help reduce this type of contention. Once again this can indicate situations where adding engines to the system can adversely affect performance.

Task switching for "Network Packet" received indicates conditions where the process completes a command and is awaiting the next one or has only received partial information and must wait for the remainder to arrive. Increasing the size of the network packet size can reduce this number.

The other related value is the "Network Packet Sent" value. Every time a task sends a TDS packet it must sleep until that activity is completed. Once again a larger packet size may reduce the number sent and reduce the number of affected context switches.

The "SYSINDEXES lookup" value is useful only in SMP environments and indicates tasks that must wait for another task to release control of a page in the sysindexes table.

This leaves the "Other Causes" category the catch basin for all switching activity not allocated to any other area. In a well-behaved situation this will become a higher number as the other causes are reduced.

Transaction Activity

The next section of the report profiles the transaction activity that occurs during the sample interval: the total number of transactions that occurred and the type of activity associated with each transaction. For OLTP applications these data can be a gold mine of information. The mix of update, delete and insert activity provides an interesting profile of the application behavior. For systems that do a lot of data update activity you will want to pay very careful attention to the section on updates to ensure that as many direct updates are done as possible. If large numbers of "expensive" updates are being done this can result in significant extra database server activity. With SQL Server System XI the conditions required to achieve a direct update have been relaxed considerably over previous versions. You will want to take advantage of these features whenever possible.

Beyond the summary information you will want to review the detailed behavior for each transaction type. This starts with the insert activity. The first section identifies inserts on heap tables. A heap table is any table that does not have a clustered index assigned. If this is the case all of the update activity occurs at the end of the page chain. This can cause lock contention on the last page. If this is occurring then the administrator may wish to assign a clustered index to the table to better distribute the insert activity to all the data pages. The section on locking behavior can help determine if this type of contention is occurring. Insert activity on tables with clustered indexes will usually disperse over the entire page chain, but another form of problem can develop. As data are added these tables and the associated indexes are quite a bit more prone to page splitting behavior. Page splitting can be a very expensive operation so this needs to be minimized. The section on "Page Splitting" will help determine if your system has developed this problem.

The percentage of total activity that is updated is identified next. This includes both direct and deferred updates. This should be reviewed to determine whether the amount of update activity is appropriate to the overall system mix. In some cases updates are very good for system performance and in others they can be detrimental.

The last section in this portion provides the delete statistics. Once again, like the update, the number and type of delete activity needs to be reviewed to ensure that they match the expected machine profile and the behavior is well understood.

The next major section in the sp_sysmon output is labeled "Transaction Management." This is a more vague way of telling you that this where the system activity with the transaction logs is located. This includes all of the activity with the user log cache (ULC) along with the log semaphores and write and allocation behavior. This section is another gold mine for experienced administrators in search of that extra few ponies hidden within their servers.

The first section of the "Transaction Management" information is the ULC information. Each SQL server connection is automatically allocated a buffer cache area used to store associated transaction log information. This is used to reduce contention for physical transaction log I/O. The size of this buffer is configurable using the "user log cache size" parameter in the sp_configure options. The information provided by sp_sysmon identifies the number of times these buffers were flushed to update the transaction log. It also provides information on what activity caused the ULC flush activity to occur.

The first reason that a ULC is flushed is that it becomes full. If this happens too frequently then a larger configured size is appropriate. The next reason is that a transaction completed. When this occurs the buffer must be flushed to ensure that the transaction information is properly committed. If the process modifies data in a different database then the current ULC is flushed for each updated database.

Any activity that modifies a "System Log Record" such as an object allocation will force a ULC flush to occur. The last section on ULC flushing is the catch-all "Other" category. Reducing the frequency of ULC flushing where possible makes this cache buffer more effective and improves the overall transaction logging behavior of the system.

The next section is also related to the ULC buffers. It indicates the behavior associated with the ULC semaphores. These are used in SMP environments to ensure that only one engine at a time is updating a ULC. This information indicates how frequently the semaphore request was immediately granted and how frequently the task had to wait for the resource to be released.

The "Log Semaphores" are used to protect the last log page where the current log update activity is occurring. This is only meaningful in SMP environments. If a high percentage of requests is forced to wait then the performance of the SMP environment will be degraded. The administrator can increase the size of the allocated ULCs or manipulate the database and application behavior to reduce the number of waits that are occurring.

The section on "Transaction Log Writes" is the total number of times the SQL Server wrote a transaction log page to disk. This occurs automatically when a page fills or a transaction commits.

The section on "Transaction Log Allocations" indicates how frequently additional log pages are allocated. This is sometimes useful for determining transaction log growth.

The last piece of transaction information is the "Avg # Writes per Log Page" This is useful for determining in a general sense the efficiency of the transaction log behavior. This is based on the previously reported write and allocation information. In an ideal world the log pages would only be written to once to fill the entire page and complete the transaction. The higher the number, the more frequently transactions are requesting that the same page be written to disk. This is the type of behavior associated with many small transactions as opposed to larger more efficient transactions.

The "Index Management" section is used to determine the amount of care and feeding the SQL Server provided to index maintenance during the sp_sysmon sample. This covers both clustered and nonclustered indexes. All insert, delete, and most update activity performed on tables with nonclustered or clustered indexes will require some maintenance on the corresponding indexes.

In general, indexes speed up data retrieval operations, but extract a penalty for data modification actions. Even where this overhead is accepted and accounted for, careful examination is required to ensure that only the minimal maintenance toll is being paid. The first index information provided is "Ins/Upd Requiring Maint." This indicates the number of modifications that potentially require corresponding index modifications. This is followed by the "# of NC Ndx Maint" which indicates the number of nonclustered indexes that were actually modified as a result of the insert and delete activity. The next category is the "Avg NC Ndx Maint/Op" which spells out the average number of maintenance actions performed per data manipulation statement. In well-performing situations then the goal is to have an average that's as low as possible, allowing the maximum number of data modifications to be performed with the minimum amount of index maintenance. This is normally accomplished by adjusting the fill factors associated with the tables and the index column construction.

The next index information provided is the "Deletes Requiring Maint." This is the equivalent section previously provided for update and insert activity except focused on the delete actions. More specifically, these values indicate the total number of delete actions that could trigger an index maintenance activity. This is followed by the "Avg NC Ndx Maint/Op" information. This provides the average number of nonclustered index maintenance actions that were required as a result of the delete statements. The goal for tuning this activity is to do the most delete actions for the minimal number of actual index maintenance actions.

The sp_sysmon output provides information on nonclustered index updates that were required as a result of page splits caused by updates to clustered indexes. This is shown as the "Row ID updates from Clustered Split" parameter. The values provided show the total number of nonclustered indexes that were affected. This is followed with the "Avg NC Ndx Maint/Op" values showing how frequently on average a clustered index page split resulted in updates to affected nonclustered indexes.

The Index Management section then proceeds to show the "Page Splits" section. This shows the total number of page splits that have occurred during the sample interval. This includes all data page, clustered index, or nonclustered index page splits. Page splitting is an activity that the SQL Server does when it needs to insert an additional row on a page but the page is already full. When this occurs the SQL Server allocates an additional page to the object and moves half the data from the original page to the newly allocated page and then proceeds to perform the requested insert on the appropriate page. In moving the rows between the newly allocated page and the original, other objects that access these moved rows would then need to be updated with their new location.

As you may have already determined all of this activity can be very time consuming and inefficient. The administrator wants to minimize page-splitting behavior as much as possible. The first line of defense for the administrator is to ensure that the data pages are allocated with an appropriate amount of blank space so that inserts and updates will have room to perform inserts without necessitating a page split.

If room exists on the page for the insert to occur then no page split is required. The default value is to 85% fill the page leaving 15% free space to perform inserts before a page split needs to occur. In environments that lean heavily on the insert and update workload, a lower fill factor may improve performance by reducing page splitting behavior. The cost of this is that each object requires more space to account for the extra free space that must be included. In essence, you're trading disk space for performance.

Additional special purpose options can be enabled depending on the exact type of index and data manipulation that is being encountered. The Sybase provided "Performance and Tuning Guide" has the most up to date information on the available options and their effects.

The next information area is "Retries" which shows the times that the SQL Server attempted to lock a split page, but could not proceed because another process already held a lock on the target. If this number is high, it indicates an unusual activity clustered around one area of the index. If this occurs then the indexes may need to be recreated to better distribute the key values.

The "Deadlock" section shows the number of times a requested page split action caused a deadlock condition. This should only happen in very rare occurrences. This is followed with the "Empty Page Flushes" values which show the number of times that an empty page that resulted from a page split was written to disk.

At certain times when an index increases over a certain side an additional index level will need to be created. This is a rare activity unless the table is being initially loaded or the index is newly created. This activity is enumerated in the "Add Index Level" portion of the sp_sysmon output.

Page shrinks occur when delete activity removes the final row of data from an index page and allows that index page to be removed from the chain. This is again a high effort task for the SQL Server to complete. If this number is consistently high then the index could probably benefit from being rebuilt to better distribute the key values among the index pages.

The sp_sysmon report then proceeds from the "Index Management" section to the "Lock Management" components. This section reports on the SQL Server locking behavior including locks, lock promotions, deadlocks, and freelock contention. The first part of the lock report is the summary view. This information is expanded later in the detail section by specific information by lock type. The summary section provides an overview of how the system locking elements are behaving. The first section within this portion is the "Total Lock Requests" information. As expected this is simply the number of lock requests received by the SQL Server during the sample interval. This is followed by the "Avg Lock Contention" section which shows the percentage of requests that encountered contention in requesting locks from the SQL Server. Obviously, the lower this number is the fewer concerns the administrator should have. If this number is higher than expected or is an appreciable portion of the overall workload then the detail section should be consulted to determine the more exact cause of the problem. The next summary section is the "Deadlock Percentage" which shows the percentage of total lock requests that resulted in deadlock conditions. If you consistently encounter deadlock conditions the causes needs to be determined and resolved to ensure effective SQL Server operation. Most times an effective resolution requires changes to the application logic to avoid these types of circumstances.

Sp_sysmon Summary

This summary section is followed by the detail information categorizing the lock requests and responses by the type of lock involved. The report shows the type of lock and how many requests were received for that type of lock and the percentage of requests that were forced to wait before they could acquire the requested resource.

The lock detail section includes this information for all of the SQL Server lock types including exclusive table, shared table, exclusive intent, shared intent, exclusive page, update page, shared page, exclusive address, shared address, and last page of heap locks. The administrator should attempt to correlate the locking requests and results to the corresponding application activity. Poor locking behavior can cripple SQL Server performance even when the overall physical resources are ready, willing, and able to please.

Resolving the problems associated with locking contention problems will frequently require some application changes. The administrator may have some flexibility in moving objects and distributing information across physical resources, but some forms of badness can only be fixed within application code. The administrator should be familiar with the various types of locks and how they are used within the SQL Server.

The administrator should also pay particular attention to circumstances where there is significant contention for the Last Page Lock on a heap table. This is the result of high levels of activity on tables which do not have a defined clustered index. This should be correlated to the overall transaction information. Quite often defining a clustered index on the data to distribute the insert activity across the whole table will resolve this problem and improve throughput. The administrator can also use table partitioning to reduce the contention and improve I/O throughput in these circumstances.

Deadlock Monitoring

The next section reports the detailed deadlock information by lock type providing deadlock conditions have occurred in the sample. To be effective, this information needs to be compared to the application activity to isolate the cause of the problem. This detail information is followed by the section reporting on the deadlock searches that were performed. The process of searching for deadlocks accounts for a significant amount of activity.

A regular housekeeper task is allocated to performing this check and issues search requests based on tunable parameters. If your system is well tuned and the occurrences of deadlocks is infrequent then reducing the frequency of checks can allow the SQL Server to devote more energy to productive work. The SQL Server will resolve deadlock problems by terminating one of the deadlocked processes. This will result in at least one unhappy camper.

The SQL Server has an internal algorithm for determining which process to remove. It is not necessarily evident that the SQL Server will terminate the process that you would have chosen if it asked you. Deadlocks are bad and should be avoided if at all possible. If your system is besieged with deadlock problems then searching more frequently may clear these conditions, thus freeing up resources and reducing the overall system lock contention. This trade-off needs to be evaluated in each circumstance. Ideally your system would encounter very few deadlocks and you can reduce the frequency of deadlock searches.   Determining whether the search effort is worthwhile can be determined by reviewing the "Avg Deadlocks per Search" to determine if the searches are mostly encountering problems or sailing right through. Searches will be skipped if the SQL Server starts a search but a previous search is still operating.

The final lock information provided is the number and types of lock promotions that have occurred. Lock escalation or promotion occurs when enough page locks are acquired that the entire table becomes locked. The threshold values for lock promotion can be tuned within the sp_configure section. Inappropriate lock promotion can result in unnecessary lock contention and deadlocking behavior.   If lock contention is high and a large number of locks are being promoted then the administrator might consider increasing the lock promotion thresholds for either specific objects or the system in general. Reviewing the lock section after modifying this behavior will help determine whether the changes made have improved the situation.

Data Cache Management

The lock section of the sp_sysmon output is followed by the "Data Cache Management" section. This major section is divided into subsections in a manner similar to the other major division. Each named cache space will have a section with information particular to its activity. As you would expect there will always be at least one section included to itemize behavior for the "default" data cache. For each cache area several types of information are presented including spinlock contention, utilization, cache searches, pool turnover, buffer wash activity, prefetch requests, and dirty read requests. The administrator who carefully tracks the data and objects bound to various cache spaces can use the sp_sysmon information to tune the cache sizes, behavior and objects for the maximum effectiveness. The cache information is usually only valid when sampled at intervals after the system has fully started and is running its production loads in the normal steady state.

Cache Report Summary

The first section of the cache report is the summary portion. This reports all the relevant statistics for the combined activity to all data cache spaces. This provides an overview of the SQL Server cache effectiveness. If problems are identified then a more careful examination of each cache component should be done to isolate the area of concern. The first interesting component is the "Total Cache Hits" statistics.

This indicates the number of times a requested data page was located in one of the cache spaces. The "% of Total" indicates as a percentage how much of the total requests for data pages were found in cache. In a well-tuned system with normal types of workload this value should be upwards of 95%. The "hits" section is immediately followed by the miss statistics. This indicates how many times a data page request had to involve a real physical I/O request. It stands to reason that these are high effort activities and should be avoided if possible. The "% of total" section when combined with the equivalent "hit" section percentage should total 100%. Adding up the number of hits and misses should yield the same number of requests reported in the "Total Cache Search" information.

Cache Turnover

The next summary section provides an overview of the "Cache Turnover." This indicates how frequently information was retrieved into cache or updated on disk from the dirty cache pages. The first interesting statistic is the "Buffers Grabbed" information. This shows the number of times a new page was entered into cache displacing a page that already existed. The removed page is supposed to be the "least recently used." By virtue of being the LRU it should also be the least likely to be required anytime soon.

A low "hit" percentage and a high number of "Buffers Grabbed" may indicate that more space needs to be allocated for the cache. The next tidbit of data provided in the output is the "Buffers Grabbed Dirty" information. This shows how often a request for a cache data page could not be met until that page was first written to disk.

If processes are consistently waiting to have cache pages allocated while the write activity is occurring then your SQL Server will be sucking slough water. The solution is probably to add additional cache space to the area that seems most affected.

Cache Strategies Used

The next section describes the activity associated with the SQL Server caching strategy. The "Cached (LRU) Buffers" is the first piece of information reported in this section. This indicates the total number of pages placed in the MRU/LRU chain for all the configured SQL Server caches. This is followed with the "Discarded (MRU) Buffers." This is the number of buffers that have been placed at the "wash marker" indicating that they can be written to disk and then used again.

The "Caching Strategy" information is followed in the report by the "Large I/O" section. The "Large I/Os Performed" shows the total number of large I/Os completed from cache. A large I/O request is for any page size created than the default 2k. The "% of Total" item shows the large I/O requests as a percentage of all the received requests. The "Large I/Os Denied" section shows how many of these requests were refused by the SQL Server. The combined completed and denied sections should add up to the "Total Large I/O Requests" reported in the last section of this portion.

This summary information is then followed by the same set of statistics reported for each individually named data cache area. The summary section information is composed of activity to each of these areas. Problems that are identified in the summary section need to be followed up with in the detail section to focus the troubleshooting activities on the areas that are performing poorly. Once again cache management is probably the best opportunity that the SQL Server administrator has to improve the overall system throughout and user satisfaction.

Detailed Cache Reporting

Some additional information is included with the detail section for each named cache space. The first item of note is the "Spinlock

Contention" value. This shows the number of times in the sample interval that an SQL Server engine had to wait for a spinlock resource to become available. A spinlock in an internal SQL Server resource used to coordinate cache access between the various SQL Server engines.

Only one engine at a time can be making updates to a cache space. If tasks are frequently forced to wait for spinlock resources then poor performance and inefficient use of the computer CPU resources is the result. Breaking the cache areas into smaller more manageable chunks can reduce the amount of contention on any single area. Each named cache area has its own spinlock resource assigned.

The next item of note in each detail section of the data cache report is the utilization section which reports the percentage of total cache requests that were directed to this specific cache area. This helps the administrator identify whether the system access is balanced and whether the right objects are bound into the cache spaces.

The overall "Data Cache Management" report is followed by the "Procedure Cache Management" section.

Evaluating Procedure Cache

Inside the procedure cache the SQL Server maintains copies of the most frequently requested stored procedures and triggers. The sp_sysmon information is used to determine how effective the cache area has been in reducing the need for the SQL Server to look on physical disk drives for the requested procedures. Generally speaking the stored procedures and triggers constitute a small amount of data and the administrator should be able to provide enough procedure cache space to prevent serious performance degradations.

The section leads off with the "Procedure Requests" data. This shows the total number of times that a stored procedure was executed. This is followed by the "Procedure Reads from Disk" which shows the percentage of total requests that could not be satisfied from the procedure cache. These requests require a physical I/O request in order to satisfy the requirement. This should be a small percentage of the total or the procedure cache component should be increased in size.

The next section is the "Procedure Writes to Disk." This reports the total number of new procedures created during the sample interval. This is typically a very low number. In fact "0" is the most frequent value reported for this parameter. The last section in the "Procedure Cache" section is the "Procedure Removals" area. This shows the number of procedures that were removed from cache because they had not been used for a significant length of time.

The next section reports the number of memory pages allocated and deallocated as part of the "Memory Management" report. The first parameter is the total number of pages allocated, and the second value reports the number of pages released as no longer needed.

This is followed by the sp_sysmon section reporting on the "Recovery Management" information. This is comprised of detailed accounting regarding the various checkpoint activities and the duration of each. The checkpointing behavior of the SQL Server process can at best be described by most administrators as "mysterious." It seems as if the SQL Server performs some miraculous activity that is rarely understood. Let's see if we can clear some of this up.

The Checkpoint Process

During the checkpoint process the SQL Server writes all pages that have been modified in cache to the physical disk ensuring that the system is completely updated. If the SQL Server has an accident before writing information to disk then the correct data must be duplicated from the transaction logs. As part of the SQL Server start-up the database data is compared against the transaction log copy and any differences are corrected. The maximum time that it takes the SQL Server to apply the outstanding updates from the transaction log is referred to as the "recovery interval."

The SQL Server monitors the number of dirty pages in cache and ensures that this information is written to disk frequently enough that the transaction log updates could be completed on system start-up within the recovery interval. Different types of checkpoint processes that can be invoked by the SQL Server. The first is the process described above which constitutes the "normal" checkpoint process. During idle cycles in the SQL Server a housekeeper process writes out dirty cache pages to disk.

This process should reduce the amount of time that a normal checkpoint will take to complete this task. If it completes writing all dirty pages to disk and only a small number of log records exist since the last checkpoint then the housekeeper issues a checkpoint command. This is a low overhead checkpoint because the housekeeper has already updated all the dirty pages. This is referred to as a "free checkpoint." The sp_sysmon output identifies the activities and effects of both normal and free checkpoints. This information can be used to tune the various checkpoint and housekeeper tasks for maximum efficiency.

Normal and Free Checkpoint Statistics

The first reported statistic in this section is the "# of Normal Checkpoints." This records the number of times in the sample interval that the normal checkpoint process was invoked. In general, this process is invoked more frequently than once per minute. The frequency is determined primarily by the "recovery interval" sp_configure setting. This is followed by the "# of Free Checkpoints" data. This records how frequently in the sample interval the housekeeper task was able to issue checkpoint command.

If your housekeeper task is invoking "free checkpoints" on a frequent basis then you can probably safely increase the "recovery interval" parameter without affecting the overall time to recovery. This is being safely covered by the housekeeper activity. The housekeeper tasks can be tuned with in "housekeeper free write percent" parameter. Review the sp_configure documentation to obtain a more complete understanding of the housekeeper tuning. The normal and free checkpoint values are followed by the "Total Checkpoints" parameter showing the combined values for both processes.

This is followed by the "Average Time per Normal Checkpoint" indicating the amount of time during the sample interval that normal checkpoints lasted. If the "normal" process is consuming too much time then it may be desirable to decrease the "recovery interval" and perform the checkpoint scan more frequently. A better method would be to increase the work accomplished by the housekeeper task and reduce the amount of work required by the normal checkpoint.

The last item is the "Avg Time per Free Checkpoint" showing the amount of time occupied performing free checkpoints. Finding more free checkpoints in general and reducing the time required to complete them will improve the overall system throughput by reducing blocking for the "checkpoint" process and freeing up resources for more productive tasks.

Managing Disk I/O

The "Disk I/O Management" section follows next in the sp_sysmon report. This provides an overview of the device and physical I/O activity. This is used by administrators to tune the system to reduce contention and delays in performing physical I/O operations. This information is provided for the server as a whole and also divided by the SQL Server engines and to specific configured devices.

The initial reported parameter in this section is the "Max Outstanding I/Os." This show the high water mark for pending I/O requests to all devices on the SQL Server during the sample interval. This is followed by the details on I/Os that were delayed for various reasons. These items can often be tuned in various aspects of the SQL Server configuration and operating system parameters.

The tunable aspects of the device I/O behavior are generally associated with asynchronous I/O parameters and the limits placed on maximum outstanding requests. The first reported cause of I/O delays is the "Disk I/O Structures." The SQL Server is configured with a fixed number of disk structures in the sp_configure parameters. When these are all in use additional I/O requests are forced to wait until one of the available structures is freed up by a completed request. Increasing the available structures can avoid causing I/O delays at the price of additional memory consumption for the new structures.

Configuration Limit Delays

This is followed by the number of delays associated with the "Server Configuration Limit." This value is set by the sp_configure command. This is normally set to the maximum that your operating system or hardware should be capable of. If you are experiencing delays in this area this assumption should be verified. You may require additional disk or hardware resources to resolve these issues.

Following this is the section on delays associated with exceeding the "Engine Configuration Limit." This is also configured by the sp_configure command. If I/O requests are being processed more or less symmetrically across all the available engines then this should be roughly the server limit divided by the number of engines with some additional factor to account for the occasional random amount of unevenness. If you're not very concerned about the engine limits then this value can be disabled or set to the server limit. The last cause of I/O delays reported is the "Operating System Limit." This reports on the configured operating system limit. If I/Os are being consistently delayed at this level then it's time to phone system operations and enlist reinforcements to improve the operating system parameters.

The delay section is followed by the "Requested and Completed Disk I/O" section. This shows the I/O requests received and completed by the SQL Server and by SQL Server engine. In most cases the requested and completed values should be very close to the same unless requests are being delayed for various reasons.

You should probably review this information over a few different sample intervals to ensure that the behavior is consistent and that the requested and completed values are close to identical. You will also wish to review the per engine statistics to determine if the requests are being balanced across the various SQL Server resources. If this is not true then you may wish to review the application behavior and determine if changes can be made to better distribute the I/O requests or application mixes to balance the load appropriately.

The report then proceeds to detail the activity by configured SQL Server device. The administrator will want to review this information to determine that as much as possible the I/O requests are balanced across the available devices and that the underlying hardware resources are allocated to the best advantage. This can be correlated to the "Context Switch" data to determine if unwanted context switching can be isolated to specific devices.

Each device section starts with the number of reads and writes that were performed to the device in the sample interval. This also identifies what percentage of the total requests each type of activity represents. This is followed by the count of total I/O requests to the device. This activity can be correlated to the statistics available at the operating system level for overall physical disk activity.

Overall disk requests need to be managed within the capabilities of the underlying disk and controller hardware to keep up with the requests issued by the SQL Server. Various techniques exist for creating devices and segments and deploying objects across these resources to more effectively manage these levels.

Device Semaphores

The device request data are followed by the "Device Semaphore Granted" and "Device Semaphore Waited" section. The device semaphores are used to control device access across multiple SQL Server engines. Obviously this is only relevant in SMP environments. Only one engine at a time can write to a device. If this level of contention is being encountered then the corrective action is to deploy more devices and spread out the various objects across as many devices as possible to reduce the amount of contention.

Once again, these situations can create situations where additional CPU or SQL Server engines can actually reduce performance. This is also an area where application design should be reviewed to determine if that has created data hotspots that could be eliminated if a different design were employed.

Network I/O Management

The final section of the sp_sysmon report is the "Network I/O Management" portion. This reports on requested and delayed network I/O requests and the size of those requests and is broken down by SQL Server engine. The section starts with "Total Requested Network I/Os." This shows the number of "Tabular Data Stream" (TDS) packets received or sent by the SQL Server. If you know the size of the packets you can determine the amount of network capacity required by the SQL Server. This information can be extremely valuable to the people who support the network infrastructure. It is okay to share this information with them. Under the right circumstances you may even be able to leverage the information into a decent lunch if you play your cards right.

This is followed by the "Network I/Os Delayed" counts. This indicates if the network request was blocked for some reason. If this is consistently the case then you should perform a more careful network analysis and review to determine the underlying cause. The TDS packets received and sent are then identified. When combined, these should equal the SQL server total. These are also combined with the number of total bytes and then the average number of bytes per packet.

If the average value is approaching the default SQL Server setting normally set at 512 then you should probably increase the maximum packet size parameters to allow client applications to configure for more effective network utilization. In other words, use fewer packets with more information. This reduces the overall network overhead and makes more effective use of the available network bandwidth.

The sp_sysmon procedure is the most valuable method of gathering specific tuning and performance information on your SQL Server. This information can and should be augmented with additional forms and types of monitoring to ensure the overall health of your system.

Other Monitoring Tools

Several excellent third-party products are available to help the system administrator maintain a grip on his operating environment and his sanity at the same time.

Sybase's SQL Monitor is a decent product. This reports on all the basic information included in the sp_sysmon report but displays the information in a more graphically friendly fashion. These third-party monitoring products can only report on information that is capable of being reported by the SQL Server. The added value for these products is in the way they present the information and additionally functions that they can enable from the underlying data. There is also a case to be made for products that incorporate the SQL Server administration and monitoring into the overall enterprise suite of tools for managing the other computer infrastructure and environment. Sybase extended quite a bit of effort during the late 1990s to make the performance information more accessible to third-party products.

An example of a product that incorporates a significant amount of SQL Server administration and monitoring in addition to its other features is the BMC Patrol product. The base product provides a good hardware and operating system support platform. This base can be extended by adding additional "knowledge modules" which provide specific management objects for additional environments.

Naturally, from the SQL Server perspective you can add a specific SQL Server module for all of the in use server versions. An Oracle module is also available and some large application modules as well. This product provides both an interactive monitoring capability, which allows the administrator to display various real-time graphs which track various elements of the SQL Server behavior. In addition the administrator can establish threshold levels and associated actions.

At a minimum the administrator can be notified of values which exceed the established thresholds by blinking red icons. These prompt the administrator to display the information and acknowledge and deal with the alert condition. This provides a mechanism for exception level reporting and management. With appropriate thresholds the administrator can respond to potential problems early on and avoid situations escalating to the point where service becomes unavailable.

Through incorporation of operating system information, more direct correlations can be drawn between the SQL Server and operating system behavior. An example would be an administrator receiving notification that an SQL server device is filled to more than 80% of capacity. The administrator can respond and add additional space to the device before any application is refused service because no additional space is available.

Platinum Technologies has a robust suite of management tools including very good SQL Server utilities. The IBM Tivoli Management Environment (TME) is an excellent open management product based on DCE specifications. Many excellent products are available that adhere to this standard and are manageable under the single environment.

Organizations with large numbers of SQL Server systems or those who are integrating the SQL Server into complex distributed computing environments should be prepared to expend some effort and cash to establish a robust and scalable management and monitoring environment for their SQL Server installations.

CHAPTER 11

T-SQL Query Performance Tuning Techniques

Optimizing T-SQL Queries

There is, of course, an entire black art and science to optimizing T-SQL queries. While I've only ever rarely seen anyone try using a magic wand, frequently there are some magic words which can do the trick!

In this chapter I want to go over the key points to remember first when writing T-SQL queries, whether dynamic or static, and then progressively get into deeper detail.

- Stored procedures
- Indexing
- Time limit
- Understanding query plans
- Using OR correctly
- DISTINCT
- Showplan and statistics I/O

Here are some guidelines to follow when putting together queries.

Stored Procedures

One of the best assets of stored procedures is that it allows you to break up complicated queries. In some cases, this is the best way to handle complex queries across many tables (five or more).

Breaking down a query involves retrieving criteria data (keys) into variables or temporary tables and then using them to retrieve the final result data. The philosophy here is that more work is required in a complex query to resolve the keys needed to return the data than the actual final data retrieve itself.

Also, only one key may be used by the optimizer per select. If you have criteria that would require two indexes to resolve efficiently, it is a good idea to break up the query.

Indexing

Effective indexing can also dramatically reduce query run time.

In general, all tables should have a unique clustered index on their natural key. If you have the following table:

```
TRANSACTION_DETAIL (
XACT_ID int,
XACT_DATE datetime,
XACT_VALUE money
)
```

the transaction id is the unique record identifier but will seldom be used in queries. Having an index of

```
TRANSACTION_DETAIL( XACT_DATE, XACT_ID)
```

will still be unique but would be helpful for all date-related rollup queries. In fact, unless you will be querying against the XACT_ID column directly, there may be no need for a unique index on XACT_ID.

When creating a compound clustered index on a table (eg. one that resolves a many-to-many relationship), place the columns with the largest domain (number of possible values) first.

Time Limit

Be aware that the SQL Optimizer has a time limit. The more complex the query, the greater the number of possible paths. If the query has too many tables, the optimizer might time-out before finding an efficient query plan. In this case, even if the optimizer stumbles on a good path once, it may not be able to find it again (see Understanding Query Plans)

In general, a query using more than four tables will time-out before the optimizer has had a chance to examine all of the possibilities. Keep in mind that the optimizer looks at views as the individual tables that they really are.

Understanding Query Plans

The SQL Server optimizer is used to determine the best path the server should follow when executing queries. This is called a Query Plan.

The SQL Server Optimizer looks at the server statistics tables when determining the plan. Theses tables are only updated when DBCC Checkalloc( ) and DBCC CheckDB( ) are run. As tables fill with data, these commands should be run to ensure that the index dispersion information in the statistics tables is up to date. Otherwise the optimizer may choose an inappropriate path. For example, if the optimizer thinks that a table has few records, it may choose to not use any indexes when executing the query. This is the kind of thing which can happen when a table is indexed prior to a great deal of insert and delete activity. Subsequent queries can "all of a sudden" perform very poorly. The DBCC commands should be run after running Update Statistics.

For ad hoc queries, a query plan is created during the query execution and is destroyed after any results are returned.

Stored procedures are a little different. The problem is this: If you create a new query plan every time someone runs a query, you could be wasting valuable CPU time, but, if you store the query plan with the query, the plan won't be updated as table sizes change.

So this is how it was resolved. SQL Server has a memory cache specifically for stored procedures. When a stored procedure is executed, the cache is checked first. If the procedure is not found OR other people are currently running every copy of it in memory, it loads a new copy into the cache and creates a fresh query plan. Every time it is called while in the cache, it will use that same query plan. All stored procedure copies will remain in cache until cache memory has been exceeded or the server is shut down and restarted. It is important to note that only one person can execute a cached copy of a stored procedure at any given time.

Using the OR statement

The query optimizer does not like ORs. If a where clause contains an OR on an indexed column, the index *will not* be used. Be aware that the IN clause is considered to be an OR. In fact, the query

```
SELECT *

FROM PRODUCT

WHERE PRODUCT_ID in (1)
```

is considered an OR and will not select the PRODUCT_ID index, but the following query will

```
SELECT *

FROM PRODUCT

WHERE PRODUCT_ID = 1
```

DISTINCT

The DISTINCT keyword in my opinion is like the GOTO keyword. It is a last resort to an improperly structured query. Many SQL generating tools use the DISTINCT keyword but this doesn't make it right.

When DISTINCT is used, an additional work table is created in tempdb and populated with the query results. This data are then checked for DISTINCTness before being returned. A regular query, running without DISTINCT will run much quicker without this overhead, otherwise use GROUP BY.

Showplan and Statistics IO

Following the above guidelines should help you to structure fairly efficient queries. If a query still runs slowly, use Showplan and Statistics IO.

Showplan is a great tool for determining whether or not an index is being selected when a query is being run in a tool such as ISQL.

Statistics IO will show you how much IO was required for each stage of query execution. If Showplan says that you are using an index for a query, Statistics IO can show which part of the query required the most IO. In general, IO is the bottleneck of a slow-running query.

Using Data Characteristics to Optimize Queries

The most important idea about characteristic functions is knowing the domain of your data and how the T-SQL functions behave in order to structure efficient queries. In some cases, the most elegant way to accomplish this is through characteristic functions.

I hacked around using characteristic ideas for a few years before hearing about SQL Forum Magazine. David Rozenstein has published a book on this topic through SQL Forum press, he and his colleagues have turned solving these problems into a science.

Because I typically work on migration projects, over the years I've run into a lot of SQL data conversion issues. These usually occur when normalizing legacy data or communicating with third-party products.

One of the most common SQL data conversions is the old Yes/No, True/False, 1/0 (bit) scenario. The following example includes a few common data conversion problems and uses the Convert( ), CharIndex( ), Upper( ) and ASCII( ) T-SQL Functions to accomplish them.

Suppose I had bulk copied in a legacy table with the format:

```
Create table Import_Data

(

Data_Id char(24),

In_Stock char(1),

Department char(1)

)
```

and I needed to insert its data in into my SQL table with the format:

```
Create table My_Table

(

Data_Id int,

In_Stock bit,

Dept_Id tinyint
```

)

By examining the Import_Data table it was noted that there are five departments (A,B,C,D,E) and the In_Stock values read "Y" or "N" (although some were null, a bit no-no). The problem was in creating a single insert statement.

Converting the Data_Id value is straightforward using the con-vert() function. As in,

```
Select Data_Id = convert(int, Data_Id)

From Import_Data
```

The In_Stock bit column took a little more thought. I needed to return a 0 if the value was empty or "N" and a 1 if the value was "Y." In this instance I was using the Sybase T-SQL version and didn't have access to a case statement. I solved this using the charindex() function. Charindex() returns the first occurance of a character in a string. Therefore, the query:

```
Select charindex( "Y", In_Stock )

From Import_Data
```

will return a 1 (or first character in the string) on an occurence of "Y" otherwise it will return a 0. If the values were "T" or "F" for true or false, the "Y" value in the charindex() statement could be substituted for a "T." Use the Upper() Function if you encounter mixed cases. Since the results are numeric values, you could even have a mixture of both. The following script illustrates these ideas and will return a 1 for a value of "Y," "y," "T" or "t," and 0 for anything else.

```
Select charindex("Y", Upper(In_Stock) ) +
```

```
charindex("T", Upper(In_Stock) )
```

```
From Import_Data
```

The last problem arose when converting the character departments into a tinyint Dept_Id value. It was determined that the easiest way to accomplish this was to convert the A department to Dept_Id 1, B department to 2, and so forth. I accomplished this using the ASCII() function. The ASCII() function will convert a single character value into an integer. Once an integer, it can be manipulated using an offset to any value you want. The easiest way to get an offset to the alphabet is by again using the ASCII() function. Putting it together, the query:

```
Select ASCII( Dept_Id ) - ASCII("A") + 1
```

```
From Import_Data
```

will return a 1 for the letter "A," 2 for "B," and so on. Again, use the Upper() function if you encounter mixed case data.

Therefore the final insert statement would be:

```
Insert into My_Table
```

```
(  Data_Id, In_Stock, Dept_Id)
```

```
select
```

```
convert( int, Data_Id),
```

```
charindex("Y", Upper(In_Stock) )
```

```
ASCII( Upper(Dept_Id) ) - ASCII("A") + 1
```

Summarizing Data

I've had a few occurrences where I needed to use values on a row to nullify summary values on that row without use of a case statement. The easiest way to demonstrate this is with a common example.

Given the following table

```
Create table Transaction_Table

(

Xact_Id int,

Xact_Amt int,

Dept_Id int

)
```

and the problem of summarizing all of the Xact_Amt column values only for department 1 and all of the Xact_Amt values but only for department 2, how can this be accomplished with a single pass through the data? This could be accomplished by executing two individual selects.

```
Select sum(Xact_Id)

From Transaction_Table

Where Dept_Id = 1
```

```
Select sum(Xact_Id)

From Transaction_Table

Where Dept_Id = 2
```

If this table only has an index on Xact_Id, this solution will involve two table scans through the data. The first thing I would do to optimize this operation is to put a nonclustered index on the Dept_Id table. By combining these selects into a single select, performance will almost double. This can be done by using the Dept_Id values at the row level to validate or invalidate the sum() aggregate function. I again turn to some of the ideas presented by David Rozenstein and have come up with the following query

```
Select sum(Xact_Amt * (1-ABS(SIN(1 - Dept_Id)) ) )

As "Dept 1 Total",

sum(Xact_Amt * (1-ABS(SIN(2 - Dept_Id)) ) )

As "Dept 2 Total"

From Transaction_Table

Where Dept_Id between 1 and 2
```

In this example, the SIN() function will return a 0 value for a correct department and a 1 or -1 value for any other department. Using the ABS() function will ensure that the value returned is always a 0 for a matching department and a 1 for a nonmatching one. Subtracting this value from 1 will switch it to 1 for a match and zero for a nonmatch. Multiplying this value by the Xact_Amt column value in the Sum() function will ensure that only the rows matching the correct department will be included in that Sum().

Although integer columns are the easiest to use when invalidating data within an aggregate function, character columns are also fairly easy once they have been converted into numeric values.

If the Dept_Id column was a single character and I needed to sum the results of department "A" and department "B," you can use the ASCII( ) function.

```
Select sum(Xact_Amt *

(1-ABS( SIN(ASCII("A") - ASCII(Dept_Id)) ) ) )

As "Dept 1 Total",

sum(Xact_Amt *

(1-ABS(SIN(ASCII("B") - ASCII(Dept_Id))) ) )

As "Dept 2 Total"

From Transaction_Table

Where Dept_Id in ("A", "B")
```

If the Dept_Id were a string value and I needed to sum for "DEPTA," and "DEPTB," I could use the CharIndex() function.

```
Select sum(Xact_Amt *

(1-ABS( SIN(1 - CharIndex("DEPTA", Dept_Id)) ) ) )
```

```
As "Dept 1 Total",

sum(Xact_Amt *(1-ABS(SIN(1 - CharIndex("DEPTB",
Dept_Id))) ) )

As "Dept 2 Total"

From Transaction_Table

Where Dept_Id in ("DEPTA", "DEPTB")
```

As you can see, this approach elegantly and effectively solves the problem of other queries against the same table and index structures.

Flipping Tables Using T-SQL

Before the advent of the relational database, host data were stored in much the same format in which they were reported. Although this method is ridged in its ability to relate table data, very little data manipulation was required when creating most reports.

While relational tables are compact and usually contain many records, most reports require turning or "flipping" a table to create wide result sets with few records. There are many ways to accomplish this using T-SQL.

Below is a real-world example of turning a table and four possible methods for solving it. The last method shows how to use a characteristic function to create a result set using only one pass through the data.

Given the table

```
GL_POSTING

Column Name          Data Type

period_id            int

account_id           int

xact_id              int

amount               money
```

and the report:

```
Posting Totals by Account
```

ACCT	P 1	P 2	P 3	P 4	P 5
1001	12,000.00	254.35	2,567.55	3,250.00	9,856.00
1002	7,000.00	12,435.54	356.65	6,890.00	5,670.00
1003	4,350.00	15,000.00	63,564.00	14,597.00	8,390.00
1004	17,000.65	354.00	3,530.00	1,568.99	835.99
1005	1,456.85	45.09	467.90	12.56	12.56

Here are some methods for creating the result set.

Use a temporary table.

Using a stored procedure, you could create a temporary table on the SQL server with the structure:

```
#temp_gl
```

```
Column NameData Type

account_idint

pd1_totalmoney NULL

pd2_totalmoney NULL

pd3_totalmoney NULL

pd5_totalmoney NULL
```

Then populate the table with distinct account ids and update each period total column with the sum of amounts for that period. The table is then selected back to the client in the correct format. Although this method allows for tuning of the individual updates to use indexes, it requires 6 passes through the GL_POSTING table.

Use Embedded Selects.

The result set could be created as a single select with 5 embedded selects as follows.

```
select distinct account_id,

pd1_total = (select sum(amount) from GL_POSTING

where period_id = 1 and account_id = p.account_id),

pd2_total = (select sum(amount) from GL_POSTING

where period_id = 2 and account_id = p.account_id),

pd3_total = (select sum(amount) from GL_POSTING
```

```
where period_id = 3 and account_id = p.account_id),

pd4_total = (select sum(amount) from GL_POSTING

where period_id = 4 and account_id = p.account_id),

pd5_total = (select sum(amount) from GL_POSTING

where period_id = 5 and account_id = p.account_id)

from GL_POSTING p

where period_id between 1 and 5
```

This method negates the need for explicitly creating a temporary table which could be valuable if called from within a transaction. Internally, however, there is very little difference in how the query is handled as compared to the first example and little or no performance improvement is realized. It is assumed that the optimizer will use an existing period_id index for each GL_POSTING pass but it is not guaranteed as in example one.

Use a Self-Join

Self-joins were invented in order to accomplish this common problem. Most relational systems support this feature. Here is how to create the same result set using a self-join.

```
Select a.account_id,

pd1_total = sum(a.amount),

pd2_total = sum(b.amount),

pd3_total = sum(c.amount),
```

```
pd4_total = sum(d.amount),

pd5_total = sum(e.amount)

from GL_POSTING a,

GL_POSTING b,

GL_POSTING c,

GL_POSTING d,

GL_POSTING e

wherea.account_id = b.account_id and

b.account_id = c.account_id and

c.account_id = d.account_id and

d.account_id = e.account_id and

a.period_id = 1 and

b.period_id = 2 and

c.period_id = 3 and

d.period_id = 4 and

e.period_id = 5

group by a.account_id
```

As in the second example, it is up to the optimizer to decide how the data is retrieved. Performance should be similar in both cases.

Use a Characteristic Function

The first three solutions are the most common but require multiple passes through the GL_POSTING table either implicitly, as in the second and third solutions or explicitly like the first one. The ultimate goal of creating an efficient result set is to have the SQL server make only 1 indexed pass through any large data tables. By examining the data closely and using the functionality and idiosyncrasies inherent in the T-SQL language, it is possible to create a select statement which makes one pass of the GL_POSTING table and only sums amounts which meet certain row level criteria. This is called a characteristic function.

In this example, we need a result set of period columns which are summed by account. The amount in each period column is only to be summed when the current row has the correct corresponding period_id. It is possible to create a T-SQL expression that evaluates to the actual amount for the correct period_id and 0 for all other period_ids.

The sign( ) Function

The sign() function is a little used T-SQL function that returns the sign of a value (not the sine of a value). It will return -1, 0, or 1 depending on whether the value passed to it is negative, zero, or positive.

The abs( ) Function

The abs( ) function returns the absolute value of a number. The command abs(sign(x)) will always return either a 0 or a 1 regardless of the value for x.

Tying It All Together

By using these functions, it is possible to create a 0 or 1 value depending on the current period_id value. If this value is multiplied by the amount before it is summed, it is possible to sum only records matching a certain period_id even though the query itself spans multiple period_ids.

```
Select account_id,

pd1_total = sum( amount * (1 - abs( sign( period_id - 1 )))),

pd2_total = sum( amount * (1 - abs( sign( period_id - 2 )))),

pd3_total = sum( amount * (1 - abs( sign( period_id - 3 )))),

pd4_total = sum( amount * (1 - abs( sign( period_id - 4 )))),

pd5_total = sum( amount * (1 - abs( sign( period_id - 5 ))))

from GL_POSTING

where period_id between 1 and 5

group by account_id
```

This query will sum the correct period values while making only one pass of records between periods 1 and 5. Of all the methods discussed, this is by far the most efficient. Amounts are only summed if the row level period_id criteria evaluates as true (1); otherwise, it is invalidated by being multiplied by zero.

Taking a Closer Look

Let's take a look at how the period 1 value is summed in sum(amount * (1 - abs(sign(period_id - 1)))).

If the current row's period_id value is 1, the expression period_id - 1 evaluates to zero. The abs(sign()) of zero is zero. 1 - zero = 1 and therefore the amount is valid and summed as the value amount * 1.

If the current row was other than period_id 1, the expression period_id - 1 would evaluate to a nonzero value, abs(sign ()) would return 1, 1 - 1 = 0 and therefore the current amount would be invalidated as amount * 0.

As long as you can create an expression that returns 0 on a match and non-0 otherwise, you can use this method to sum multiple columns, each of which requires different row level criteria. This example used an integer key which is the easiest to use in an expressiong but with a little manipulation, any data type can be used.

Since stumbling onto the idea of characteristic functions, I try to use them as often as possible. They are great for any query that involves turning a table, creating descriptions based on key values and most other processing which requires doing different things depending on the current row.

Characteristic functions; learn them, live them, love them, and before you know it you too will be amazing yourself and confusing your friends.

CHAPTER 12

Open Client

Sybase has committed to developing and deploying client/server-based products. They have always recognized that they exist in a heterogeneous world and more recently have offered products which provide for integration of more than just clients with a server.

The Sybase approach to client/server has been to emphasize the need to access data across local-area networks (LANs) and wide-area networks (WANs). Data may be distributed or replicated according to the needs of the business.

Additionally, Sybase has offered coexistence with many different communications topologies and protocols. They have a flexible approach to communications through their net-libraries (which are described in more detail later).

Also, the Sybase approach to client/server is based on modularity. You can plug and play the components you need for your particular application, environment or objective. Their offerings are not bundled into one-size-fits-all packages.

It is important to recognize that Sybase has grown because the marketplace wants and has wanted open systems in a practical sense. What started out as a necessity (SQL Server was offered with open access because there was no time to develop a toolset), became an advantage.

Third parties make better tools than do the database vendors. Users and developers will always find requirements that can only be met by building a customized solution.

Sybase has built this capability into their SQL Server product with their DB-Libraries, which are now called Open Client libraries. Based on past performance, there is no reason to suspect or fear that Sybase will turn their backs on this capability and lock third-party tools and vendors out of their product offerings with undocumented features or hooks.

The flexibility of the Open Client approach to client/server is clearly demonstrated in this example. As a result of the modularization of components, any third party application, such as PowerBuilder or Visual Basic, can connect to an SQL Server regardless of the communications hardware used.

This is very different than pre-client/server solutions.

The application is written with DB-Library calls contained in within it. These calls are provided by the Open Client libraries provided by Sybase and linked into the application by the developer when it is written.

Once compiled and distributed, when the application looks for an SQL Server, Open Client actually looks for services provided by Net-Library. These libraries are installed on the client workstation which is to run the compiled application and are configured to talk to the specific communication software and hardware used for that client.

Examples of Windows-based net-libraries that work with different communications protocols include Net-Lib for LAN Work-Place for DOS (wnovtc) or for PCTCP (wftptc).

In turn, these communications protocols can sit on top of commonplace Ethernet or token ring hardware or more exotic X.25, ISDN, or FDDI connections.

The number of third-party products is growing by leaps and bounds. Because of the inexpensive and relatively easy method of making an application SQL Server-aware, software developers for tools usually make SQL Server a natural connection

Products that incorporate Open Database Connectivity (ODBC) can also connect to SQL Server; however, this connection is accomplished by translating the database calls through ODBC then to Open Client, which adds an additional step and adversely affects performance.

Most vendors of popular data retrieval or manipulation products opt for to write direct SQL Server access into their applications

Net-library was a means of ensuring that SQL Server could take advantage of multiple networking protocols without Sybase having to get into the networking business.

DB-Library applications have been written without regard for connectivity, which is managed totally by net-lib.

By placing the management of the connection in the hands of the communications package vendors, users can configure their systems to connect concurrently to all manner of services without adversely affecting their database access. Another advantage of this approach is that communications package vendors can be changed without any impact on the Sybase client/server application itself.

Companies that have decided to migrate from Windows 3.x to Windows 95, for example, can migrate their communications layers from third-party vendors, such as FTP or Novell, and simply use the Microsoft-supplied TCP/IP or named pipes communications. For a firm with many thousands of Sybase connected PCs, this can add up to a pretty penny!

In previous publications, we have provided applications along with the books. In fact, in the CD-ROM enclosed with this book is one of those applications: an updated DBA@Win. By far the support calls we received have been for support of Net-Lib connectivity to SQL Server. If you are a dyed-in-the-wool administrator, hopefully you will be able to use this chapter to send out the applicable pages to your user community when those same questions arise. If you're not used to the vagaries of Sybase connectivity, this chapter should help in diagnosing and troubleshooting your own client/server communications blues.

Net-Lib 4.2

Like any good news organization, I am going to lead with the hottest story: the most recent net-library procedure that I have available as I write this. Installing SQL Server clients with Sybase provided net-libraries gives you the advantages of staying completely within their toolset. However, in my opinion, this doesn't actually get you much, because the provided tools haven't been in the same class as their Microsoft competitors nor is installation as straightforward as it should be, especially for a company that has been providing these install routines for almost a decade. In any case, I guess if it were self-explanatory you wouldn't need this book and then where would I be? So here goes...

SQLEDIT

One of the new features of the System 10 for NT was an upgrade in the way clients were added and managed. To accomplish this, a new utility was supplied to make configuring a number of servers and connection info easier. This utility was called SQL EDIT.

FIGURE 12.1. SQL Edit utility for configuring net-library details

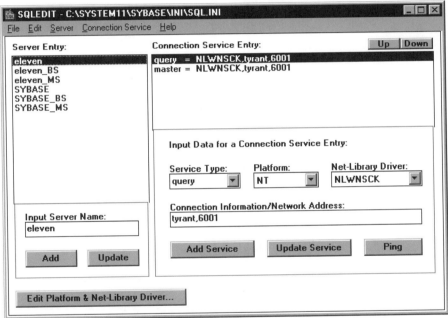

You should note a couple of key items shown in Figure 12.1. First, it is divided into the Server Entry panel on the left and the Connection Service Entry definition on the right. It is not obvious, but you have to click on the server you wish to edit in order to bring up the associated connection service information.

This can be a little frustrating when you are trying to delete connection services, because if you haven't moved the mouse over and clicked on the connection service panel, you start deleting server names. Oh, and there is no multiple-level undo; you can undo the last action only. In any case, it's better than using notepad to edit an ini file, so I guess we should all be thankful for that.

Through SQL Edit you can set up each client to access any number of servers by name. This is very similar to previous ways of tying together named servers with net-lib program names, network addresses and query ports, except that now the addresses are written to a new file – SQL.INI.

SQL INI

The SQL.INI file can be written to directly, though typically this is not advised. Go through SQLEDIT to change or add server info. The SQL Edit program writes the appropriate addresses in the sql.ini file in the format shown in Figure 12.2.

FIGURE 12.2. Sample SQL.INI entries

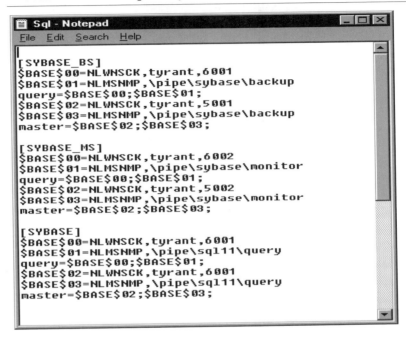

```
Sql - Notepad
File  Edit  Search  Help

[SYBASE_BS]
$BASE$00=NLWNSCK,tyrant,6001
$BASE$01=NLMSNMP,\pipe\sybase\backup
query=$BASE$00;$BASE$01;
$BASE$02=NLWNSCK,tyrant,5001
$BASE$03=NLMSNMP,\pipe\sybase\backup
master=$BASE$02;$BASE$03;

[SYBASE_MS]
$BASE$00=NLWNSCK,tyrant,6002
$BASE$01=NLMSNMP,\pipe\sybase\monitor
query=$BASE$00;$BASE$01;
$BASE$02=NLWNSCK,tyrant,5002
$BASE$03=NLMSNMP,\pipe\sybase\monitor
master=$BASE$02;$BASE$03;

[SYBASE]
$BASE$00=NLWNSCK,tyrant,6001
$BASE$01=NLMSNMP,\pipe\sql11\query
query=$BASE$00;$BASE$01;
$BASE$02=NLWNSCK,tyrant,6001
$BASE$03=NLMSNMP,\pipe\sql11\query
master=$BASE$02;$BASE$03;
```

In this case, you see the net-lib configuration information for a
Windows NT-based client for the Sybase SQL Server and its associated Backup Server and Monitor Server. Tyrant is the host
name of the NT server where SQL Server is running. It was not
necessary to specify the IP address, although this would have
worked through SQL EDIT as well.

Additionally, you can see the format for the named pipes address.
The default for the early versions of System XI for NT was
\pipe\sql\query, as it is for the Microsoft version of SQL Server
6.5. Because I have both loaded on my laptop (tyrant), I decided to
name the Sybase pipe sql11\query to avoid any confusion. More
recent versions install \pipe\sybase\query as the pipe address.

TIP: If you have trouble when installing open client for Windows NT, install only the TCP/IP version first. Add the named pipes version after the server is up and running. I noticed on server installs that the open client for named pipes took precedence over the TCP/IP address and that the install routine would fail unless only the nlwsck driver was specified.

SQL Advantage

When I got my first version of Adaptive Server Enterprise 11.5, I noticed that, as usual with a new release from Sybase, the install routine and client were different than previous versions. As this book is intended to be relevant to virtually all Sybase releases, I've included the new approach here as well.

First, one of the interesting things about the client install is that it comes on the distribution CD for the server product itself. That might not normally be unusual, except in this case the CD was for the AIX version, so to run the setup routine under Windows 95 and NT seems a bit strange.

In any case, it works. When you are presented with the first screen asking for installation options, select all files rather than runtime only. Once it copies the necessary files to disk, you will have to reboot (even if it doesn't ask you to, you better do so). Then you will see a few new Sybase entries on your start button. These include DS Edit, OC OS config, and SQL Advantage. These are the new utilities for installing and configuring net-libraries, Open Client configuration, and isql/w, respectively.

The DS Edit option looks like the figure below when first launched.

FIGURE 12.3. DS Edit options

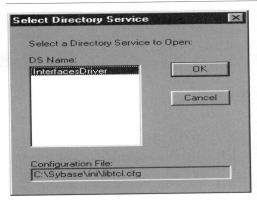

The default entry is the interfaces driver that allows you to configure which communications protocol to use with Open Client. Click on OK and you will see the next screen.

FIGURE 12.4. DS Edit Interfaces Driver

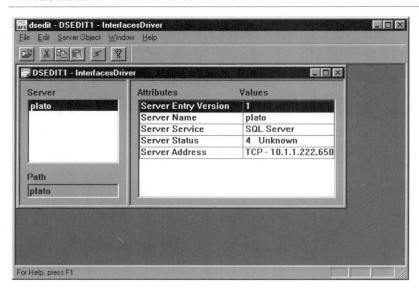

Here you see the replacement for the sql config utility of previous System 10 and XI versions. By double clicking directly on the server address, you can edit the IP address, query port number and so on. Or use the server object menu item to invoke the add/ edit options.

The little red lightning bolt button is used to call sybping, a handy bit of integration to ensure you have appropriately configured your client.

As always, you have to be able to "ping" the server before you can do any useful work, so once that's accomplished you can move to the next item – OC Config.

FIGURE 12.5. The Open Client Configuration Utility

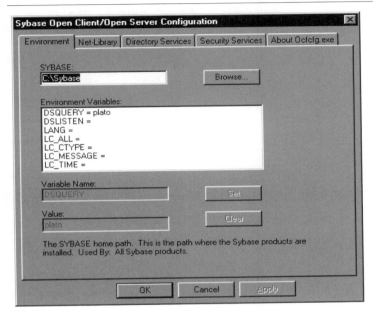

In the bad old days, you would add the DSQuery environment variable in the autoexec, but with 32-bit Windows products, obviously another approach was needed. The OC Config utility lets you set these as shown in the figure above.

Additionally, you can configure different communications protocols for Net-Library as demonstrated in Figure 12.6.

FIGURE 12.6. Net-Library configuration through OC Config

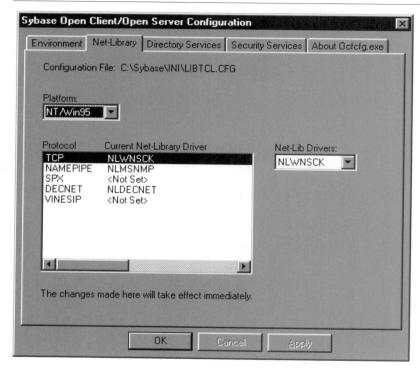

The key advantage to the new configuration utilities is convenience – at long last something that has been designed to work with the 32 bit Windows environments.

Another item that has long needed replacing is isql/w. SQL Advantage is offered in this area. When you first start up SQL Advantage you see the following screen.

FIGURE 12.7. SQL Advantage

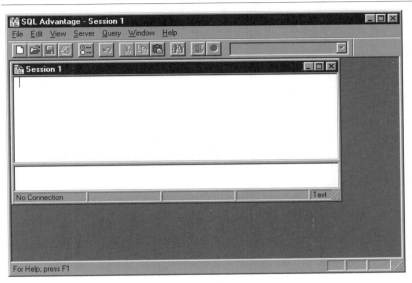

The major disappointment I found with SQL Advantage was its apparent inability to read straight text files with the suffix.sql. It seems that Sybase thought SQL Advantage should have its own format for sql files, which doesn't work for those of us who are constantly moving sql scripts from Unix to NT to 95 and back again.

Microsoft Open Client

Here things start to get interesting. Many people don't actually like working with the Sybase Open Client libraries. Not only is the isql for Windows provided by Sybase vastly inferior to the Microsoft version, but the mssql libraries are not licensed (although the number of client connections to a Microsoft SQL Server are chargeable per license.) This means that you can freely distribute the MSSQL net-libraries but you may not do so with the Sybase versions. Whatever your preference, I thought it might be a good idea to provide a rundown on both!

On Disk 2 of the Microsoft BackOffice CD set, there is a directory called mssql. This contains the Open Client setup utility, as well as the net-libraries and SQL Server utility programs such as isql. They work just fine with a System XI server and in some cases are superior to their Sybase-supplied counterparts.

The way to set up an NT- or 95-based PC with the Microsoft client libraries is to run w3dbver.exe. Launching this executable gives you the screen in Figure 12.8:

MS SQL Client Installation

Along with BackOffice 2.5 installation routines for installing Microsoft SQL Server, there are new installation routines for installing clients using the Microsoft net-libraries

FIGURE 12.8. The Microsoft SQL Client Configurator

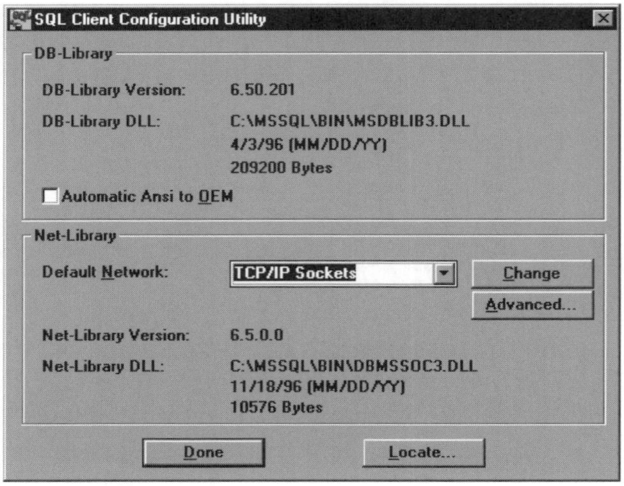

In this case, the application had been installed in the mssql directory and provided its own dblib dynamic link library, msdblib3.dll Clicking Advanced gives you a screen where you can associate a given communications method with the appropriate net-library. For example, the Windows Sockets TCP/IP communications driver loaded when you add support for TCP/IP to a Windows PC, has the entry in Figure 12.9:

FIGURE 12.9. Setting the Winsock TCP/IP net-library configuration

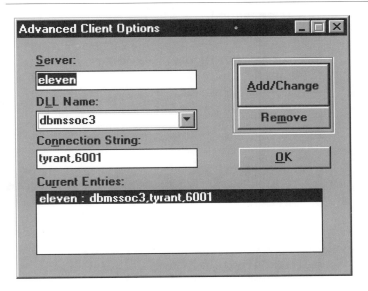

In this case the server name is eleven, the dbmssoc3 dll has been specified and the address is again tyrant with the query port number as 6001. This points to the same Sybase SQL Server called Sybase under SQL Edit, but the net-library used to connect the client to the server is the Microsoft dbmossc3.dll.

Unlike Sybase, Microsoft continues to store the SQL Server address to net-library values in the win.ini. This can be a little strange under Windows NT, since not much else gets kept there, but in the example below you will see how you could manually use sysedit to bring up win.ini under NT and change or add server address information for the Microsoft net-libraries.

FIGURE 12.10. WIN.INI Entry for MS SQL Clients, including System XI Servers

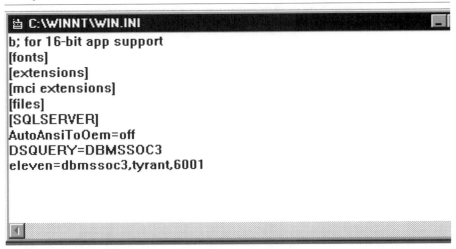

```
📄 C:\WINNT\WIN.INI                                          ▬

b; for 16-bit app support
[fonts]
[extensions]
[mci extensions]
[files]
[SQLSERVER]
AutoAnsiToOem=off
DSQUERY=DBMSSOC3
eleven=dbmssoc3,tyrant,6001
```

There you have it, like the older versions of net-lib such as 1.0, the win.ini entry SQL Server maintains all of the addressing for Windows clients using microsoft supplied net-libraries accessing either System XI or SQL Server 6.x.

Upgrading Net-Library Versions

There is an upgrade option available under SQL Edit. I suspect this was intended for people upgrading their Sybase net-library versions from version 1.0 (Supplied with SQL Server 4.x), rather than Microsoft-supplied net-libraries (see Figure 12.10). However, the procedure is the same in both cases.

FIGURE 12.11. Importing older net-library configurations

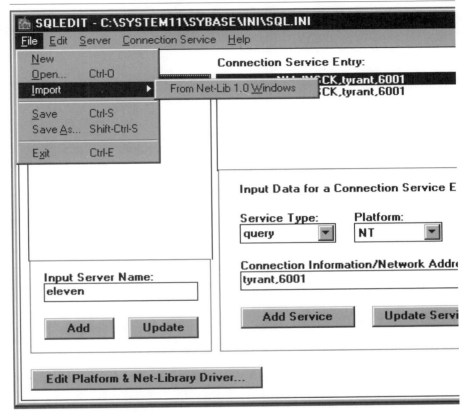

Those of you upgrading from 4.x versions of Sybase SQL Server to System XI may want to use the import feature of SQL Edit, especially if you have many different server entries on each client. Selecting the upgrade option gives you the following dialog box.

FIGURE 12.12. Upgrading Net-library 1.0 entries using SQL Edit

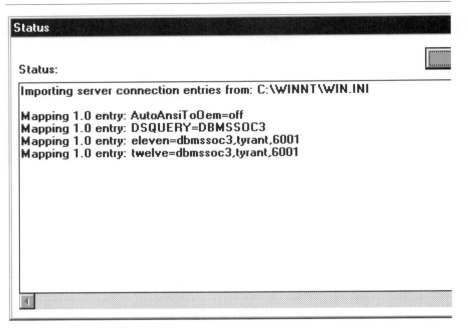

As part of my fascination with interoperability between Windows 95 and NT, I went ahead and upgraded the server addressed specified in the win.ini.

When I went back into SQL Edit to check and see what this actually accomplished, I have to admit not much had changed. The server list contained new entries for DSQUERY and twelve, but the net-library and connection information had to be entered manually.

Net-Libraries 1.0

Since this work is intended as a more comprehensive reference guide for users of Sybase technology, I thought it might be a good idea to include all of the net-lib configuration options, including the more archaic ones from the Windows 3.x world.

As you will notice, for a long time the Net-lib installation routines were DOS based. I have had no idea why this was the case, I guess Sybase was a bit rooted in the command line interface until the takeover of PowerBuilder (or was that until being taken over by PowerBuilder,<grin>). In any event, the basic steps for installing net-libraries can be seen in the following set of screen captures beginning with Figure 12.12.

FIGURE 12.13. The traditional installation routine for 1.0 net-libraries

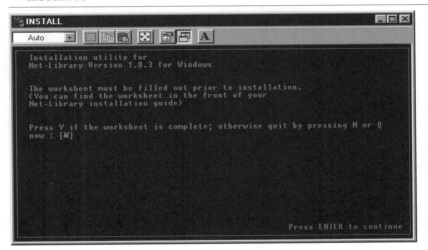

MMmhmmm, doesn't that look good! I actually went to the bother of capturing all the screens following this one, but on second thought I'll spare you. The worksheet items that have to be completed are identified through this screen. It appears at the end of the interrogation to ask you if you don't agree and want to start over.

FIGURE 12.14. Completed Net-library 1.0 Worksheet

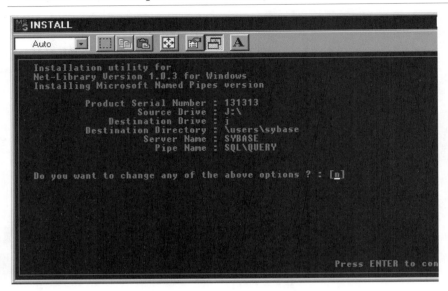

While the newer SQL Edit approach may take a little getting used to, it's much better than running sybclenv.bat!

Summary

In this chapter you were introduced to the Sybase client configuration utilities, past and present. Additionally, we covered where to find the underlying configuration files and what they contain.

You should also be more comfortable with the distinctions between the Microsoft SQL Client net-libraries and the Sybase Open Client net-libs. Yes, they perform the same functions, they work largely interchangeably together, but no – they are not the same.

Sybase was overdue to create a new and improved client configurator over the DOS-based Net-Lib 1.0 installer. Keeping Sybase-related entries in the SQL.INI file also helps to avoid confusion for anyone connecting to both Sybase and Microsoft SQL Servers.

The role of net-libraries is especially important when managing connections with PC clients to a large population of servers. Smaller sites may frequently set a client up once and forget pretty much about it. I hope this chapter helps as both a good refresher and introduction to the new ASE 11.5 based utilities if you haven't already seen them.

CHAPTER 13

CT-Library versus DB-Library

In this chapter I take you through the uses and features of both CT-Library and DB-Library. These two APIs allow you to connect client applications to SQL Server, but they handle a number of things very differently. In this chapter I cover the following areas:

- Client libraries
- DB-Library
- Implementing DB-Library applications
- CT-Library
- Implementing CT-Library applications
- Future directions

Client Libraries

Part of Sybase's appeal is its openness in terms of programming tools. Sybase provides function libraries for a wide variety of development tools and platforms. I prefer this method over embedded SQL because it doesn't require things like proprietary compilers, precompiling or weird linking. I can pick a compiler that I'm comfortable with and gain access to SQL Server data by calling functions. First, let's take a look at the role of a client library.

The Sybase Server communicates to its clients using a proprietary protocol called Tabular Data Stream (or TDS). The base requirements for a client library must then be the ability to connect to a server, negotiate a mutually agreeable version of Tabular Data Stream, execute T-SQL commands and provide access to any results. For many years all of this functionality and more has been available in DB-Library.

DB-Library

DB-Library is a set of programming functions that allows for client access to Sybase Server. The DB-Library function set has been around since the inception of Sybase itself. Functions are available for connecting to a server, executing SQL commands and accessing result sets.

Query results are efficiently buffered and read into an application row by row much like a forward only cursor. Result values can either be copied automatically into program variables using the dbbind( ) function or accessed directly using dbdata( ). Data definition functions are available to determine number, type and size of result columns allowing for generic result processing. Server status, error messages and compute columns can also be accessed using DB-Library functions.

Using these functions alone allows a programmer to create powerful front-end applications which can be compiled and run on a wide variety of platforms. But wait, if you buy the DB-Library Application Programming Interface you also get the following extra functionality at no extra charge!

Sybase and Microsoft Compatibility.

If you use either pre-System 10 Sybase DB-Library or Microsoft DB-Library, your application will be able run against both Sybase and Microsoft SQL Servers. Not all CT-Library functional calls are supported by Microsoft SQL Server or versions of Sybase SQL Server prior to System 10.

Two Phase Commit

The DB-Library Two Phase Commit functions allow an application to implement transaction processing on multiple servers. If a table is updated successfully on Server A but failed on Server B, Server A is rolled back.

RPC Library

The RPC functions allow for more efficient calling of stored procedures. Using the text buffer approach to execute Transact-SQL commands works fine for dynamic SQL commands but is not efficient if a query is run many times. This is because the server needs to parse, compile, and optimize the T-SQL commands before they can be run.

Putting recurring queries into stored procedures will eliminate these steps. Sybase provides memory cache specifically for stored procedures. Because of this, there is a good chance that when you request a Stored Procedure be run, it has already been parsed, compiled, loaded into memory, and optimized.

By requesting a stored procedure using Transact SQL (as in "execute sp_who sa"), the request itself still needs to be parsed and compiled. Not only that, the application must convert any non-string parameters into strings only to have the server convert them back again.

The RPC library solves all of these problems by allowing the programmer to bypass the Sybase Server's T-SQL language handler entirely when requesting stored procedures (aka RPCs). Parameters are passed in their native data types and DB-Library also provides functions for retrieving output parameter values. Any result sets generated by the Stored Procedure are processed by the application as if they were generated using normal T-SQL commands.

Bulk Copy Library

The "Select into/Bulk Copy" database option, when turned on, allows tables to be populated without being logged. This is particularly helpful when populating large tables in a database that has a small log file. In order for a Bulk Copy operation to run in a nonlogged mode, there cannot be an index on the table being populated. This is a moot point when looking at "Select into" since this operation will always create a new table without an index. When working with large tables, it is usually much quicker to drop all indexes on the table, populate it with BCP and then rebuild the indexes than to copy the data in with the indexes already built.

The client utility "BCP.EXE" was written using the Bulk Copy functions. In many cases, this utility is excellent as is for copying data into and out of server tables. If an application is generating a large amount of data which is to be inserted into a Sybase Server, the BCP functions provide an efficient mechanism for accomplishing this task.

Cursor Library

Server side cursors have been available since the introduction of Sybase System 10. The DB-Library command set was enhanced to provide access to this functionality.

Miscellaneous Functionality

Additional functionality includes automatic data conversion and automatic conversion of NULLs to programmer-defined values. These are both very helpful to application designers. Depending on the platform, some DB-Library functions have asynchronous counterparts.

Data types such as Datetime and Money are returned to an application as complex structures. Although DB-Library provides functions for viewing and manipulating these values, they are easier to work with if they are converted to string and float values. Representing NULL in an application (especially NULL numeric values) can also be a problem.

Implementing DB-Library Applications

Implementing basic DB-Library is fairly straight forward. The following examples are in C but the basic functionality is implemented across languages.

DB-Library uses two global message handlers. The Server Message Handler is called each time the SQL Server issues a server message. The Error Message Handler is called any time that DB-Library encounters an error. It is up to the programmer to define and install these message handlers. Both handlers are called with error level information. Checking the error severity within the handler will determine if it is an informational message (e.g., "Database context changed to master") or a show-stopper ("Login failed").

The following code example demonstrates the steps required to process a query using DB-Library. This includes:

- Installing the message handlers
- Creating a server connection
- Issuing a T-SQL query
- Processing the query results

This example retrieves name, type, id, and crdate from the sysobjects table in the master database. The results are sent to the standard output device.

When accessing return values, it is a good habit to define local variables using the DB-Library defined types. Some types, such as INT are processor dependent. Using the DBINT type instead will ensure platform independence.

```
/*

**This DB-Library example illustrates how to connect
**to a server, execute a select and print out the
** result rows.

*/

#include <stdio.h>

/*

** Include the appropriate header files depending

** on Sybase or Microsoft DB-Library

*/

#ifdef SYBASE

#include <sybfront.h>

#include <sybdb.h>

#include <syberror.h>
```

```
#else

#include <sqlfront.h>

#include <sqldb.h>

#endif

/* Forward declarations of the error handler and
message handler.

*/

int err_handler(DBPROCESS*, int, int, int, char*,
char*);

int msg_handler(DBPROCESS*, DBINT, int, int,
char*);

main()

{

DBPROCESS*dbproc;/* server connection structure.
*/

LOGINREC*login;/* Login information structure. */

/* These are the variables used to store the
returning data. */

DBCHARcrdate[DATELEN+1];

DBINTid;
```

```
DBCHARname[MAXNAME+1];

DBCHARtype[TYPELEN+1];

RETCODEresult_code;

   /* dbinit() must be called before any other DB-
Library function */

dbinit();/* initialize dblib */

/* Install the user-supplied error-handling and
message-handling

* functions. They are defined at the bottom of this
source file.

*/

dbmsghandle((DBMSGHANDLE_PROC)msg_handler);

dberrhandle((DBERRHANDLE_PROC)err_handler);

/*

** Get a LOGINREC structure and fill it with the
necessary

** login information.

** dblogin() will allocate a login record and the

** DBSETL...() macros are used to set the login
properties.
```

```
*/

login = dblogin();

DBSETLUSER(login, "UserName");

DBSETLPWD(login, "Password");

DBSETLAPP(login, "example1");

/*

** Get a DBPROCESS structure for communicating with
** SQL Server.

** This structure is referenced any time you need
** to communicate with the server.

*/

dbproc = dbopen(login, "Myserver");

/*

** Use the dbcmd() function to set the query text
** in the command buffer

*/

dbcmd(dbproc, "select name, type, id, crdate ");

dbcmd(dbproc, "from master..sysobjects");

/* Execute the command buffer on the server */
```

```
dbsqlexec(dbproc);

/*

** Process each command until there are no more.

** dbresults() is called once for each result set
** returned from the query

*/

while ((result_code = dbresults(dbproc)) !=
NO_MORE_RESULTS)

{

if (result_code == SUCCEED)

{

/* Bind program variables. */

/* dbbind() specifies where column values are */

/* to be copied each time the dbnextrow() */

/* function is called */

dbbind(dbproc, 1, NTBSTRINGBIND, (DBINT) 0, name);

dbbind(dbproc, 2, NTBSTRINGBIND, (DBINT) 0, type);

dbbind(dbproc, 3, INTBIND, (DBINT) 0, (BYTE *)
&id);
```

```
dbbind(dbproc, 4, NTBSTRINGBIND, (DBINT) 0,
crdate);

/* Now print the rows. */

while (dbnextrow(dbproc) != NO_MORE_ROWS)

{

printf

("%s %s %ld %s\n", name, type, id, crdate);

}

}

}

/* Close our connection and exit the program. */

/* dbexit() closes all active dbproc connections
and */

/* frees up resources allocated by dbinit() */

dbexit();

return(STDEXIT);

}

/* DB-Library error handling function */
```

```
int err_handler(dbproc, severity, dberr, oserr,
dberrstr, oserrstr)

DBPROCESS*dbproc;

intseverity;

intdberr;

intoserr;

char*dberrstr;

char*oserrstr;

{

    printf("DB-LIBRARY error:\n\t%s\n", dberrstr);

if (oserr != DBNOERR)

printf("Operating-system error:\n\t%s\n",
oserrstr);

if ((dbproc == NULL) || (DBDEAD(dbproc)))

return(INT_EXIT);

return(INT_CANCEL);

}

/* DB-Library server message handling function */
```

```
int msg_handler(dbproc, msgno, msgstate, severity,
msgtext)

DBPROCESS*dbproc;

DBINTmsgno;

intmsgstate;

intseverity;

char*msgtext;

{

printf

("SQL Server message %ld, state %d, severity
%d:\n\t%s\n",

msgno, msgstate, severity, msgtext);

return(0);

}
```

CT-Library

Sybase System 10 which offered, among other things, server side
cursors for the first time, represented an increase in client functionality over previous server versions. Because of this extended
functionality a new version of Tabular Data Stream was required.

At this time, the Sybase developers took a good look at the DB-Library API and its counterpart, Open Server Library which is used to create Open Server applications. Although these two products offered different functionality (one was used to create Client applications and the other to create server applications) there were overlaps in the basic connection and TDS handling routines. Thus, CS-Library was created.

CS-Library contains all of the basic connection and TDS handling functionality common to Client and server applications. It is used with CT-Library to create client applications and with OSLibrary to create Open server applications.

Sybase System 10 and later now offers the DB-Library and CT-Library/CS-Library APIs for creating client applications. However, when programming with DB-Library version 10 or later, a macro-conversion header must be included to convert the code to CS/CT-Library calls before compiling.

CT-Library itself differs little differences from DB-Library which was also extended to allow for cursor processing. The CT-Library functions parallel the DB-Library functions so closely that upgrading your DB-Library skills to CT-Library should be fairly straight forward.

Because of the CT-Library/CS-Library architecture, server connections are now broken into 2 parts, Localization information (platform, language, connection information) and the connection itself. CT-Library also offers asynchronous queries and the ability to execute and process multiple queries simultaneously on the same connection.

Implementing CT-Library Applications

Creating basic applications with CT-Library and CS-Library is similar to DB-Library. The first difference that you will notice is the change in the connection structure. Where DB-Library had one structure (the DBPROCESS structure) to manage the server connection and SQL command buffer, CT/CS Library has broken this into a Context structure, a Connection structure and a Command structure.

CS-Library also introduces the CS_ DATAFMT structure. This is a generic structure used to describe parameter and result column information.

The following synchronous query example is written in C and parallels the DB-Library sample shown earlier in this chapter as closely as possible for comparison. It will connect to a server, issue a select against the sysobjects table and display the results to the standard output.

Note that functions and data types beginning with "CS_" belong to CS-Library and functions and datatypes beginning with the prefix "CT_" belong to CT-Library.

```
/*

**This CS-Library/CT-Library example illustrates how to

** connect to a server, execute a select and print out

**the result rows.

*/

#include <stdio.h>

#include <ctpublic.h>

/*

** Define a global context structure to use

*/

CS_CONTEXT *context;
```

```
/* Client message and server message callback
routines: */

CS_RETCODE   clientmsg_callback();

CS_RETCODE   servermsg_callback();

#define MAXCOLUMNS 4

#define MAXSTRING 41

/*

** Main entry point for the program.

*/

main()
{

    CS_CONNECTION    *connection;   /* Connection structure */

    CS_COMMAND        *cmd;          /* Command structure    */


    /* Data format structures for column
descriptions: */

    CS_DATAFMT               columns[MAXCOLUMNS];

    CS_INT               datalength[MAXCOLUMNS];

    CS_SMALLINT          indicator[MAXCOLUMNS];
```

```
CS_INT            count;

CS_RETCODE        ret, res_type;

CS_CHAR           name[MAXSTRING];

CS_CHAR           type[MAXSTRING];

CS_CHAR           crdate[MAXSTRING];

CS_INT    id;

/*

** Get a context structure to use.

*/

cs_ctx_alloc(CS_VERSION_100, &context)

/*

** Initialize Open Client.

*/

ct_init(context, CS_VERSION_100);



/*

** Install message callback routines.

*/
```

```
    ct_callback(context, NULL, CS_SET,
CS_CLIENTMSG_CB,

            clientmsg_callback);

    ct_callback(context, NULL, CS_SET,
CS_SERVERMSG_CB,

            servermsg_callback);

  /*

  ** Connect to the server:

  **      Allocate a connection structure.

  **      Set user name and password.

  **      Create the connection.

  */

  ct_con_alloc(context, &connection);

  ct_con_props(connection, CS_SET, CS_USERNAME,
"UserName",

            CS_NULLTERM, NULL);

  ct_con_props(connection, CS_SET, CS_PASSWORD,
"Password",

            CS_NULLTERM, NULL);

  /*
```

```
    ** This call actually creates the connection:

    */

    ct_connect(connection, "Myserver",
CS_NULLTERM);



    /*

    ** Allocate a command structure to use to
create the query.

    */

    ct_cmd_alloc(connection, &cmd);



    /*

    ** Set the T-SQL value of the message command

    */

    ct_command(cmd, CS_LANG_CMD,

"select name, type, id, crdate from
master..sysobjects",

            CS_NULLTERM, CS_UNUSED);

    /*
```

```
** Send and execute the command.

*/

ct_send(cmd);



/*

** Process the results of the command.

*/

while((ret = ct_results(cmd, &res_type))==
CS_SUCCEED)

{

    if (res_type != CS_ROW_RESULT)

break;

    /*

    ** We're expecting exactly four columns.

    ** For each column, fill in the relevant

    ** fields in a data format structure, and

    ** bind the column.

    */
```

```
/* Name column */

        columns[0].datatype = CS_CHAR_TYPE;

        columns[0].format = CS_FMT_NULLTERM;

        columns[0].maxlength = MAXSTRING;

        columns[0].count = 1;

        columns[0].locale = NULL;

        ct_bind(cmd, 1, &columns[0], name, &datalength[0],

                        &indicator[0]);

    /* Type Column */

        columns[1].datatype = CS_CHAR_TYPE;

        columns[1].format = CS_FMT_NULLTERM;

        columns[1].maxlength = MAXSTRING;

        columns[1].count = 1;

        columns[1].locale = NULL;

        ct_bind(cmd, 2, &columns[1], type, &datalength[1],

                        &indicator[1]);
```

```
/* ID column */

   columns[2].datatype = CS_INT_TYPE;

        columns[2].format = CS_FMT_UNUSED;

        columns[2].maxlength = CS_UNUSED;

        columns[2].count = 1;

        columns[2].locale = NULL;

        ct_bind(cmd, 3, &columns[2], &id, &datalength[2],

                        &indicator[2]);

  /* Create date column */

        columns[3].datatype = CS_CHAR_TYPE;

        columns[3].format = CS_FMT_NULLTERM;

        columns[3].maxlength = MAXSTRING;

        columns[3].count = 1;

        columns[3].locale = NULL;

        ct_bind(cmd, 4, &columns[3], crdate, &datalength[3],

                        &indicator[3]);

        /*
```

```
    ** Now fetch and print the rows.

    */

    while(((ret = ct_fetch(cmd, CS_UNUSED, CS_UNUSED,

        CS_UNUSED, &count))

        == CS_SUCCEED) || (ret == CS_ROW_FAIL))

    {

        /*

        ** We have a row, let's print it.

        */

        printf("%s %s %ld %s\n", name, type, id, crdate);

    }



    /* All done, free up connection and allocated resources.

    */

    ct_cmd_drop(cmd);
```

```
                ct_close(connection, CS_UNUSED);

                ct_con_drop(connection);

                ct_exit(context, CS_UNUSED);

                cs_ctx_drop(context);

                return 0;

        }



        /
        *************************************************
        **************

        **

        ** callback functions

        **

        *************************************************
        **************/

        /*

        ** clientmsg_callback()

        **

        ** Type of function:
```

```
** example program client message handler

** Installed as a callback into Open Client.

**

** Returns:

** CS_SUCCEED

**

*/

CS_RETCODE CS_PUBLIC clientmsg_callback(context,
connection, errmsg)

CS_CONTEXT*context;

CS_CONNECTION*connection;

CS_CLIENTMSG*errmsg;

{

/* Display the message to stdout */

printf("\nOpen Client Message:\n");

printf("Message number: LAYER = (%ld) ORIGIN =
(%ld) ",

CS_LAYER(errmsg->msgnumber), CS_ORIGIN(errmsg-
>msgnumber));
```

```
printf("SEVERITY = (%ld) NUMBER = (%ld)\n",

CS_SEVERITY(errmsg->msgnumber),

CS_NUMBER(errmsg->msgnumber));

printf("Message String: %s\n", errmsg->msgstring);

/* Check if operating system error

if (errmsg->osstringlen > 0)

{

printf("Operating System Error: %s\n",

errmsg->osstring);

}

return CS_SUCCEED;

}

/*

** servermsg_callback()

**

** Type of function:

** example program server message handler

** Installed as a callback into Open Client.
```

```
**

** Returns:

** CS_SUCCEED

*/

CS_RETCODE CS_PUBLIC servermsg_callback(context,
connection, srvmsg)

CS_CONTEXT*context;

CS_CONNECTION*connection;

CS_SERVERMSG*srvmsg;

{

/* Display the message to stdout */

printf("\nServer message:\n");

printf("Message number: %ld, Severity %ld, ",

srvmsg->msgnumber, srvmsg->severity);

printf("State %ld, Line %ld\n",

srvmsg->state, srvmsg->line);


/* Check for additional information
```

```
if (srvmsg->svrnlen > 0)

{

printf("Server '%s'\n", srvmsg->svrname);

}


if (srvmsg->proclen > 0)

{

printf(" Procedure '%s'\n", srvmsg->proc);

}

/* Display the message text */

printf("Message String: %s\n", srvmsg->text);

return CS_SUCCEED;

}
```

Future Directions

I have used DB-Library for over 6 years. As a programmer, I was looking for something platform independent to leverage my skill set. I found it with Sybase, C, and DB-Library. Over the years I have written client applications that were deployed in DEC/VMS, Intel/DOS/Windows, and Unix environments. With minimal coding changes if any, data access functionality written for one platform could be compiled and deployed on another. The Sybase Servers themselves have also run on a wide variety of platforms.

When Sybase got together with Microsoft to create SQL Server 4.2, I was in heaven. Finally I could develop and test powerful client/server applications at home very inexpensively and then roll them out into multimillion dollar installations.

Sybase System 10 and Microsoft SQL Server 6.0 were both released after the breakup of the Sybase/Microsoft alliance. Although both still support DB-Library clients, only time will tell how long this will continue. Much of my client experience has been with Microsoft Windows SDK and MFC against Sybase and MS SQL Servers. I have therefore decided to stick with DB-Library for the time being. I still have the functionality supplied by CT-Library because asynchronous queries can be accomplished within DB-Library by using worker threads.

One of the drawbacks of both CT-Library and DB-Library is that neither is object oriented. This allows them to be compiler independent and is actually a plus when trying to resolve the "Should I use CT-Library or DB-Library?" question. To use either one efficiently in an object-oriented environment such as C++, they need to be wrapped into objects. Using this layered approach when developing Sybase Server applications allows the programmer to easily change the client interface without the need to modify the application itself.

In the case of Microsoft Windows, the wrapper is provided as ODBC. This is a generic database interface and does not provide all of the Sybase Client Library functionality. If you require more functionality or want to trim down the ODBC layer, it is fairly straightforward to create your own connection management and query processing objects (it took me about 2 weeks). Using either method will insulate your application from the problem of which physical connection mechanism to use and allow you to concentrate on the application itself.

CHAPTER 14

Using Open Server

As a systems designer, I have gravitated to using Sybase products in the past because of the ingrained features which support integration of multiple heterogeneous clients and server data sources.

More than just marketing bumpff, this Sybase capability has long been reflected deeply in its products and strategies. In the real world, there isn't room for just one database engine any more than there is room for just one client environment.

In some cases, it has been desired by customers to migrate completely off their traditional legacy systems. However, when you begin dealing with tables consisting of millions of rows and client connections numbering hundreds, it is just impractical to try to migrate everything with the big bang approach. It is far more practical to spend a little extra time, effort, and money, and put the new technology in place in phases.

What this means is that, say, the consolidated General Ledger application may continue to run on a "big iron" mainframe, while the first reporting applications are moved onto Sybase client/

server systems. We have worked a lot with DataWarehouses where the production data remained in the legacy world where decision support was the first application introduced on Sybase.

Over time, of course, the strategy usually calls for the applications to be migrated one by one, as the resources are made available. To accomplish this, integration with legacy systems is mandatory. One of the reasons why we wanted to write this book was because of our experiences in using various flavors of SQL Server in achieving just that objective.

In various other books and articles I have written, I've specifically addressed the need to perform competent data modeling at both the logical and physical level. As a developer, you need a validated, stable data model before you start wasting your valuable time and effort on programming, referring to columns whose names change weekly or accessing tables which disappear.

As an administrator, you must have a map of your database, down to the device level, in order to tease the greatest performance out of your application. Everyone knows that even with the hardware performance gains we've enjoyed over the past twenty and more years, queries always evolve to max out the batch window, let alone ad hoc query standards.

With the introduction of legacy systems integration, there comes a need to map data to its sources of origin, frequently normalizing the data as well.

With replication services comes a need to identify publishers and subscribers of data. Enterprise data dictionaries are the rosetta stone of decision support and distributed systems navigation.

In this section of the book, we deal with the various Sybase tools which are sold to assist you in managing the integration of relational technology with legacy assets. Beyond that, we look at how you can take advantage of this technology to move to distributed and mobile computing applications.

No book is going to be able to be highly relevant to your organization's needs and challenges. There is no substitute for proper analysis and design. It is my sincere hope that you will get some ideas on how this technology can be applied in your environment, as well as a sense of an approach to mastering that technology yourself. And if there's anything we can do to help, give us a call!

There are advantages and disadvantages to the way Sybase has isolated the database engine from the operating system. Yes, security is vastly improved. True, performance can be optimized much more easily. However, while the approach Sybase has taken with Open Client allows excellent integration from the client application into the server, it is still awkward to integrate from the server out.

This is primarily due to the need to make operating system or external application calls based on data changes in the server. In some cases, you want to be able to trigger more than just an additional stored procedure or SQL operation based on a given insert, delete or update. This is essentially what people are referring to when they use the term "WorkFlow."

In this chapter you will gain an appreciation for how workflow can be implemented using Sybase tools, including the traditional Open Server toolset.

Work Flow Automation Defined

As advances in technology hurtle forward, there has been an increasing need to pull together the various data and systems in place throughout organizations. While this requirement exists for even small organizations, large multinational companies are in a position to realize the greatest efficiencies from tightly integrated, data driven applications which communicate over a wide area.

Why? Simply because in a small organization you can look over the top of your cubicle and yell, "Hey Joe, we're out of pencils. Can you pick some up while you're out?" In a conglomerate you can yell all you want but it's not likely to work out as well.

Let's look at a practical example. Some organizations take advantage of its buying power to negotiate lower prices as a matter of policy. To accomplish this a purchase order system might trigger an e-mail to inform a centralized purchasing officer that someone in the company has requisitioned a hundred thousand dollars worth of widgets from supplier Y. Knowing in the past fiscal year the company had already bought a hundred thousand dollars worth of widgets from supplier X could allow a purchasing agent to get a price based on buying two hundred thousand widgets.

On the other hand, this could be a false economy because widgets from supplier Y are completely different from widgets from supplier X. Its not our job to second guess what the users want to do with the data, from a design and development perspective its more important to figure out how to link a purchase order system to your e-mail.

Inter-Application Integration

Let's take the most straightforward example of where we would use open server. We have two applications running on the same physical server.

Typically, this would be a situation where the Sybase SQL Server made an operating system call, perhaps a daemon in unix or sending a message to the console. But the basic arrangement works something like the figure below:

FIGURE 14.1. A Simple Open Server Arrangement

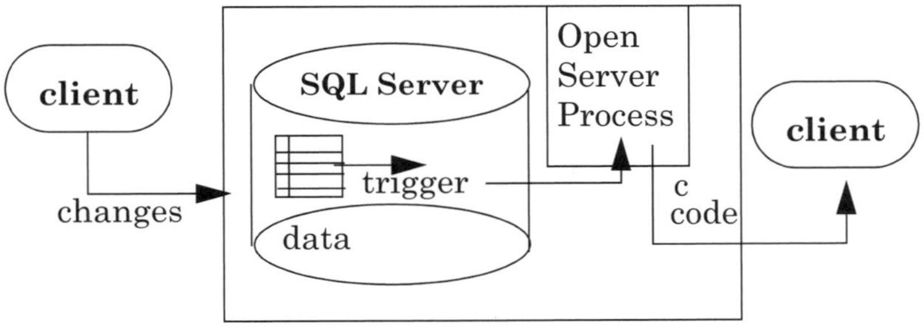

As you can see, a client application changes data, which sets off a predefined trigger. The SQL in the trigger executes a stored procedure belonging to the Open Server. This is handled identically to remote stored procedures, syntactically by prefacing the stored procedure name with the server name, i.e.
`execute open_server.database.dbo.sp_wake_up.`

The Open Server process is a separate operating system process which accepts T-SQL calls such as execute but allows inclusion of code to be executed instead of being limited to SQL. Supported languages for Open Server include C, Cobol, and Ada. For support for other languages, talk to your Sybase rep. The most common language for writing Open Server applications is either C or Cobol depending on which host environment you are trying to integrate.

This is a very powerful offering which can solve a great many application problems in a client/server setting. The example discussed so far has been for an extremely simple situation where you need data driven actions taken by a program or an operating system. Open Server allows you to accomplish this, but it is highly useful for coordinating multiple SQL Server environments, implementing bullet-proof security, or integrating database engines from a variety of vendors. This particular topic is covered in greater detail later in this section.

Before getting into the specifics of how to set up an Open Server for Systems XI, let's look at a more complex requirement which can be solved handily by Open Server technology.

Let's say you have a critical application which demands users be able to log into a server any time, day or night. Synchronizing the database engines themselves can be accomplished with replication, two phase commit, or even dump/load functions through bcp, syb_backup or a third party utility. For our purposes the data is "relatively stable," the requirement is for full server redundancy and transparent switching between them.

Think about that for a second. Using Open Client, you know that an application can abstract much of the addressing of any given server into a name, but how would you make logging into a server transparent for any given user? For that matter, let's say we're not talking about one user, but we're actually talking about several hundred.

Jim Munro, the Open Server guru at our company worked on a problem of this nature several years ago. In fact, this is a real world example of a problem he solved using this technology. The way he approached it was to create a login server using Open Server which had the smarts to ping the primary login server and if no answer was received, to proceed to the next server in the list.

The topology for that application looked something like the following figure:

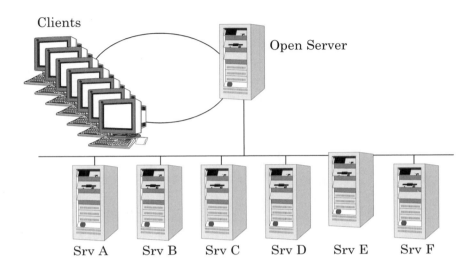

Clients

Open Server

Srv A Srv B Srv C Srv D Srv E Srv F

FIGURE 14.2. Multiple SQL Server topology using Open Server

Other criteria can be used instead of simply pinging a server. If you had rules of thumb for your application about maximum numbers of users per server, you could count the number of connections used and allocate server resources that way.

Certainly this adds a layer of complexity to the system and potential delay from a user perspective. But these costs are inherent in integrating multiple servers anyway, and it is possible to write your code in a tight and efficient manner reducing, if not eliminating, overhead and response time delays.

Setting Up Open Server

Okay, so now you have an idea of where to use Open Server. Let's take a look at exactly what you have to do to set up this puppy.

First, you will need an environment for writing the Open Server application. Specifically, you need an Open Server license from Sybase and a compatible compiler. During the creation of this book, the folks at Sybase were kind enough to provide us with an Open Server license for our Microsoft C/C++ environment running on Windows NT 4.0.

Incidentally, we picked the NT platform for the Open Server application because we liked the price/performance. We saw a terrific opportunity for synergy between big Unix servers running production database applications and some Open Servers running on highly cost effective (read cheap) NT servers. Something to keep in mind if you get anywhere near budgets at your organization.

Anyway, let me turn things over here to Jim.

Open Server Defined

I've been asked many times "What is an Open Server?" and there are really two parts to that answer.

Open Server as an application is a multi-threaded Server Process which appears to Sybase clients and other Sybase Servers to be another Sybase Server. An Open Server will accept client connections, process Remote Procedure Calls and Transact SQL commands and can send back result sets and other Sybase related information such as output parameter values, error codes, and messages.

When a SQL Server executes a stored procedure on another SQL Server, it uses a Remote Procedure Call. This RPC facility is much more efficient than sending T-SQL commands since it bypasses the SQL Server's language handler entirely. Parameters are sent in their native format which negates the need for server parsing and data conversion.

Although an Open Server can accept T-SQL language statements from a client exactly like a SQL Server, the parser and interpreter must be coded by the programmer. Because of this fact, most Open Server functionality is achieved via RPCs.

All processing within the Open Server is coded in a third generation language. Open Server as seen by the developer is a set of programming libraries which provide functions for emulating Sybase Server behavior. Supported languages for Open Server include C, Cobol, and Ada. For support for other languages, talk to your Sybase rep. The most common language for writing Open Server applications is either C or Cobol depending on which host environment you are trying to integrate. By giving the programmer this level of access to the Sybase environment, remote procedures running on an Open Server can access any other third-party library functions.

The Open Server tool kit out of the box does not include any actual database functionality. Open Server has been offered as a method for augmenting Sybase Server functionality and not for replacing it. A typical Open Server application works in conjunction with at least one Sybase Server. By using Open Client, an Open Server application can act as a client to the Sybase Server in order to service its own client's requests.

This is a very powerful offering which can solve a great many application problems in a client/server setting.

Open Server Applications

There are many uses for Open Server in a typical enterprise solution. In fact, you could be running one now without realizing. Sybase offerings including Monitor Server, Replication Server and Omni Server are in fact canned Open Server applications. These applications work in conjunction with SQL Server to enhance SQL Server functionality while minimizing any extra SQL Server processing requirements. An Open Server runs as its own separate operating system process. It can reside anywhere on the network which allows for a distributed processing environment.

Open Server is highly useful for coordinating multiple SQL Server environments, implementing bullet-proof security or integrating database engines from a variety of vendors.

More Inter-Application Integration

Let's take another example of where we would use Open Server to enhance an existing SQL Server installation. ABC Company has an existing SQL Server installation which is running an Order Entry System. To streamline the workflow within their organization, the Credit department needs to be notified of any orders over $10,000.00 as soon as they are placed. The company has an existing e-mail system with a programming interface which they wish to use for notification.

Their solution was to create an Open Server and code a single RPC called sp_send_mail. The RPC is called from the insert trigger of the ORDERS table if the TOTAL_AMOUNT column value exceeds 10,000. The RPC includes parameters for supplying recipient name and the message text which are assembled within the trigger. The RPC then uses API calls to create and sent the mail message. If a mail message cannot be created within the

RPC, an error is returned and the trigger rolls back the entire insert. This is important in ensuring that the message was sent.

Now that the company had a generic mail creation stored procedure they were able to implement workflow across the organization. This tight integration between organizational data and mail allowed them to streamline the entire process from Order Entry to Shipping and track the progress between.

Middleware

Before getting into the specifics of how to set up an Open Server for Systems XI, let's look at a more complex requirement which can be solved handily by Open Server technology.   The above example used Open Server to extend SQL Server functionality. Clients still log into the SQL Server and RPC calls are made from there using the stored procedure syntax `execute OSNAME...sp_name`. Open Server can also serve clients directly. Clients can log into an Open Server directly and access other SQL Servers or Open Servers from there.

In this scenario, you have a critical application which demands users be able to log into a server any time, day or night. Synchronizing the database engines themselves can be accomplished with replication, two phase commit, or even dump/load functions through bcp, syb_backup or a third party utility. For our purposes the data is "relatively stable," the requirement is for full server redundancy and transparent switching between them.

Let's examine this problem. Using Open Client, you know that an application can abstract a lot of the addressing of any given server into a name, but how would you make logging into multiple servers transparent for any given user without having to change the user's server name and addressing information?

For that matter, let's say we're not talking about one user, but we're actually talking about several hundred. You are not going to be able to publish a policy that says something to the effect that if Server One is down, then try Server Two. Real world users tend to have a low confidence in any computing solution that involves that sort of hit and miss activity.

I encountered this problem several years ago and the solution was to have all clients log into an Open Server. This server checked on the availability of the Primary SQL Server. If it was available, client requests were routed there. If the server was not available, requests were routed to the backup SQL Server. One of Open Server's benefits is a feature called Pass-Thru Mode. While in this mode, an Open Server can send and receive Tabular Data Stream packets without needing to unpack and examine them. Pass thru mode maintains Sybase user name and password security. Even though there was an extra layer between the client and the SQL Server, response time was not noticeably affected.

Other criteria can be used instead of simply pinging a server. If you had rules of thumb for your application about maximum numbers of users per server, you could count the number of connections used and allocate server resources that way.

Open Server can also be used to encapsulate business processes which affect multiple SQL Servers. For example, an 'sp_add_product' Open Server RPC could be coded to ensure that new products are added to all departmental servers, mimicing Replication Server functionality by using the Open Client two phase commit library. The RPC could also notify marketing via e-mail of the product's availability.

Registered Procedures

Another powerful feature of Open Server is Registered Procedures and Notification Procedures. These features are available to Open Client applications. In the traditional client-server environment, a client makes a request to a server and processes the results of that request. If the information that the client has requested is not yet available, nothing is returned.

Registered Procedures provide a mechanism for notifying a client when an action has occurred such as a stock price changing, a table being modified, etc. A client executes this procedure knowing that the data is not yet available and supplies the server with a function to execute when it is.

Notification Procedures are System Registered Procedures which allow clients to dynamically request notification of the execution of other Registered Procedures on the Open Server. For example, a client can request to be notified any time that a user executes the procedure "sp_who."

System Registered Procedures

Any Open Server automatically provides clients with several Registered Procedures. These procedures are used to return Server status information and to allow for the dynamic creation of Notification Procedures.

One familiar procedure is 'sp_who' which displays information about all threads running on the server. Another registered procedure "sp_ps" returns a subset of this information.

Unlike SQL Server which provides the stored procedure 'sp_help,' Open Server uses the registered procedure 'sp_reglist' to return a list of all available registered procedures.

Setting Up the Development Environment

Once the Open Server Setup Wizard has been run, you will need to modify your compiler's "INCLUDE" and "LIBRARY" paths in order to use the Open Server API.

Versions 1.0 and 2.0 of the Open Server were a complete API and Open Servers used DB-Library only if they were acting as clients themselves with other Open or SQL Servers.

Since System 10, Sybase has taken the common connection management components of both DB-Library and OS-Library and created a new connection management library called CS-Library. This library is used both for CT-Library client applications and Version 10 Open Server applications. A second library, Server-Library, contains all of the server specific functions.

Installing an Open Server

An Open Server application is an executable program launched as an Operating System background task. Depending on how it has been coded, parameters may need to be passed to supply things like Server Name, Log File Name, etc.

Version 1.0 and 2.0 Open Servers read a file (INTERFACES or WIN.INI) in order to determine which port, socket or pipe to use when listening for client requests exactly like pre-System 10 SQL Servers. Version 10 Open Servers make use of the new SQL.INI file to accomplish this.

Create an entry in the appropriate file in the same manner that you would add a new SQL Server entry. When the Open Server is executed, it will check the file to determine to which port/socket/pipe to attach.

Structure of an Open Server Application

Open Server Architecture

Open Server is a multi-threaded server application. It contains an internal message queue of event requests which is automatically maintained. Any time a client connects, disconnects, or makes a request, an event message is added to the queue. Messages can also be added to the queue programmatically from within the Open Server itself. When the server retrieves a message from the queue, it calls the event handler associated with the message.

Event handlers are callback functions which are usually installed when the Open Server is being initialized. Events include execute RPC requests, execute SQL text, server start, server stop, server errors and client connect. Most standard events have default handlers associated with them. For example, the default handler which is called when a Client tries to execute SQL text will return the message "No Language Handler Installed." To extend the functionality of the default handler, the programmer creates a new callback function and installs it using either the srv_props or srv_handle function depending on the specific event. The new handler replaces the handler previously installed. In general, the handler for any specific event can be changed at any time during the execution life of the Open Server.

The steps involved in creating a basic Open Server are as follows:

1) Allocate a CS-Library Context Structure

2) Install a CS-Library error handler

3) Set any other context or localization properties.

4) Associate the context structure with the Open Server and set the version.

5) Install the server error handler

6) Set any other server properties.

7) Initialize the Open Server internal structures.

8) Install any necessary event handlers (RPCs, client management, text handling, etc.)

9) Run the server.

Once the server begins running it will scans the message queue for event requests. Any time a message is found, the server will execute its associated event handler. Most messages are inserted into the message queue at the same (MEDIUM) priority and are serviced on a first in first out basis. Any messages with a HIGH priority will be moved to the front of the queue. An example of this is a Cancel Query request from a client. On the flip side, messages with a LOW priority will remain in the queue until all MEDIUM and HIGH priority messages have been serviced. This is handy for user-defined background maintenance tasks.

Skeleton Open Server Application

The following code fragment illustrates the main() function of a basic Open Server application. Originally shipped as the OSINTRO.C sample, it has been enhanced to provide basic error handling functionality. A detailed explanation of each of the above nine steps follows.

```
/*

**          Sybase Open Server Version 10.0
```

```
**        Confidential Property of Sybase, Inc.

**          (c) Copyright Sybase, Inc. 1993

**          All rights reserved

**

** OSINTRO.C

**

**This program takes the minimum steps necessary to
** initialize and start an Open Server application.

*/

#if       (USE_SCCSID)

static char       Sccsid[] = {"%Z% %M% %I% %G%"};

#endif   /* (USE_SCCSID) */

/*

** Include the operating system specific header files required
** by this Open Server application.

*/

#include          <stdio.h>

/*

** Include the required Open Server header files.

**
```

```
**      ospublic.h       Public Open Server **structures,
typedefs, defines,

**                      and function prototypes.

**

**      oserror.h       Open Server error number defines.  This
** header file is only required if the Open Server application
** wants to detect specific errors in the Open Server

**                      error handler.

*/

#include        <ospublic.h>

#include        <oserror.h>

#include        "OSLib.h"

/*

** Local defines.

**      OS_ARGCOUNT       Expected number of command
** line arguments.

*/

#define OS_ARGCOUNT     2

/*

** This is the main entry point for this sample Open Server
application.

** The following arguments are expected on the command line:
```

```
**

**      OSName       The name of the Open Server application.

**                   This name must exist in the interfaces file

**                   defined by the SYBASE environment variable.

**

** Returns:

**      0                    Open Server exited successfully.

** 1    An error was detected during initialization.

*/

int     main( argc, argv )

int argc;

char *argv[];

{

CS_CONTEXT          *cp;                     /* Context
structure.              */

CS_CHAR             OSName[MAX_SERVERNAME];      /* Open
Server application name.         */

CS_CHAR     logfile[512];  /* Log file name.
*/

CS_BOOL             ok;                      /* Error control
flag.             */
```

```
/* Initialization.
*/

ok = CS_TRUE;

/*

** Read the command line options.  There must be
one argument

** specifying the server name.

*/

strcpy(OSName, argv[1]);

if (OSName == char(*)NULL)

return (CS_FALSE);

/*

** Allocate a CS-Library context structure to
define the default

** localization information. Open Server will also store
global

** state information in this structure during initialization.

*/

if(cs_ctx_alloc(CS_VERSION_100, &cp) == CS_FAIL)

{
```

```
(CS_VOID)fprintf(stderr, "%s: cs_ctx_alloc
failed", OSName);

return(CS_FALSE);

}

/*

** Default Open Server localization information can be changed

** here before calling srv_version using cs_config and
**cs_locale. Open Server uses CS-Library internallyfor data
**conversion so all applications should install a CS-Library
**error handler if they are interested in receiving data
**conversion errors.

*/

cs_config(cp, CS_SET, CS_MESSAGE_CB, (void
*)&cs_err_handler, sizeof(int), NULL);

/*

** Set the Open Server version and context information.

*/

if(srv_version(cp, CS_VERSION_100) == CS_FAIL)

{

/*

** Release the context structure already allocated.

*/
```

```
(CS_VOID)cs_ctx_drop(cp);

(CS_VOID)fprintf(stderr, "%s: srv_version failed",
OSName);

return(CS_FALSE);

}

/*

** Install the Server error handler

*/

srv_props(cp, CS_SET, SRV_S_ERRHANDLE,

  (void *)&server_err_handler, sizeof(int), NULL);

/*

** Default Open Server global properties can be
changed here

** before calling srv_init.  We just change the
default log

** file name to use the name of this Open Server.

*/

/*

** Build a new Open Server log file name using
`OSName'.
```

```
*/

(CS_VOID)sprintf(logfile, "%s.log", OSName);

/*

** Set the new log file name using the global SRV_S_LOGFILE

** property.

*/

if(srv_props(cp, CS_SET, SRV_S_LOGFILE, logfile, CS_NULLTERM,

(CS_INT *)NULL) == CS_FAIL)

{

/*

** Release the context structure already allocated.

*/

(CS_VOID)cs_ctx_drop(cp);

(CS_VOID)fprintf(stderr,

"%s: srv_props(SRV_S_LOGFILE) failed\n", OSName);

return(CS_FALSE);

}
```

```
/*

** Initialize Open Server.  This causes Open Server
to allocate

** internal control structures based on the global
properties set

** above.  Open Server also looks up the OSName in
the

** interfaces files.

*/

if(srv_init((SRV_CONFIG *)NULL, OSName,
CS_NULLTERM)

== (SRV_SERVER *)NULL)

{

/*

** Release the context structure already allocated.

*/

(CS_VOID)cs_ctx_drop(cp);

(CS_VOID)fprintf(stderr, "%s: srv_init failed\n",
OSName);

return(CS_FALSE);
```

```
}

/*

**        Install Event handlers

*/

if ( srv_handle((SRV_SERVER *)NULL, SRV_START,
start_regproc)

== CS_FAIL )

{

(CS_VOID)cs_ctx_drop(cp);

(CS_VOID)fprintf(stderr, "%s: srv_handle
failed\n",

OSName);

return(CS_FALSE);

}

/*

** Start up Open Server.

*/

if(srv_run((SRV_SERVER *)NULL) == CS_FAIL)

{
```

```
(CS_VOID)fprintf(stderr, "%s: srv_run failed\n",
OSName);

ok = CS_FALSE;

}

/*

** Release all allocated control structures and
exit.

*/

(CS_VOID)cs_ctx_drop(cp);

return(ok ? CS_TRUE : CS_FALSE);

}
```

Allocate a CS-Library Context Structure

CS-Library is used to manage low-level client and server connections. Open Server Library versions 10 and CS-Library work tightly together in much the same manner as CT-Library and CS-Library. A CS_CONTEXT structure must be allocated for the Open Server in order to store necessary localization information. Localization information refers to such things as character set, language and currency definitions. This structure is also used by Open Server as a place to store global state information. Even if you decide to use DB-Library as a connection mechanism within your Open Server instead of CT-Library, the server libraries still require the CS-Library context structure.

```
CS_CONTEXT        *cp;

/* Context structure.            */

if(cs_ctx_alloc(CS_VERSION_100, &cp) == CS_FAIL)

{

(CS_VOID)fprintf(stderr, "%s: cs_ctx_alloc
failed", OSName);

return(1);

}
```

Use the cs_ctx_alloc() function to allocate the CS_CONTEXT structure. The version parameter defines the highest level of Tabular Data Stream that CS-Library will try to negotiate when accepting client connections.

Install a CS-Library Error Handler

The commands cs_config() and cs_locale() are used to set CS-Library configuration and localization information, respectively. At a minimum it is recommended that you install a CS-Library message handler.

```
/*

**Default Open Server localization information can be changed

**here before calling srv_version using cs_config and
**cs_locale.
```

```
** Open Server uses CS-Library internally for data conversion
**so applications should install a CS-Library error handler if
** they are interested in receiving data conversion errors.

*/

cs_config(cp, CS_SET, CS_MESSAGE_CB, (void
*)&cs_err_handler,

sizeof(int), NULL);
```

cs_err_handler is a callback function. CS-Library will call this function if any CS-Library errors occur. An example of a CS-Library error handler follows.

```
/*

** CS_ERR_HANDLER

**

**This routine is the CS-Library error handler used by this
**Open Server application. CS-Library calls it whenever an
**error occurs.

**      Here we simply log the error text and return.

*/

CS_RETCODE CS_PUBLIC cs_err_handler(cp, msg)

CS_CONTEXT       *cp;

CS_CLIENTMSG     *msg;

{
```

```
CS_CHAR          mbuf[CS_MAX_MSG*2];      /* Message
buffer. */

/*

** Send the message to stdout.

*/

fprintf(stdout, "CS-Library error %ld/%ld/%ld/%ld
- %s\n",

CS_LAYER(msg->msgnumber),

CS_ORIGIN(msg->msgnumber), CS_SEVERITY(msg-
>msgnumber),

CS_NUMBER(msg->msgnumber), msg->msgstring);

/*

** Log any operating system error information.

*/

if( msg->osstringlen > 0 )

{

fprintf(stdout,

"CS-Library Operating system error %ld - %s.\n",

msg->osnumber, msg->osstring);
```

```
}

return CS_SUCCEED;

}
```

A CS-Library error handler is always called with two parameters. CS_CONTEXT is the Open Server's context structure and CS_CLIENTMSG is a message structure. In this example only the CS_CLIENTMSG structure is examined, but the CS_CONTEXT is also useful for retrieving Open Server Name and other information. The CS_CONTEXT structure parameter contains the error message number and text as well as any Operating System error and its text. Use the CS_... macros to extract individual status values from the msgnumber member.

Set Any Other Context or Localization Properties.

In this example, the only CS property we are setting is the error handler function name. If there is any other CS configuration or localization information to be set it must be done before the context structure is passed to the Open Server for registration.

Associate the Context Structure with the Open Server and Set the Version.

Use the Server Library function srv_version() to set the Open Server's context structure and version.

```
/*

** Set the Open Server version and context
information.

*/
```

```
if(srv_version(cp, CS_VERSION_100) == CS_FAIL)

{

/*

** Release the context structure already allocated.

*/

(CS_VOID)cs_ctx_drop(cp);

(CS_VOID)fprintf(stderr, "%s: srv_version failed",
OSName);

return(CS_FALSE);

}
```

If this function fails, it is good practice to deallocate the
CS_CONTEXT structure using cs_ctx_drop() before returning.

Install the Server Error Handler

It is recommended that any Open Server application has a Server
error handler installed as well as a CS-Library error handler.
This callback function is called by Open Server anytime Server
Library generates an error. The Server Library function
srv_props() is used to set and get Open Server properties and is
used in the example to set the error handler to the user callback
function server_err_handler.

```
/*

** Install the Server error handler
```

```
*/

srv_props(cp, CS_SET, SRV_S_ERRHANDLE,

 (void *)&server_err_handler, sizeof(int), NULL);
```

Server error handlers are called by Open Server with a number of parameters for a number of reasons. This simple example examines the operating system error number and severity parameters. A complete error handler should determine if the error was caused by a client connection and, if so, send an informational message to the client.

```
/*

** SERVER_ERR_HANDLER

**Open Server calls this routine whenever an internal error
**occurs. The arguments passed in describe the error number,
**severity and error string, as well as which thread,
**if any, was active when the error occurred.

**      We deal with the different error severities as follows:

**      SRV_FATAL_SERVER        This error means that Open
**Server hit an unrecoverable error. We try to log it and
**return.

**      SRV_FATAL_PROCESS       This severity indicates that a
**thread hit an error that will cause the thread to terminate.
**We log the error and return.

**      SRV_INFO This is an informational error. If the given

**thread is an active client thread, we send the

**error information that client via a message.

**
```

```
** Parameters:

**       server          - The Open Server server running.

**       sp              - The Open Server thread that got the
**error.

**       errornum        - The Open Server error number.

**       severity        - The error severity.

**       state           - The error state.

**       oserrnum        - The operating system error number, if
**any.

**       errtext         - The text of the error message.

**       errtextlen      - The length of the errtext message

**       oserrtext       - The text of the operating system
**error message.

**       oserrtextlen    - The length of the errtext message.

**

** Returns:

**       CS_CONTINUE      Continue with this Open Server.

**       CS_FAIL          Exit the Open Server application.

*/

CS_RETCODE        CS_PUBLIC
server_err_handler(server, sp, errornum, severity,

state, oserrnum, errtext, errtextlen, oserrtext,

oserrtextlen)
```

```
SRV_SERVER      *server;

SRV_PROC        *sp;

CS_INT          errornum;

CS_INT          severity;

CS_INT          state;

CS_INT          oserrnum;

CS_CHAR         *errtext;

CS_INT          errtextlen;

CS_CHAR         *oserrtext;

CS_INT          oserrtextlen;

{

/*

** Is it an operating system error? If so, log it.

*/

if (oserrnum != SRV_ENO_OS_ERR)

{

/*

** Log the error.
```

```
*/

fprintf(stdout, "OPERATING SYSTEM ERROR: %d:
%s.\n",

oserrnum, oserrtext);

}

/*

** Is this a fatal error for the Open Server
application?

*/

if (severity == SRV_FATAL_SERVER)

{

/*

** Try to log the error, and return.

*/

fprintf(stdout," FATAL SERVER ERROR: %d/%d/%d:
%s.\n", errornum, severity, state, errtext);

return SRV_EXIT_PROGRAM;

}

/*
```

```
** Did a thread get a fatal error?

*/

if (severity == SRV_FATAL_PROCESS)

{

/*

** Log the error, and return.

*/

fprintf(stdout,

"FATAL CONNECT ERROR: %d/%d/%d: %s.\n",

errornum, severity, state, errtext);

return CS_CONTINUE;

}

/*

** Let's log the error.

*/

fprintf(stdout, "ERROR: %d/%d/%d: %s.\n",

errornum, severity, state, errtext);

return CS_CONTINUE;
```

```
}
```

Set Any Other Server Properties.

Another function of srv_props() is setting the server's log file name. Since Open Server runs as an independent process, the Message Log is an important mechanism for logging error messages and debugging information.

A typical Open Server application will route all CS-Library errors and Server Library errors to the Message Log file.

```
if(srv_props(cp, CS_SET, SRV_S_LOGFILE, logfile,
CS_NULLTERM,

(CS_INT *)NULL) == CS_FAIL)

{

/*

** Release the context structure already allocated.

*/

(CS_VOID)cs_ctx_drop(cp);

(CS_VOID)fprintf(stderr,

"srv_props(SRV_S_LOGFILE) failed\n");

return(CS_FALSE);

}
```

Initialize the Open Server Internal Structures.

An Open Server is started with 2 main functions, srv_init() and srv_run(). srv_init() is used to initialize the internal Open Server structures and srv_run() is used to initiate the Server message handling loop.

```
/*

** Initialize Open Server. This causes Open Server to allocate

** internal control structures based on the global properties set

** above. Open Server also looks up the OSName in the

** interfaces files.

*/

if(srv_init((SRV_CONFIG *)NULL, OSName, CS_NULLTERM)

== (SRV_SERVER *)NULL)

{

/*

** Release the context structure already allocated.

*/

(CS_VOID)cs_ctx_drop(cp);
```

```
fprintf(stderr, "%s: srv_init failed\n", OSName);

return(CS_FALSE);

}
```

Install Any Necessary Event Handlers

This includes any RPCs, client management or text handling your application may need.

Open Server must be initialized before any event handlers can be installed. In this example, a handler is installed to respond to the SRV_START event. When the server first begins running it generates a SRV_START message. In this case the user function start_regproc() will be called in response to the SRV_START message.

Many Open Servers use the Server Start Event to install RPCs and other message handlers.

```
/*

**      Install Event handlers

*/

if (srv_handle((SRV_SERVER *)NULL, SRV_START,
start_regproc)

== CS_FAIL)

{

(CS_VOID)cs_ctx_drop(cp);
```

```
(CS_VOID)fprintf(stderr, "%s: srv_handle
failed\n",

OSName);

return(CS_FALSE);

}

}
```

Run the Server.

The srv_run() function is what begins the actual message processing. Once srv_run() has been called, all execution takes place within the event handling routines.

```
/*

** Start up Open Server.

*/

if(srv_run((SRV_SERVER *)NULL) == CS_FAIL)

{

(CS_VOID)fprintf(stderr, "%s: srv_run failed\n",
OSName);

ok = CS_FALSE;

Server Configuration using srv_prop()

Events and Handlers
```

Logging Messages

Registering Procedures

The SRV_STOP Event

And voilà, now you have a working Open Server process!

CHAPTER 15

Omni Connect

OMNI SQL Gateway

One of the key architectural features of the Open Server environment is that it allows the addition of features that are not normally provided in the SQL Server product. One of the most significant possibilities is the ability to translate data from other environments and allow it to be accessed as if it were a SQL Server using all of the well-known client access mechanisms. Sybase recognized this capability early on and began marketing internally developed products that incorporated this level of function. They were not the only ones who recognized this opportunity.

A smaller company, MDI, also developed and marketed data translation products based on the Open Server architecture. Sybase later purchased MDI and incorporated its primary product line into its own. They even shelved some of their own products that were less capable than the equivalent MDI product. Sybase also reworked its connectivity strategy to become more consistent and coherent. The connectivity products that Sybase is now marketing are much higher quality and more easily understood.

The cornerstone to the connectivity products is the OMNIServer Gateway. This product is positioned as the universal server through which clients can access all of the non-Sybase data resources transparently. It's a little like a data proxy server. A client requests data from the OMNIServer who in turn translates that request into a specific data request from another server. The OMNIServer returns the required information to the original client who requested it. The client is never aware that any other resource was required except the OMNIServer. The OMNIServer obtains data at the request of the client.

The OMNIServer itself contains no tables or user information. It keeps track of resources that are in other environments and presents them as if they were local databases and tables, etc. This allows the OMNIServer to function as a data integration and warehouse environment.

Data that may reside on several different application servers, for instance, can be accessed and even joined through the OMNIServer environment for decision support operation. The client signs into the OMNIServer environment as if it were any other SQL Server environment. The regular Open Server features are used to allow the OMNIServer to understand and respond to these regular client requests. The client is unaware that the information they requested may have been provided from another server.

This capability alone makes the OMNIServer product popular with large enterprise-oriented organizations. They can allow their SQL Server application environments to be structured in a manner directly suited to the intended application use. They can then provide a structured access to this information for other applications using the OMNIServer.

This is often more effective than becoming concerned about enabling and maintaining the appropriate remote connection security on each individual SQL Server. The individual administrators do not need to be concerned about what trust relationships are established and individual ids and security privileges. They can share public data to whatever degree desired by allowing the OMNIServer to publish it on their behalf.

Most organizations would encourage all users to become valid OMNIServer logins and then manage individual user permissions by groups to the various application databases, tables, and views. This simplifies administration and allows a consolidated control point for data access.

Another common usage of the OMNIServer is to allow organizations an easier migration to an enterprise data model. This is especially useful for organizations where departments or applications have been developed without a consistent and coherent enterprise data model and plan.

As a result, the organization is left with a legacy problem to be dealt with in their conversion to an enterprise data model. The OMNIServer allows them to repackage this existing legacy data into objects more consistent with the new model. This can be done immediately without compromising the integrity of the existing application systems.

On it's own, the OMNIServer product is a capable and valuable product. It becomes even more strategic when combined with the other OMNIConnect products such as OMNIConnect Oracle or OMNIConnect for DB/2. These products are Open Server-based products. However, they translate requests from Open Client applications into native requests to the underlying database environment. The target systems perform the operation and return to the client a result just as if a SQL Server had answered the request. This process of translating T-SQL requests into other database dialects is a key capability provided by the Open Server libraries.

Extended to an enterprise solution this allows an organization to ubiquitously deploy the Open Client libraries across the organization and allow those clients universal access to all their data sources. By standardizing on the Open Client data access, an organization can standardize and simplify their client workstation environments. This can reduce costs and improve support.

When combined with the OMNIServer product that allows these other OMNIConnect services to be defined through it both a simplified client and server environment are created. All clients make data requests exclusively with the Open Client access to the OMNIServer. The OMNIServer relays the requests to the designated enterprise or application server and responds appropriately to the client.

As elegant a solution as this is on paper it raises an interesting question. Why hasn't this universal approach been more successful in the real world? Do these products work as advertised? The answer is yes with a couple of qualifications. As usual the devil is in the details. The OMNIServer and OMNIConnect products do work for most things at most times.

Unfortunately, there are a couple of hang-ups. The first is that not all functions that would be available in the native environments are available in the OMNI world. Not every feature works in exactly the way a normal human being would expect. We of course refer to these unexpected features as bugs.

The second significant limitation is performance.

Omni Performance

There are occasions for which there is just no equivalent SQL Server command to translate into for the remote system. The real deal is that as soon as you have one exception to the universal access rule the whole value of the thing comes into question. Of course, this doesn't have to be the case it can be a managed situation based on need. However, once a precedent is established it becomes much more difficult to manage.

The folks at Sybase have sensibly provided a Pass Thru Mode, that allows the gateway products to ignore any translation steps and pass the client request verbatim to the server and the response back in the same manner.

The theory would be that once in awhile when a request is untranslatable then a passthru call is practical. Once this facility is used to any significant degree the question of how practical the universal client access metaphor is will reappear. This becomes a lot more pressing when some of the performance implications are considered.

As everyone is aware, none of this translation or proxy data retrieval service is free from a performance perspective. Client requests are retrieved at the OMNIServer where they are parsed and interpreted as regular T-SQL statements. Then the appropriate request is made to the remote server, which again proceeds through the same process of parsing and optimizing before returning a result set.

If the OMNIServer is doing a join, then this process is repeated many times with the OMNIServer producing the joined result set. As can be expected, this introduces some overhead into each request. The OMNIConnect products, by introducing a translation step to convert the T-SQL requests into a native format, also introduce a performance penalty.

The OMNI products are intended to simplify access and management, but they do extract a performance penalty for this functionality. It's a funny thing but programmers and users are pretty sensitive to such things. They are amazingly uninterested in paying the performance fee for their convenience.

Another issue to be aware of is that these solutions must be evaluated for suitability to intended use. This is a fancier way of saying just because you can do it doesn't mean you necessarily should. Take an example of an organization that's aggressively moving into the distributed world and trying to facilitate this process by providing a bridge back to their legacy DB/2 data. They figure this OMNIConnect for DB/2 product as the cat's meow for such a project. All's good at this point. It seems sensible enough. Then they define their 10 million row customer detail history file to the OMNI environment and send out a corporate memo declaring it open season.

The next day Joe Salesman walks in, sees the memo and fires up his trusty 486/25 and decides to go hunting. His MS/Access program seems just the weapon for such an opportunity. He defines a join between the DB/2 customer detail file and the marketing customer master to see if there are any real customers that marketing doesn't know about. Of course, he does this join using the OMNIServer. The next sound you hear will be the other system users yelling to each other "Is the network down?" This noise will cascade down the hall for a few moments.

Next will be the OMNIServer administrator screaming while running down the hall to the server room to restart the server after it melts like cheddar cheese over nicely grilled hamburger. Finally, there is the subtle PC bell tone of the little 486/25 popping up an error window to tell Joe Salesman his hard disk is full. Not a pretty picture, is it? You may want to carefully consider the larger implications to your environment before determining whether these types of solutions are appropriate for you. Of course, with planning and common sense these types of scenarios are avoidable and can be managed appropriately. This can only be applied if you're aware of the fact that they should be.

A couple of issues that fall into the category of features that you wish were excluded from the products. These are things that you should be aware of when using these products.

It is possible, and in some cases desirable, to use the OMNIServer environment to perform initial or large data loads in the distributed environment without using the Sybase "Bulk Copy Utility." Both tables are defined to the OMNIServer and the data is migrated or copied using a "SELECT INTO" statement. This works really well in many situations. Problems can occur as the data sizes increase because this operation runs in a single transaction with no other controls on it. This can cause the database log for the target table to fill up and place the process into "log suspend" status.

This can be a problem when the data sets are large or the database consists of the single table to be loaded and the transaction log is only a small percentage of the overall size. You can get the table with 10% of the data and the log will fill up. You could make the log the same size as the database, but that seems a little wasteful for ordinary operations. Using the BCP program an administrator can control the transaction commit behavior and insure that the transaction logs don't fill up.

Another feature to be aware of with the OMNIServer and OMNI-Connect products is that indexing behavior on views may not work as expected. In the normal operation of a SQL Server, when queries are made of view the indexes from the underlying tables are used to efficiently satisfy the request. In the OMNI environments this may not always be true. When views are defined in the OMNIServer and the base tables and indexes are accessed through the OMNIconnect products, then it is very likely that you will encounter extremely poor query optimization. The default behavior for the OMNIServer environment is to go and obtain all the data in the base table first and then apply any filter criteria. This will make performance unacceptable for large tablesets.

These products provide a very nice architectural fit, but they do need to be implemented with care and planning. They definitely work and are robust enough for production environments, but cautious implementation is advised. These products are ideal examples of the types of features and capabilities that the Open Server product from Sybase incorporates.

Summary

OMNIConnect is a key product under the Sybase family for integrating heterogeneous data sources with one client configuration – Open Client. The problem is one of complexity and performance.

Using OMNIConnect, it is possible to make accessing far-flung corporate data very easy. It's easy. In fact, it's almost too easy. Without proper planning and administration the costs in terms of network traffic and system workloads can get out of control. One must be cautious about employing these solutions to avoid setting unreasonable and unachievable expectations.

CHAPTER 16

Replication & Data Synchronization Strategies

Distributed inventories require that you be able to book or allocate product (data) held on another site Rep Server. You could use asynchronous stored procs to ensure you were actually successful in booking off the remote inventory and replication would communicate the changed data out to the other centers.

Over half of the initial uses for Rep Server were warm standby sites. The product is now a little over 4 years old, and new uses for the features are beginning to be used. Applications are now being designed to take advantage of Rep Server capabilities. The biggest original users were investment banks on the East Coast of the United States interested primarily in warm standby servers.

Replication server is a key driver for a high-speed link within an enterprise such as ATM. Replication Server could easily drive corporate implementation of high-speed network switches from one site to another, especially where you are linking major headquarters, say, Houston, Calgary, and London for an Oil & Gas multinational.

Routes can be established that allow you to propagate multiple sites from centralized headquarters, for example, New York to London and subsequently from London on to Lisbon, Paris, Bonn, and Vienna. This allows you to select appropriate underlying communications channels rather than having to tie all of those sites back directly to New York or wherever a master server was located.

Concepts

Distinctions between distributed and replicated data:

- Distributed data is a single image of the database maintained across multiple servers.
- Replicated data is copied from a designated primary or master copy held across multiple servers.

Rep server was designed to support warm sites for disaster recovery and propagation of data across a large organization to allow access locally (including mainframe data). The key architectural benefit of replication is the ability to move data off to other servers, whether for performance (reducing number of users sharing a box) or access time (moving WAN access to LAN access).

Distributed data looks at the model of master copies across multiple sites, Replication Server looks at how to copy that data from server A to server B and servers C, D, and E, if appropriate.

Synchronous versus Asynchronous Changes

Synchronous data management across multiple servers is best characterized by two phase commit. Either all the changes are applied or none of them are. Asynchronous changes may or may not be applied immediately depending on issues such as the network being up, timing, etc. The state consistency is affected by the mode of change, in other words, comparing the primary to replicate data gives you an indication of whether synchronous or asynchronous applies (tight consistency or loose consistency).

Tight consistency requires atomic transactions across servers. If the update, insert, or delete fails, all changes are rolled back. Locks are maintained until all changes are successfully completed. TP monitors like Tuxedo, Encina, Top End, and CICS look after tight consistency across multiple heterogeneous servers, such as DB/2, Oracle, and Sybase.

Loose consistency applies where data are not required to match on all servers at any given time. Under usual operations and green light status for all servers and connections the norm may be a few seconds. (Distributed networking to allow replicated data across servers in Thailand, Malaysia, and elsewhere, for example.) Manufacturing data provided by globally distributed operations where the network may be down for any number of days due to phone system failures and other environmental difficulties.

The expected length of potential downtime must be modeled as part of the Rep Server topology. "Heartbeat" utilities will provide statistics on latency or how old the data is on any given server. System architects should design the system with a "steady-state" view of the amount of data to be replicated. Will down time translate into bottlenecks so that the link will be clogged when it comes back up? How much data will be transferred? These sorts of issues must be modeled when determining the best Rep Server architecture.

Rep Server topology design is cross-disciplinary; it spans app design, network management, server administration, capacity planning, database administration, plus architectural approaches. To do it well requires that the system designer be familiar with a wide range of issues.

While Replication Server is an asynchronous method of replicating data, other methods include:

- Database dump and load
- BCP
- Transaction log transfer

These other methods are all snapshot treatment of tables, which is to say, point in time oriented not transaction oriented.

The Replication Server product from Sybase is designed to augment or replace these methods.

Definition of Rep Server

Rep Server provides continuous, asynchronous transfer of log records to replicate databases. The Log Transfer Manager is a process responsible for managing this update process so that all logged transactions are applied to replicate databases. This provides transactional consistency, all data are kept in a consistent state within a specific transaction. Where a transaction updates multiple rows, all changes are applied to replicants. The replicant can subscribe to subsets of the base tables to propagate only changes to desired rows. (For subsidiary business units, this would replicate only changes to rows with data concerning that business unit for example.) This can be handled at the row or specified table level.

Benefits

Several major benefits accrue from using the Replication Server approach.

Fault tolerance is supported in both the network and servers as latency allowed in the replication. Database Servers from multiple vendors is supported through combination of Rep Server with Open Gateways.

Drawbacks

Application transparency: Rep Server may move data according to time/change criteria, but the application is typically required to be aware of the status of the replicated data.

Asynch stored procedures allow queries to be performed locally against replicated data and changes to be applied against the remote primary server.

Primary Data

All data to be replicated must have a designated primary row. Primary tables contain at least one primary row but may also contain replicated data. Primary databases contain primary tables. Bidirectional replication may be architected for disaster recovery sites where a particular direction may only be activated in the event of a disaster. The warm site does not propagate data back unless activated by an emergency; however, the design must allow for restoration of data from backup site to previous primaries when they are brought back on-line.

Sybase manages this process with their tech support applications. All customer data are maintained primary in Emeryville, the Burlington office can request this data, there is a location code to be stored for each row that indicates whether it is EME data or BUR. However, as a design characteristic, there must be a unique key for any table to be replicated. Usually this is enforced with a unique primary key.

Rules for Managing Loose Consistency

There must be a primary row and you must know who owns the row. This *may* only be for a particular transaction, if the owner of the data changes as the record moves from processing site to processing site.

Sybase does not prevent you from allowing all data to be replicated everywhere. This means it must be dealt with in the architecture. However, there are some limitations on this...if you replicate Emeryville data, for example, to Burlington and then back, you could have an endless loop. However, the TLM only applies changes made by other than the maintenance user, all replications are recorded under the authority of the maintenance user thereby ensuring that such an endless loop does not occur.

There can be multiple replicate copies at a particular site or within a single server. However, replicated rows should not be updated by an application unless they are designated both primary and replicated rows. Replicate tables do not have a path for forwarding changes to other servers holding these rows as replicates.

Replication may be based on a where clause to provide for table fragments (joins are not supported). To replicate columns only you designate an entire column (only one per version 10 Rep Server), this is known as a projection.

Sample Applications

To meet the various requirements that a customer might have, these application architectures can be deployed.

Design Considerations

A large component of Rep Server topology design is determining which communications channel to use. In some cases it will be more cost effective to route a replication through two servers rather than to do it directly point to point, simply because of the amount of data and the speed of the link. A route from Vancouver to Montreal may involve a stop in Toronto since both of them require access to primary tables. This works better when considering four or more sites. T1 links are faster (obviously) than 56 KBPS links. This underlying communications topology including bandwidth forms the skeleton for your Rep Server application.

For querying replicated tables and updating another server with designated primary tables, you may use remote stored procedures. Or you can create a replication definition on the remote server that does not actually update the data but records the fact that the stored procedure fired and then replicates those changes to the designated primary as part of the TLM process. The changes are not applied locally, they are made against the primary and later replicated back to the local data where the user made the update to the Rep Server definition.

Applying changes to multiple copies of the data and then replicating those changes throughout your system will yield unpredictable results. It may be possible to model this or make business decisions about it, but most likely you will want to manage it as part of the Rep Server architecture.

Also, you could choose to make the changes locally, but put a pending flag on it. This could be handled either as a ready flag or with a table containing the primary keys of the pending rows.

Distributed Primary Fragment

Depending on the amount of locally designated primary data, replication can manage subscriptions of subsets of various servers. However, to update the data of another server data, they would have to log in remotely.

Corporate Roll-Up

The corporate head office would subscribe to all primary data and data would be replicated to a central server where "the big picture" can be seen, while local users can treat the data as completely local with LAN performance. This would mean that you would roll out read-only copies of the data for decision support or data warehouse requirements.

Warm Standby

Due to latency, transactions may not be applied at the point of fail-over. The traditional view of a HOT SITE standby requires that no transactions may be outstanding. The warm standby is also often used for decision support unless and until a failure occurs at which point it becomes the designated primary.

Rep Server Systems Architecture

Here we go into the specific components which make up a typical Replication Server environment. Even those of you with a great deal of experience with the Sybase SQL Server product may be surprised at the number of new elements and procedures introduced as part of the Rep Server product.

Keywords and Concepts

Publish Source Data: This means to define columns and rows to be available for replication

Subscribers copy published data to their local databases

Materialization is the synchronization of the primary and the replicate databases. It is the process by which the subscribed rows are moved into the replicate tables.

The Players

These are the components that make up a Replication Server environment

- PRS – Primary Replication Server – (an OPEN Server application)
- PDS – Primary Data Server
- PBD – Primary Data Base
- RDS – Replication Data Server
- RDB – Replicated Data base
- LTM – Log Transfer Manager (an Open Server application)
- SD – Stable Device (a raw partition where the LTM maintains its queues)
- RSSD – Replication Server System Database (installed on a 4.9.2 + SQL Server)

- RSI – Replication Server Interfaces (lists Replication Servers to data server connects)
- DSI – Data Server Interface (lists data server to Replication Servers)
- ID Server – One Rep server must maintain the details on all other servers and databases.

The Process

To establish that a table should be replicated,

1. sp_setreplicate titles, true in the PDB

2. create replication definition at PRS

3. create subscription at RRS

This materializes the subscription. The table must preexist on the replicated database or an error will occur and the transaction will be suspended.

The initial materialization can pull all of the data down into the RDB or you can choose bulk materialization.

Generally over a slow line you would want to load the data through some gross means such as tape to disk then use the bulk copy utility to move data into the replicate database.

Performance Tip

If you are going over a WAN, you should implement an RRS, instead of specifying the remote database directly, because this will allow you to buffer (cache) changes onto the SD of the Replicate Replication Server. If you have two servers linked over, say, FDDI you can use the PRS to manage the replication.

ID Server:

Is installed automatically on the first RS system and must be running when new RSs and DBs are added.

Key Installation and Startup Files

rs_install_systables.sql loads system tables in RSSD during install.

file_name.parms contains parms used for RS installation.

file_name.stderr stores console messages.

file_name.cfg contains all necessary startup parameters.

file_name.log contains error and warning messages.

RUNSERVER you guessed it – run Rep Server.

Sites, Connections, Routes & Domains

Each Rep Server is considered a site even on the same box as another RS. Connections are from an RS to a replicate database. Each RDB is one connection.

Routes are from one RS to another, they may have specified hops and may be indirect as well as direct, A to C by B. Routes are directional, and bidirectional traffic requires two routes.

All RSs tied by routes to each other are considered a replication domain. You need one ID server per domain.

The Replication Servers have a unique set of commands to work within the system databases for that Rep Server. You may connect to it using isql, as long as the name is in the interfaces file and it is up.

Replication Server Manager

This is a Windows-based monitoring package for Rep Server. Rep server is seen as a pretty complicated product. One of the customer demands was for a GUI-based management tool for working with Rep Server. The RSM was intended to provide systems administration facilities, though internal Sybase people feel it is not good for this. For monitoring however, it is seen as highly useful. Also included is a heartbeat monitoring facility for latency.

One of the major drawbacks to RSM is the ability for anyone with access to RSM to review the sa passwords for any server that supports replication. This is a "security nightmare."

Future releases of Replication Server will come with a Tivoli management utility to assist in management of Rep Servers and associated components.

Tricks & Traps

User-defined datatypes cannot be replicated, the underlying datatype only is replicated. This should not be a problem in as much as defaults and rules will format the entry on the primary row, not the replicated rows.

Text and image data are not replicated because they are not logged. However, there are ways of accomplishing this, though not with the stock product. This feature should be available with version 10.2 of Rep server.

Views can subscribe to replication.

Truncate table is a nonlogged operation and is *not* a good idea to perform on a table for which replication has been defined, since it will put the rep and primary tables out of synch, or at worst screw up the LTM.

If the stable queues fill up you can lose data. However, the usual behavior is for the transactions to write into the outbound queue should the connection be suspended between the PRS and RRS. There is a performance implication where the transaction is written to disk twice for the inbound and outbound queues. However, without writing these transactions to disk twice, recoverability could not be ensured in the event of a broken link.

Rep server for NT does not work with anything under 4.9.2. You can replicate to a 4.2 or Microsoft SQL Server, but you can not get an LTM to run against it. Instead you need Sybase SQL Server System 10. Microsoft Open Server is (ODS) which is based on version 1.0 of the Sybase Open Server product and remember that Microsoft does not support CT-Library. In some cases you might actually need to put an Open Server wrapper around the Microsoft SQL Server in order to translate the CT-Library calls to DB-Library.

TDS is the mechanism by which the client and server speak. Sybase is at TDS 5.0 whereas Microsoft is at version 4.2.

Keep an up-to-date backup of your RSSD, new subscriptions, routes, error_classes or replication definitions should not be made without making a backup. Recovering an old RSSD is a real nightmare to recover (similiar to a master database recovery). Mirroring the database makes the most sense.

You do not want to try to replicate tables which are not owned by DBO. Rep Server assumes tables are owned by DBO and does not have a mechanism anywhere for specifying the owner of tables within a given database.

Replication Command Language

The Rep Server has its own parser and its own language. Like T-SQL extra white space is ignored, it is case sensitive for identifiers and character strings and it uses the System 10 conventions for commenting /* */ and ANSI style --

Replication definitions are created using RCL:

Create replication definition NAME with primary at server.dbname with all tables named 'tablename' (replicated contents) primary key(column name <can be composite key>) searchable columns(stor_id,ord_num)<optional>

The where clauses of a SQL query can only be applied against searchable columns. If you do not intend to search the columns prior to replication, don't define them as searchable as there is some overhead associated with defining these searchable columns.

The parser will choke on reserved words in column names unless surrounded with double quotes.

Rules Governing Creation of Rep Definitions

- Must be uniquely named.
- One rep def per primary table.
- Primary and replicate tables must have the same name (unless modified through a function).
- Columns must be present in table and names & datatypes must match.
- User defined datatypes cannot be replicated (the underlying types must match).
- Stored procedures and their parameters may be replicated as well as rows.
- Cannot replicate from views.
- Cannot drop rep defs to which subscriptions have been defined.
- Views can subscribe to a replication definition (only one underlying table may be updated).
- Must have run sp_setreplicate, true on the table in the PBD.

Subscriptions

- Created in the SSD as well as rep defs.
- Allows you to subscribe to rows and columns based on criteria (where clause – no joins).
- After the subscription definition, you must materialize it, which propagates the data. Ongoing operation is known as continuous replication.

- Defined at the RRS which manages the database to receive the replicated rows.

Timing on materialization must be worked out to avoid materializing, then replicating the same transactions. Replication will not be initiated until materialization brings the data to a relatively consistent state.

Select * with holdlock will ensure that data have not been changed while the materialization is performed. Not issuing the holdlock allows changes to be made prior to replication activation which means those transactions will be lost. This is known as atomic materialization. (By extension placing the database in RO mode will *really* take care of this!)

Materialization over a WAN is generally just too slow, typically Sybase does manual (bulk copy) materialization. Datatools allows object level backup or logical backup across versions so this product would be quite useful for the materialization process.

Create Subscription will perform this materialization and is the simplest for an operator, but the most expensive in terms of network traffic, and locks maintained on both the primary and replicate tables.

The rows to be replicated gang up in a materialization queue maintained on the RRS until a marker arrives allowing the rows to be replicated. The marker is placed in the log on the transaction log on the PDB. The materialization queue has to be as large as the table to be materialized. (This is one of the reasons bulk materialization is chosen.)

Incremental atomic materialization is a variation that performs the materialization (writes) in batches of 10 rows. This allows access to the replicate database. The queue size and concurrency requirements for the PDB remain the same as for atomic materialization. However the RDB's log can be truncated between batches.

Automatic NonAtomic Materialization

The process is the same as other forms of materialization, but no holdlock is issued on the primary table and changes may be made to the primary table which will make the states inconsistent between the replicate and the primary tables.

Bulk Materializations

Define Subscription, Activate Subscription, then Validate Subscription. This is the fastest means of installing Replication. This method is especially useful for moving OLTP databases into DSS databases if the OLTP database is down for a couple of hours.

No network traffic required (at least for the materialization, if you bcp over the network or ftp obviously there will be network traffic).

The validation process will review the data on the primary and the replicate to ensure consistency.

Subscription Behavior

Where you have defined a subset of the primary table data to be replicated some updates may become deletes or inserts. A book publisher who updates an address to be WI will be a delete in a replicated database of CA publishers, this is known as migrating a row out of the subscription. Moving to CA would migrate the row into the subscription.

You may have set up valid rep defs, subscriptions, etc. However, if for any reason the insert into the target table fails, the connection between the primary Rep Server and the Rep Server is suspended. This can be seen by issuing the admin who_is_down in the RRS. The transaction remains in the Rep Server log and as soon as you reestablish the connection with the resume connection to NYDS1 command, the transaction attempts to start again.

Subscription Checklist

A number of steps must be performed prior to issuing a subscription for replicated data. This includes mostly the installation and setup of the Rep Server databases and objects. All permissions must be set correctly, rep definitions created and sp_setreplicate run. (For a complete list see 5-29 in Rep Server Guide, Vol. 1.).

To successfully create the subscription and get it to run I had to perform the following tasks:

- Create a table in pubs7 – djw_titles.
- Log in into the PRS – TKRS1.
- Create replication definition djw_titlesdef.
- Login into NYDS1.
- Create a blank table of titles called djw_titles.
- Login to NYRS2.
- Create subscription definition for djw_titlesdef.

This worked because the PRS (TKRS1) had been set up with a route to the RRS (NYDS2), which propagated my replication definition as soon as it had been established.

The manual process requires three steps in the initialization of a subscription rather than simply creating it, which is automatic. The Define Subscription, Activate Subscription, and Validate Subscription commands are used when you wish to use bcp to populate your tables.

First you need to create your replication definitio;, as I've indicated earlier you must list all of the columns if that's what you want replicated and certainly if you do not specify replication of all columns on the target table those columns not to be replicated must allow nulls. (Hmmmm!)

After that, you define your subscription in the RRD, and check the subscription. This is in the Rep Server so only commands like define, check, activate, and admin will work. You connect to the

Rep Server using isql which gets a little confusing, because you see the same 1> that you get with the isql connect to a real SQL Server.

To get the Rep Server to move data across you need four isql sessions (maybe five if you want to use bcp or check what time class gets out):

- isql -Usa -STKRS1 (the Primary Rep Server)
- isql -Uuser16 -STKDS1 (the Primary Data Server)
- isql -Usa -SNYRS2 (the Replication Replication Server)
- isql -Uuser16 -SNYDS1 (the Replication Data Server)

To check the status of subscriptions, you log into sessions 1 and 3, which will give you the status of the subscription on the primary and on the Replication Servers. However, all the definitions go into session 3 and are propagated back to the primary server as part of the route.

To check the status of routes and replication definitions, you log into sessions 2 and 4 and use the REPLICATION-SERVERNAME_RSSD, which is an annoying naming convention, but which puts you into the systems database for the REP Server. The convention for stored procedures in REP Server is rs_, such as rs_helproute, rs_helprep.

The LTM is typically named DATASERVER_REPLICATED-DATABASE_LTM.

Steps for Installing Rep Server:

1. Query tables in the primary database (select name from sysobjects where type ="U" >fileout).

2. Determine tables to be replicated, move list into file.

3. Create shell script for I in 'cat tables.repdef' <do>.

4. repdef >$I.repdef.

5. isql -Usa -SPRS <i.repdef.

6. For j in repdef define validate check subscriptions <do>.

7. isql -Usa -P -SRRS <<EOF.

8. $1 subscription $2{2} _S1 for ${2} _RD1 with replicate at RDS.rdb <go> <<EOF.

This uses the repdef shell script for generating replication definitions developed by Sybase, and it automates the creation of the definitions and subscriptions. This presupposes no one else is on the box, and that you will create the empty tables on the RDB, and bcp or otherwise populate the tables on RDB prior to launching the replication process. There is also a utility for recreating tables on the Replication Server without having to do so manually (dumpdd). This pumps out schema definitions from existing tables.

Functions and Function Strings

Replication Server will allow replication of data from SQL Server to flat files or to other database formats (managed by Open Server). This requires mapping of commands from T-SQL to commands intelligible by other programs. You do this with functions and function strings.

The PRS does not send T-SQL to the RRS. An update, for instance, is not update table set, etc. because of the need to describe the update in relation to the subscription criteria. Migrating data out of the subscription means deleting rows where a column has been updated but the new value falls outside the criteria for inclusion under the subscription. This is handled through the Log Transfer Language, and this is generated by the Log Transfer Manager and passed to the PRS and then on to the RRS as a function instance (a specific request with parameters).

This is the mechanism that is used to replicate data outside the SQL Server environment. However, to do this you must write the LTL to translate the generic Log Transfer Language into something digestible by the heterogeneous server. Even within homogeneous SQL Server environments T-SQL is not used. These functions can be user defined and can be used to trap functions like update and perform them as stored procedures (for example) if desired.

User Defined Functions and Asynchronous Stored Procedures

Consider this situation: There are three servers – one in New York, another in London, and a third in San Francisco. The requirement is for all updates to be made in New York but all users connect to their local SQL Server and run the same application.

To deal with updates in SF and London which make the data effective in NY, you must have two versions of the stored procedures. If you use synchronous stored procedures, i.e., rpc, the performance would likely be unacceptable. The other way to handle it is to replicate the stored procedure and its parameters to the server in NY.

The users in NY use the stored procedures directly. The stored proc to be replicated is a function, and needs to be added to the function class. When a user in SF or London uses the stored procedure, the sp with parameters is a function instance.

In this situation, the users in SF and London would not see the changes they made directly due to the lag time between the replication of the stored proc and the replication of the data in NY. The changed data rows would have to be replicated from NY to SF and LON before queries would show the data.

A UDF (user defined function is always tied to a particular rep def. It is called by executing a replicated SP with the same name and parameters as those for the function.

UDFs are defined at the primary (name and parameters, not actions) and defined at the PRS. They cannot be named rs_ (try uf_ instead).

Benefit

One benefit is there is less overhead in network traffic because you are sending only name and parameters. With inserts and updates you must transfer the entire row image (before and after for updates).

This mechanism allows you to ensure that all updates are applied to one server and one server alone without connecting the clients to the remote application.

Asynchronous Stored Procedure Behavior

You execute Asynchronous stored procs at the replicate. The proc must be defined with the same name and param as the UDF and marked for replication with sp_setreplicate. The proc is executed at the RDS but does not have to do anything, replicate data should not be changed because the data will be replicated from the primary through normal means. The execution of the asynch proc only needs to be recorded in the log. Any actions should be non-invasive to the replicate table but may record things in audit tables, printing messages etc.

For asynch. stored procs, you must establish an LTM on the replicate server to pick up the fact that the stored procedure was executed and replicate that back to the primary where it is actually performed. Frequently the RRS stored proc writes the changes to a pending table which is a duplicate table of the replicated data (i.e. a third table). This can be used to determine whether the replicated stored proc succeeded or failed or was pending. (Perform a union against the pending table and the replicated data table.)

The replicated stored procedure process is convoluted because you cannot yet define rep defs for database objects other than tables. Future releases of Rep Server will support directly defined rep defs. (This is true where you wish to push out the definition of the stored proc vs. its action or the row image once the proc has been actioned on the primary.)

Error Handling In Rep Server

Several error logs maintained as part of Rep Server implementations. The data server would record disk or log full messages for example. Errorlogs are alsomaintained for the LTM and for the PRS SD.

If you enter bad syntax the error message comes back to the isql or other session.

Lack of permissions are recorded in the data server log, either on the RDS or PDS.

Exceptions are logged in the RSSD (held in tables).

If you issue a resume connection to XXXX.yyyy skip transaction, the transaction causing the connection to go down is stored on the DS RSSD in rs_exceptshdr, rs_exceptscmd, rs_systext. The transaction does not get discarded.

rs_exceptslast contains info on the last logged transaction. If you had to skip the tran as part of resume the connection you get identity of the last tran from rs_exceptslast and then the text of the transaction from rs_systext. This will allow you to reapply the transactions that were lost.

(The systems tables in Rep Server are ugly, ugly, ugly. Check the join column for rs_exceptscmd and rs_systext cmd.id = parentid . Not only that but rs_ stands for functions, i.e., rs_update and for tables rs_systext. What in the world is that about?)

You can change the error actions from the default by creating an error class and associating the connection with that class. You may modify a connection to use a particular class by suspending the connection, then using the assign action command to assign a particular set of tasks to the error class you created. This associates the action with an error message. Then you alter the connection to XXXX.yyyy set errorclass to your errorclass.

Monitoring Rep Server

RSM which is supplied with every Rep Server, can be used, or a command line interface through isql or some other utility can be used (admin health, admin who_is_up).

RSM is actually useful for setting up heartbeat and latency monitoring.

Admin is run from the isql connect to the PRS or RRS itself. Admin commands include:

- who_is_up
- who_is_down
- who
- health
- version
- echo "string"
- pid
- quiesce_force_rsi
- quiesce_check
- log_name
- disk_space
- set_log_name

Quiesencing Rep Server:

When you want to bring Rep Server down you must first:

1. Quiesce the Log Transfer Managers (stop stuff coming in).

2. Unload the outbound queues (get rid of the stuff you got).

3. Write the replications to the RDBs (write it out to destination).

4. Bring the Rep Server down (shutdown).

You quiesce the server if you want to make alterations to; route topologies, database connections, replication definitions, or subscriptions.

Managing the Stable Device

The purpose of the stable device is to contain the messages for the inbound and outbound queues. It holds all messages until they are sent. Stable devices are made up of partitions. Each partition consists of 1 MB segments. There are 64 16k blocks in a segment. A segment cannot be deallocated until all blocks are deleted. You use sysadmin commands to deal with blocks:

- sysadmin dump_queue
- sysadmin sqm_unzap_command
- sysadmin sqm_zap_command

For Unix files as the stable device, the stable device must exist before running the rs_install. Use touch or cat null > sdd.dat to create it.

Capacity Planning

You can work through the calculations for how much stable storage you need based on your assessment of the rows transferred as part of a "typical" transaction. The stable device might fill up if the connection is down, in which case you need to add disk device to the stable device. To do this:

add partition logical_name on '/dev/rdsk/cxtxdxsx'. Use one partition per raw device.

Your key considerations for capacity planning include:

- Volume of data to be replicated.
- Update rate.
- Number of sites.
- Row width of replicate tables.
- Length of column names.
- Length of parameter names.
- Width of parameters for replicated functions.
- Number of modifications per second.
- Typical transaction duration.
- Length of time you want buffer queues when destination is unavailable.

Performance Issues

If you place your logs on a solid-state device (or on a very fast disk) you will boost the performance of your Replication Server, since this is one of the key areas that Rep Server must manage, because it polls the log for eligible transactions, the faster the better. Placing tempdb on a solid-state device yields very high performance increases, but placing the stable device on it would be overkill.

Database Dumps

You can coordinate dumps of replicate databases and the PRS to a "known point of consistency." This is handled by creating a function string (actually altering) rs_dumpdb and mapping the rs_dumpdb function to all Rep Servers with subscriptions for the database. In the Rep Server course example, a stored procedure was created to allow specification of different dump devices across multiple Rep Servers.

The stored procedure was associated with the function rs_dumpdb so it was executed instead of the default function string.

If you wanted to build error handling into this process you can define a user defined error and then assign an action to that error message, ie. print warning, retry later, select a backup device.

Recovering from Failure

The Replication Server will recover automatically from:

- Network failures.
- Machine crashes (not disk).
- Dataserver exits (no logged trans lost).
- Rep Server shutdown.
- LTM shutdown.

It will not recover automatically from:

- Bad interfaces file.
- Stable device full.
- Stable device failure.
- Primary database log truncated.
- Unrecoverable primary database failure.
- Unrecoverable RSSD failure.

With the secondary truncation point, a dump tran with truncate_only will only dump back to the secondary truncation point. If you override that with DBCC settrunc("ltm", "ignore") and force the dump tran with truncate your SQL Server will work fine, but Rep Server will choke when the LTM looks for the secondary truncation point, which it thinks is still there, even though it was truncated by the dump tran. Complex recovery procedures are then required. This might be done if you had to continue production server operation and needed the log cleared.

If you have routes with Replication Servers passing data along, if any of the stable device partitions crash (this does not apply to the primary Rep Server) then the upstream Rep Server will keep all changes sent on for a default of 2 hours. You can increase this with the save_interval option which increases the recoverability, extends the amount of time the link can be down without losing transactions and requires more disk space to hold the outbound queue.

If a partition becomes corrupt, you can extend it using the mechanism discussed earlier. It is recommended that you quiesce the Rep Server to ensure that nothing is inbound while the queue is being rebuilt.

If you need to reload the database and transaction logs from dump files, you must load the database into a temporary database, issue a SCAN command to the ltm, load a transaction dump and continue scan and load tran until there are no more transaction logs to be loaded.

Users and Security

One of the common complaints about early Rep Server versions included password unencryption and other security holes were considered big drawbacks of the product. The following logins were required to manage a REP Server implementation:

- LTM login to the database to be logged (usually sa).
- LTM to Rep Server.
- RSSD access login (sa).
- <passwords must match between the PRS and PDS_RSSD>.
- logins for Rep Server for logins to Replicate Data Servers.
- DSI connection for Rep Server to Data Server.

The maintenance user must not be sa to avoid major problems with ignored transactions. The maintenance user is specific to a Rep Server install and shouldn't be any real person's id. Maintenance users are set for each database to be replicated.

If this is violated, it can be difficult to determine why replication isn't occurring properly. However, you DO NOT WANT to specify tables for replication that are not owned by DBO.

The associated passwords and user id's are set up in parameter files which are called by rs_install when you install REP Server.

rs_setup_db is run after rs_install. Both of these procedures will provide default user names and passwords. The ids are:

- sa.
- DB_DBO_user used by LTM to read db tran log for replication.
- RSSD_DBO_user used by LTM to read RSSD tran log to replicate systems tables.
- RSSD_prim_user used by Rep Serv for system table update to be replicated to other sites.
- RSSD_maint_user used by Rep Server for system tables updates not to be replicated to other sites.
- LTM_admin_user used to log in and shutdown LTM for RSSD.
- RS_RS_user used by other Rep Servs to log in to PRS.
- LTM_RS_userused to read tran log for RSSD used to read tran log for PDBs.

All of these ids are maintained in rs_users which is a human readable file in RSSD with the password column unencrypted. For this reason you want to restrict access to RSSD to the SYBASE user, like starting SQL Server itself with the startserver –f flag.

When replicating stored procedures you do not use the maintenance user id, which is what you use when replicating data; instead, you have to send the replicated stored procedure with a valid id for the database in which it is to be executed (i.e., PDB).

Permissions

Within the create user process you can also grant {sa | connect source | create object | primary subscribe to user} or they can be revoked as well.

- sa permission can be passed onto other logins.
- Create objects allows creation of rep def's subscriptions etc.
- Primary subscribe allows creation of s subscription for primary data managed by the RS.
- Connect source allows connection of RS for log transfers required by LTMs.

Summary

From this chapter you should have a good overview of the Replication Server architecture and its characteristics. This chapter has been written primarily for those who are working with Rep Server or expecting to work with it for the first time.

Managing data replication has been a key area of development within Sybase for several years. The Replication Server product is a very powerful way of ensuring data consistency across multiple servers in various geographic areas.

CHAPTER 17

SQL Anywhere & Mobile Computing

One of the more interesting things about the Powersoft/Sybase merger was the acquisition of the Watcom database product. At the time, people in the know saw this as a very shrewd way for Sybase to address their lack of a DOS-based product.

In the following years, Sybase did indeed leverage the Watcom product, renaming it SQL Anywhere and positioning it as a small footprint DOS compatible SQL database engine. This opened up the world of mobile computing for Sybase users, but it also created some opportunties for software developers who had to deal with Netware or other DOS-like operating systems.

In some cases, Sybase has pursued a strategy of positioning SQL Anywhere in place of reliance on SQL Server 6.x. Where an application needs the services of a relational database, but may in fact need to run on a resource-poor server (or even concurrent with the application on a workstation), SQL Anywhere is the answer offered by Sybase.

A True Story

One customer of mine had been using a mainframe file set supported by a service bureau and accessed using the venerable Focus query tool. After assessing their customer base, the service bureau put out an announcement that the new minimum access and storage charges were going to be about triple what the customer had been paying. After agreeing to disagree, the service bureau downloaded the data onto umpteen zillion diskettes and packed them off to the customer.

I got involved shortly after the customer had a consultant load the data up onto their Netware server using SQL Anywhere. The requirement was for any research analyst to be able to access the data, but not be able to make changes to it. An additional wrinkle was that the data had been provided by another organization and because personal demographic data were involved there were some confidentiality and protection of privacy concerns.

As it turned out, the antiquated 486/Netware 3.12 environment on which SQL Anywhere had been targeted was not going to do the job. So we fished around for a different solution.

Specifically, we took an available Pentium workstation which had a couple of gigabytes of free space, configured it to support file sharing and loaded the SQL Anywhere engine onto it. Then we installed PC/Focus clients on new laptops for the research analysts and set them up with ODBC connectivity.

In this way, an underutilized workstation became a server while ensuring data could be accessed from a central point of control.

However, as you might expect, this situation was not one that was going to last. Not only was speed an issue while working with larger databases, but the research analysts wanted to be able to access the database from home and at meetings off-site.

To accomplish this, within the constraints of ensuring data integrity, we wrote the databases onto CD-ROMs with our handy HP SureStore and turned the analysts loose with read-only copies. True, we could have simply marked the databases as read only or designated the server-based system as the master, but management was comforted by the idea that it was technologically impossible to change data values on the CD.

To give you an idea of the features and functions of SQL Anywhere, let me take you through the process of the installation and configuration of the databases as we did above.

Installing SQL Anywhere Professional

The installation process is quite simple, actually. There are a few options for which you may want to plan ahead. Installing the server environment and simple client tools requires about 80 megabytes of space depending on the options you select.

The first screen (Figure 17.1) shows the installation options:

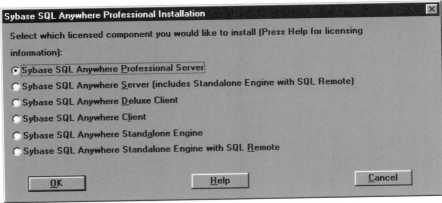

FIGURE 17.1. The SQL Anywhere Installation Menu

To set up a server, with all of its tools and widgets, you select the Professional Server (this includes the development environment NetImpact Dynamo). The meat of the package is simply the stand-alone engine plus SQL Remote, but you can slim down your installation to clients as needed. We'll cover the features of SQL Remote a little later, but for now, assume that if you want to move databases from one SQL Anywhere stand-alone server (i.e. a notebook user) to another, you'll want either SQL Anywhere Professional or Option 2, just the engine with SQL Remote.

Figure 17.2 shows you just what you're getting into:

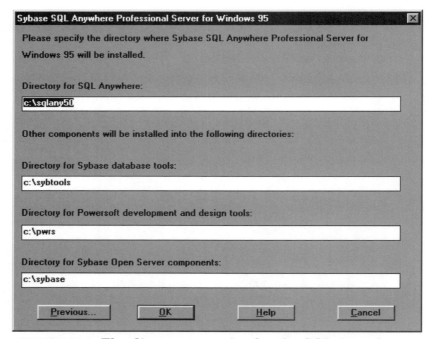

FIGURE 17.2. **The directory entries for the SQL Anywhere cornucopia of tools**

Don't worry, you have the option of deselecting these in the next screen. In the interest of brevity, I've skipped a couple of screens, but here in Figure 17.3 you can see the first selection option activated - SQL Anywhere optional components.

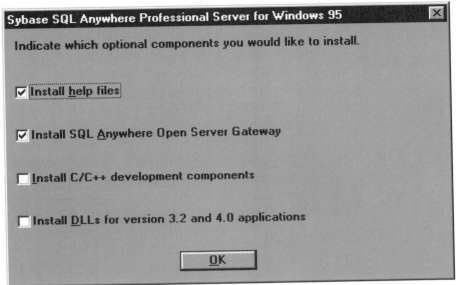

FIGURE 17.3. Optional SQL Anywhere Install Components

The key point of interest here is that you can load up the .dll's needed for compatibility with earlier Watcom databases, as well as the Watcom C/C++ compiler and tools. As an aside, we used the Watcom compiler for a few projects and the developer's thought it took a little getting used to but ultimately decided it was a good toolkit. For the purposes of this chapter, we're going to avoid all the trimmings and just look at the database features and functions.

For those of you who like statistics, the server and Sybase central tool needed only 11.2 MB, once I deselected the NetImpact and InfoMaker options.

The installation routine has what is to me a kind of wierd ending in that, where it presents a successful completion message and then leaves you at the initial installation screen. I was distracted at one point and ended up starting the installation process over because I thought it "didn't take." In any case, the installation routine creates a program group and modifies autoexec.bat and config.sys (even on Win 95 and NT) and a reboot is required to get up and running.

Starting a SQL Anywhere Server

One of the first things that struck me as interesting about SQL Anywhere is that there is no master database or meta data about databases. Instead you start the database engine with an associated database name. The cool thing is that as long as you have a path to the database, you can start it up. This means that unlike SQL Server, which has to know all about the database, devices, users, logins and so on, SQL Anywhere lets you start the engine up on your machine and pull the data in from "anywhere."

That being said, there were a couple of somewhat strange things we had to deal with when we were solving the research analyst problem. I mentioned earlier that we were sharing the data, in fact, we were using SQL Anywhere databases that had been set up by someone else. They had opted for the largest page size for the database (4096 bytes). As a result, every time I tried to start the database on my SQL Anywhere server, I got a message saying the database page size was too big.

This meant I needed to set a flag for SQL Anywhere, specifically the maximum page size for any database had to be set. Finding out exactly how to accomplish this wasn't as straightforward as I would have liked. On the other hand, as the expression goes, "It's easy once you know how..."

SQL Anywhere uses the dbeng50.exe program to start the database engine. On the command line an example of the syntax would be:

```
C:\sqlany50\win32\dbeng50.exe
c:\sqlany50\sademo.db
```

This calls the database engine and identifies the location and name of the sademo database. To start the database with a gross page size of 4096, you have to add the -gp switch. Like so:

```
C:\sqlany50\win32\dbeng50.exe
c:\sqlany50\sademo.db -gp 4096
```

On the NT version you can configure the service to automatically start with that switch through the GUI based configuration tool. Handy that. In any case, once I modified the startup string in keeping with the above, no more problem. On start up, the engine process under Windows 95 looks like that shown in Figure 17.4.:

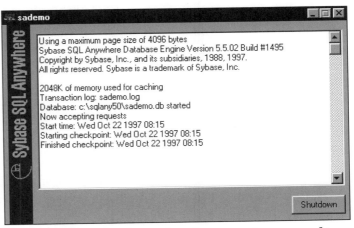

FIGURE 17.4. SQL Anywhere database engine console

The console fires up then minimizes on the taskbar to stay conveniently out of the way.

Client Tools & Utilities

Two main utilities are shipped with SQL Anywhere professional, a variation of isql and something called Sybase Central. Isql is very similar to the interface shipped with the earlier Watcom product and not nearly as funky as the w/isql utility that ships with System XI for Windows NT.

SQL Anywhere ISQL

For those of us who would rather type than click, isql is still the fastest way to ship SQL to a Sybase server, including SQL Anywhere. If you have not worked with SQL Anywhere in the past, Figure 17.5 will give you an idea of how the tool is laid out.

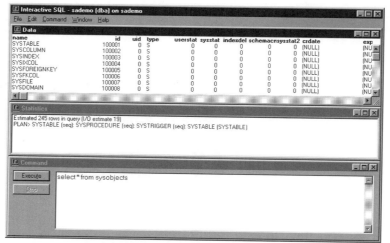

FIGURE 17.5. Isql Query and output from SQL Anywhere

The statistics window in the middle gives you a sense of the system activity generated by the query, the sql syntax at the bottom is where you enter commands and the result set shows up at the top.

The file menu is pretty much what you would expect, giving you the ability to save SQL queries and open them. Disappointingly, the ability to save data rows is not supported. I think this is a pretty serious weakness in the usability of the tool from a developer's standpoint. Most developers are generally quite interested in result sets.

One of the edit menu options lets you insert table and column names by browsing them, rather than having to rely on either memory or your never-handy physical data model map.

Sybase Central

Possibly more interesting than isql is the Sybase Central utility. This application is a GUI based "mission control" approach to manipulating data and databases. The main screen is shown in Figure 17.6:

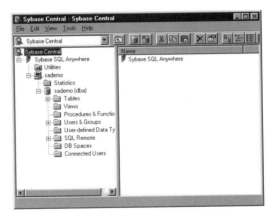

FIGURE 17.6. Sybase Central for SQL Anywhere

The now traditional Explorer-like interface on the left allows you to browse database resources as well as structure.

To expand on that you can see how the contents of the database is listed in the right-hand panel when you activate the tables option in the explorer tree (Figure 17.7).

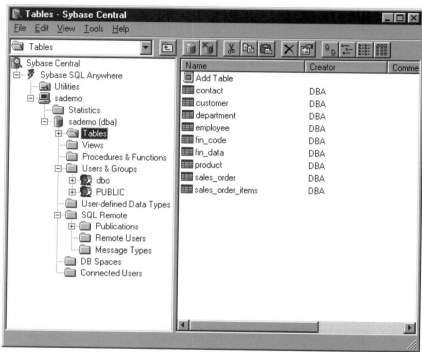

FIGURE 17.7. Fully exploded view of database tables using Sybase Central

One of the neat features in Sybase Central is the use of wizards to create database objects such as views and stored procedures. If you are used to working full time in an environment like SQL Server and only occasionally support people using SQL Anywhere, it's handy to be able to step through the wizards rather than try to remember the differences in syntax.

Utilizing the Utilities

You can use the isql command line to perform all database administration functions, but Sybase Central offers a point-and-click approach to the most common ones.

Once you connect to a database, you see on the left panel a utilities folder. Figure 17.8 shows the options available to you.

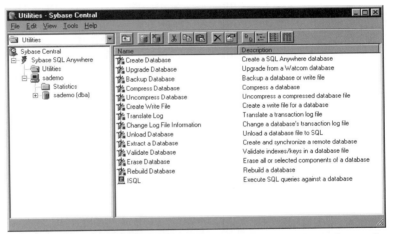

FIGURE 17.8. The Sybase Central Database administration utility options

isql can be called up directly and this is useful if you expect to submit any sql statements to your database. Okay, more than useful, essential. However, the create database and backup utilities are more typically more easily handled through Sybase Central.

Additionally, you may "unload" or "translate" the contents of a database or transaction log into SQL statements. This is the equivalent of a "save as SQL" function. The only other function that is not self explanatory (or, worse, a repeat of the help file) is the "Extract a remote database" command.

SQL Anywhere offers a very attractive ability to manage the propagation of data across many local, remote, or mobile servers. Architecturally, the big challenge with this is keeping the data in synch. The extract command is used to accomplish this.

The first step is to create the "consolidated" or master database. Master in this case means that all of the data belonging to the database are contained and potentially available for subscription. All other SQL Anywhere databases subscribe to some or all of the data. Where a network connection is available to a running consolidated database, the extract command will run a database wizard which steps you through the updating and synchronization process.

Sybase Central Wizards

Like all Windows wizards, the application asks you questions and steps you through the process of creating, say, a stored procedure. For example, one of the most frequently used systems procedures in Sybase is sp_help. For whatever reason, this stored procedure is not shipped with SQL Anywhere. So for our purposes, I thought I would take you through the use of the wizard to create one.

From Sybase Central, expand the database in which you want to create the stored proc and click on procedures and functions. This will show you the existing procedures as well as give you the option of creating new ones through the wizard or from a template. Selecting the wizard gives you the screen shown in Figure 17.9.

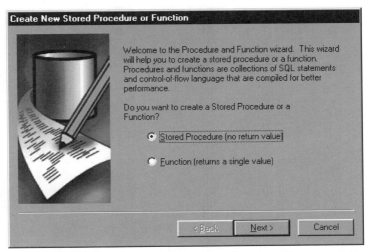

FIGURE 17.9. The SQL Anywhere stored procedure creation wizard

The stored procedure will either return a result set, or simply return a result code, 0 or 1, success or failure to perform the desired activity.

The next screen gives you the opportunity to name the procedure and owner for the proc. Execute permissions can be granted or changed after the stored procedure has been successfully created. This is handled through isql in a manner very similar to working with SQL Server.

However, the following step is somewhat more interesting, so I'm including it as Figure 17.10 for you to review.

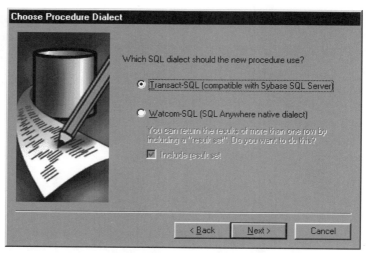

FIGURE 17.10. SQL Anywhere stored procedure creation wizard dialect options

To me, this was very interesting, because writing stored procedures is a very important element of any Sybase developer's repertoire. The idea that you can use the wizard to create SQL Server-compatible stored procs is quite appealing. Even more attractive is the opportunity to recycle existing stored procs written for the Sybase server environment. To that end, I wanted to test the limits in this version for the T-SQL compatibility of SQL Anywhere.

Before doing this, however, I wanted to do a dead simple walk-through of the wizard. When asked for syntax for sp_help, select name, type from sysobjects was entered. After bringing up a wordpad like view to confirm the syntax in the stored procedure template, I was asked if I wanted to test the procedure using isql. Testing? Sure, why not think I. The test results were inconclusive. When I simply cut and paste the .sql from sp_help on Sybase system XI into the stored procedure create wizard's editor, it kept telling me it was not a valid create statement. So I fired up isql and tried it that way.

By the way, I think it's worth noting that the editor looks to me like a great tool for checking stored procedure syntax as you go. I thought it might be nice to include a screen capture of it, but I realized that without a four-color press you simply weren't going to get much from the figure. Take a look for yourself, if you get a chance.

Back to our procedure...after a little cleanup, the proc compiled without complaint. When I tried to run it, of course it couldn't find a table named spt_values, which is fine. I wasn't really expecting identical meta data structures; instead, we wanted to test the T-SQL compatibility, right?

All in all, I was reasonably impressed with SQL Anywhere and its support for T-SQL commands. The biggest downfall really is that the structures are so different you really do have to learn a completely new database environment. At the same time, for anyone looking to write and test stored procedures either at home or on the road, provided you have an identical structure to your user database in Sybase, I suspect that much of the work will be transparently reusable. The benefits of immediate response time and a portable small footprint, true client/server relational database engine strikes me as well worth any potential incompatibilities in scaling up to a Sybase server.

CHAPTER 18

Third-Party Tools

At one point I thought we should include a review of our favorite third-party tools for the Sybase server arena. Then it dawned on me that maybe you would prefer to actually have a useful third-party tool included with the book! To that end, we have released a version of our dbAgent utility. Typically, this product is available only as part of our STARS (Server Troubleshooting, Administration and Remote Support) service subscription. But as a reader of this book, what the hey, you're almost family anyway.

Introducing dbAgent

dbAgent is a database utility for managing and automating many database maintenance operations as well as capturing and reporting resource allocation information. dbAgent is a 32-bit application which runs on Windows NT and can access all versions of Sybase SQL Server and Microsoft SQL Server.

dbAgent can be executed in one of two modes.

As an application, dbAgent is used to run SQL queries and scripts interactively, report on resource allocation, configure automation options and manage local and remote NT Schedulers. Interactive Mode is the default behavior for dbAgent.

When dbAgent is called with the proper parameters, it will automatically log into a SQL Server and run predefined database management and allocation capturing functions. When triggered by an NT Scheduler in Automation Mode, dbAgent can be used to run maintenance functions automatically at predefined intervals. A combination of databases and maintenance options is called a Configuration. Any number of Configurations can be created. The id of the Configuration to be run is passed as a parameter when running in Automation Mode. This allows for the scheduling of different maintenance functions running at different time periods.

Interactive Mode

In this mode you can use dbAgent as a replacement for wisql (see the short summary of Sybase supplied utilities in chapter 12).

Logging In

To perform any database access in Interactive Mode, a user must first log in (see Figure 18.1). This dialog box is located under "File/Login…." dbAgent will automatically populate the Login dialog box with the last server name and user name used.

After a successful Login, all dbAgent options are made available to the user.

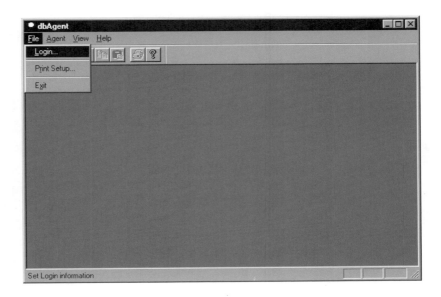

FIGURE 18.1. The dbAgent login screen

The Login dialog can be accessed at any time during a user session. After logging into a different SQL Server, all previous reports remain in dbAgent and all subsequent reports and queries will access the new server. This provides the ability to configure and report on multiple servers within a single user session.

dbAgent was created using the Microsoft version of DB-Library. In order for dbAgent to find a remote SQL server there must first be a registry entry for it. Use the Microsoft 'Client Configuration' utility (WINDBVER.EXE) to add a new server into the registry (Figure 18.2).

Or you can add servers by clicking the servers button on the log in screen. You will need to add the appropriate Net-Library and connection string. For a TCP/IP server, try dbmssocn, hostname (or IP address), query port.

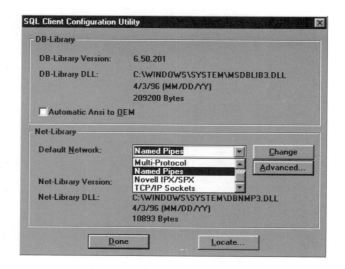

FIGURE 18.2. Configuring the connection type

Once you have selected the transport protocol you wish to use to connect dbAgent to your server, you specify the name, address, and query port of the target servers by clicking the advanced button.

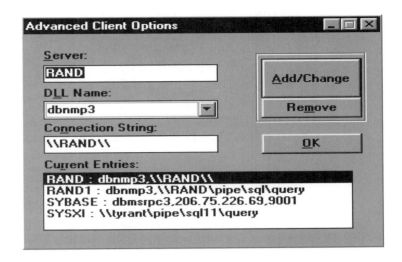

FIGURE 18.3. Setting connection information

dbAgent Windows

dbAgent is a Multiple Document Interface (MDI) application. All child windows of the application are Notepad-like text documents.

Text documents can be opened and edited within dbAgent and basic cut/paste and save functionality is available. Any report windows which are created by dbAgent can also be saved as text files.

When closing child windows or exiting the application, you will be prompted to save any reports or messages created during the session.

The Message Log Window

The Message Log Window is a special dbAgent window. This window is automatically created the first time you log into a server using dbAgent and will remain there until your dbAgent session has been completed.

The Message Log Window is read-only. This means that the contents cannot be changed. The Close button has also been disabled on this window because dbAgent always needs a place to put any server or error messages it may receive.

Message Log data may be cleared from within dbAgent. This is performed via the "Edit/Clear Message Log" menu option.

Message Log data may also be saved using the 'File/Save As' menu option just like any other dbAgent window. When dbAgent is running in Automation Mode, this window is automatically saved for troubleshooting and monitoring purposes (Figure 18.4).

FIGURE 18.4. dbAgent message log window

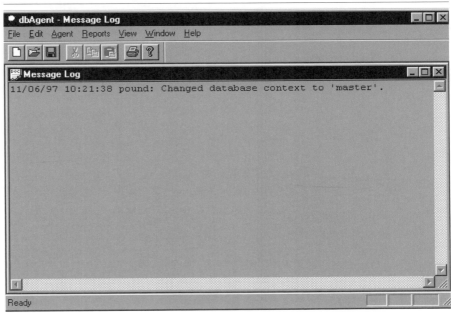

Executing SQL Commands

After connecting to a SQL Server, SQL commands and Scripts can be run using 'Execute T-SQL Commands' dialog. This dialog is accessed from the 'Agent/Execute SQL…' menu option and can remain open throughout the user session. If you log in to a new server while the dialog is open, any new commands will be executed on the new server.

Any Transact SQL commands may be entered into the Command Window or edit portion of the dialog box. Command batches are separated by 'go' statements. Query output is formatted much like 'isql' or 'wisql'.

Commands are executed using the Execute button. Output of the queries can either be routed to the 'Message Log Window' or a new window. 'Message Log Window' is the default output window. 'New Window" will create a new output window each time the 'Execute' button is pressed. This is handy for executing report-type stored procedures and saving the output separately. When using the 'New Window' option, all Server and Error messages resulting from queries are still routed to the 'Message Log Window." Most Sybase and SQL Server data types are supported in the query output.

The 'Show Rows' checkbox adds the number of rows returned from each query to the result output. This is handy when checking the number of rows returned in a select.

The Clear button is used for clearing the Command Window. This is handy when executing large scripts.

The Open button will launch the "File Open" common dialog box. Use this option to read a Script File into the Command Window.

Generating Reports

All allocation reports are found under the 'Reports' menu option. To generate any report, you must be logged into a SQL server containing the STARS_SUPPORT database and at least one "Capture Run" must have been previously executed.

Object 'Size' reports will report on object allocation information for a single Capture Period.

Object 'Growth' reports will report on allocation changes between two Capture Periods.

The common 'Set Report Criteria' dialog is launched whenever any report is selected. This dialog allows you to select Capture

Period ranges and databases. Different selection options are available depending on the requirements of the specific report.

After a Report has been run, a new window is created and populated with the results. This report can then be saved as a text file.

Automation Mode

dbAgent also functions as a batch or script scheduler, somewhat like cron in Unix.

Running dbAgent in Automation Mode

When dbAgent is executed without parameters, it is running in Interactive Mode. When executed with the -An parameter, dbAgent will run in Automation Mode. Where, -A is the Automation switch and n is the run Configuration Id to be used by dbAgent.

Running a predefined set of maintenance routines is called a "Capture Run." Running dbAgent in Automation mode is required when automating Capture Runs.

Typically, the NT Scheduler is used to run dbAgent in this mode.

When running in Automation Mode, dbAgent retrieves the last Server Name, User Name, and Password found in its INI file in order to connect to a SQL Server. These values are resaved after every successful login when running in Interactive Mode. Passwords in this file are encrypted and can only be entered using the dbAgent "File/Login" dialog. If a different copy of the dbAgent executable is used when running in Automation Mode, it is important for its INI file contains the correct Login information.

After a successful login, dbAgent retrieves Capture Run configuration information from the Server's STARS_SUPPORT database using the supplied Configuration Id parameter. All maintenance options set for the supplied configuration are then run. All messages returned by the SQL Server during an automated run are logged under a predefined file name. The log file name is saved with the configuration information allowing different log file names for each configuration.

Capture Runs can also be run Interactively by selecting the Run button while in the "Configure Capture Runs" dialog.

Configuring Automated Runs

Actions taken within a Capture Run are configured using the 'Configure Capture Runs' dialog box. This is accessed from the 'Agent/Configure Capture...' menu option while running in Interactive Mode.

The 'Run Configuration' section of the dialog specifies the current configuration. The configuration number found here relates to the value passed to dbAgent during an automated run. A saved configuration may be retrieved and viewed or edited. The 'Delete' button will delete the current Configuration. If all Configurations are deleted, a new configuration will automatically be created. The 'New' button is used to create a new configuration. New configurations are empty and must be configured in the 'Database Processing' section.

The Database Processing section is used to set which options are run during a Capture Run and which databases those options will process. The message log file for automated runs is also specified here. The 'Browse' button may be used to specify file name and path. Keep in mind that the path to this file is relative to the instance of dbAgent running in Automation Mode. This is important if you are configuring a Capture Run remotely which will be run using a different copy of the dbAgent executable.

The 'Run Capture' checkbox is used for capturing resource allocation information about the selected databases during a run to create data for the Reports section of dbAgent.

Other maintenance options include DBCC(CheckAlloc),
DBCC(Checkdb) and Update Statistics. CheckAlloc and Checkdb
are required in order to ensure that allocation information is correct. When specifying the 'Single User' option, all databases other
than 'master' and 'tempdb' will be placed in Single User Mode
before any other maintenance options are run.

When running the Configure Capture Runs dialog the first time,
no databases will be found in the list. Use the 'Refresh' button to
populate the STARS_SUPPORT database with a list of all databases. The 'Refresh' button will also need to be pressed any time a
new database has been added to the Server which requires maintenance.

When creating a new Configuration, no databases are initially
selected. Any number of databases may be selected for maintenance. The All and None buttons are handy for selecting or deselecting all databases from this list.

The Run button is used to run the currently selected configuration immediately. Output from the run is sent to the Message Log
window but is not logged to the file specified in the configuration.

The Schedule button is used to access the 'Schedule Jobs' dialog.

Using the NT Scheduler

The 'Schedule Jobs' dialog is a complete interface into the NT
Scheduling Service. This dialog is accessed either by the 'Agent/
Schedule Jobs' menu option or using the Schedule button while in
the 'Configure Capture Runs' dialog.

To access the NT Scheduler, the Schedule Service must be running on the selected NT Server and the user must have administrative privileges.

The 'Scheduled Jobs on (server)' list shows all jobs scheduled on the current server. When the 'Schedule Jobs' dialog is initially opened, jobs are displayed for the local NT Server. To access the jobs scheduled on a remote NT Server, type the name of the NT Server into the 'Server' section of the dialog and select the 'Refresh' button. Jobs on the local server can be selected by explicitly typing the server name or leaving the Server name entry blank.

Selecting a specific job in the 'Scheduled Jobs' list will display the settings for that job.

The 'Edit Scheduled Command' section of the dialog specifies the time and command to be scheduled.

'Time' is expressed in the 24-hour format "00:00" in 1 minute increments. If the current time is greater than the scheduled time, the job will run the following day.

'Cmd' is the actual executable to be run by the Scheduler. This is where you would enter the dbAgent executable name (dbAgent.exe) and path without parameters if you are creating an Automated dbAgent job. Any executable (*.exe, *.bat, *.com, *.pif, *.cmd) can be entered here. Keep in mind that if you are scheduling a remote NT Server, the path name is relative to that server. Use the Browse button to locate an executable via the 'File Open' dialog. The absolute path name will ensure that the correct executable will be run. This can be obtained through the Neighborhood Network portion of 'File Open' or entered manually in the form \\ServerName\ShareName\ExeDirectory\ExeName.ext.

'Parms' specifies any parameters required by the application specified in 'Cmd'. This is where you would enter the "-An" argument when scheduling an automated dbAgent.exe Capture Run. Each parameter is separated by a space and entered as if they were being entered at the Command Prompt.

Any combination of Day of Month, Frequency, and Day of Week will be accepted by NT Scheduler for any job. The job will always execute at the same time for each Day of Month or day of Week selected.

The 'Frequency' determines how often the job will be run. If 'One Time' has been selected, the job will be removed from the NT Scheduler's queue after each selected period associated with the job has been run once. If 'Periodically' has been selected for the job, it will be run continuously at the configured intervals until it has been deleted from the Scheduler manually.

Any number of days in the month can be selected for a scheduled job. If a Day of Month is selected which is less than the current day of month, it will be run in the following month.

Any number of days in the week may also be selected for a scheduled job. If a Day of Week is selected that is less than the current day of week, it will be run in the following week.

The Add button will schedule a new job on the currently selected NT Server using the displayed settings. A job is modified by selecting it from the list, deleting it, changing the settings and adding it back in as a new job.

The Delete button will delete the currently selected job from the scheduler queue. Settings displayed on the dialog are not affected by a delete and can be reused to add a new job.

Installation

In order to run the dbAgent application you require:

- The dbAgent executable (dbAgent.exe)
- NT Server Version 3.5 or greater
- Microsoft's 32-bit MFC 4.0 DLLs installed
- Microsoft's 32-bit Net Library DLLs installed
- Dial-up networking must be installed on each client

The INI file dbAgent.ini will be automatically created the first time the application is executed.

The STARS_SUPPORT database must be created on any SQL Server which requires running maintenance routines or creating allocation reports. These are the steps necessary for creating and populating the STARS_SUPPORT database.

- Create a database called 'STARS_SUPPORT' minimum 2 MB
- Run the USG_TBL.SQL script to create the STARS_SUPPORT tables
- Run the rest of the .SQL scripts to create the necessary stored procedures (NEXT_ID.SQL first).
- Run any scripts with the extension '.MS' if you are installing dbAgent on a Microsoft SQL Server.
- Run any scripts with the extension '.SYB' if this is a Sybase Server installation.

Enjoy!

Summary

dbAgent is a registered product of WNS, the company that employs the writer. We at WNS have found dbAgent to be a highly useful utility for database administrators and developers alike and we hope you like it, too.

It should go without saying, but past experience and expectations tell differently. While the version of dbAgent included on the CD is not crippled or a 'lite' version, until you sign on as a STARS subscriber, there is no technical support of any kind for this product. If you like what you see, and would like the most recent release, or access to our troubleshooting database, by all means look us up at www.wns.com or call 1-800-387-8722 for information about the commercial product.

CHAPTER 19

Adaptive Server IQ

Whenever I hear the expression "Data Warehouse," I immediately flash back to that scene from Raiders of the Lost Ark. Maybe you remember it; some guy is wheeling away a crate into a vast storehouse of potentially interesting things. The voiceover is a line given by a government official; "Top men are working on it."

Sound familiar? A vast storehouse of interesting stuff (data) and a query billed as high performance, but backed up by an overworked guy just months from retirement. The traditional performance dilemma of the traditional DataWarehouse.

This is one of the reasons why I like the Adaptive Server IQ so much. The idea behind it was to radically improve the ad hoc query performance of a Decision Support Systems data store. Whether you call it a data mart or data warehouse, typically the differentiation is one of hardware and row count, rather than wait time on a query.

For this reason, the scalability of IQ appeals. It can run on an NT server or on a honking RS/6000 SP like the one that defeated Kasparov in '97. Take your pick. Still, I have to admit it was all marketing hype to me until a couple of Sybase guys took me out back and explained the facts of IQ life. The benefit of said experience I am attempting to pass on here.

IQ – The Objectives

Sybase originated in the OLTP world, as we have already established or know from long familiarity with the Epstein and Hoffman lore. The problem is that OLTP and DSS are diametrically opposed from a technical standpoint. Short bursts of update or write traffic is vastly different than the long selects of ad hoc queries.

Naturally, while you could conceivably try to buy one architecture to fill both bills, in actuality you are going to need to separate servers with appropriate optimizers to really get the job done. This is exactly what Sybase had in mind when they came up with the IQ product.

Maturing Decision Support Systems

The archetypal DSS server is not in the business of supporting real time writes. For a while now, DSS servers have been collections of data pulled from a variety of originating data stores. Perhaps through replication, but more likely through the time honored tradition of writing out some variant of a txt file and ftp'ing it across the network, then using bcp to upload the data.

And why not? Most decision support requirements are not up to the minute. They are batch or period oriented. There are many reasons to wait until a period is closed by the powers that be (usually the Accounting Department) allowing everybody to agree to the same division or period subtotals.

This makes boardroom arguments over who has the right data rather moot.

Focus on the Data Warehouse

One of the key areas Sybase has identified as strategic for their product line is the Data Warehouse. The short definition of a Data Warehouse is a replicated collection of data from operational systems, designed chiefly for queries and decision support.

By replicated, I do not necessarily mean through replication server, though that's an elegant way to do it. In this case replicated means that the queries are not running up against a production database or application. Periodic data is closed off and transferred to a data store where it is available for queries.

Whether your organization refers to it as a Datawarehouse, Data Mining or Business Intelligence, the requirement is to provide speedy access to large data stores. Traditionally, the hard part is the need to anticipate the type of queries and tune them to run with acceptable performance.

This is not the view of a data warehouse that Sybase has been working toward. As they have stated it, a data warehouse must support complex, ad hoc queries, with the highest performance.

On-line Analytic Processing and Relational On-line Analytic Processing (OLAP and ROLAP, respectively) support consolidation and drill down of data in real time. With the ever increasing requirement to reduce time to market, information has to be converted out of data, on-line rather than in batch mode.

DSS – An Example

IBM has been promoting an unexpected real life connection discovered at one of their customer sites as a result of what they call 'Data Mining'. It turns out that in grocery stores across America, there is an early evening spike in sales of both baby diapers and beer. The cause was traced to new fathers sent out after work to replenish the household diaper supply. While there, many of them picked up a six pack of beer. Using this business intelligence meant that the grocery store chain could ensure that beer and diapers were either placed together or never had sale prices applied at the same time. This kind of support for category management can make a developer a hero, especially with a marketing department!

The Query from Hell

Let's consider the underlying data access needed to uncover this kind of buying pattern. First, you have to use the transaction data to get down to the product level, location and time of the sale. Depending on the time period over which you project the query, this could be many millions and billions of rows. Not your average SQL query to say the least.

It is precisely in this kind of situation that AdaptiveIQ shines. For the sake of convenience, I'll refer to the diaper/beer query in the following explanation of how IQ provides bitwise indexing and the huge increase in performance along with it.

Solving the Performance Problem

Unstructured queries are a very real challenge to successfully address. There is more than one way to skin a cat, however, and here you will see some of the options open to you.

Hardware

There are several traditional ways to approach queries against large data stores. Throwing hardware at the problem as long been a favorite. Increasing the power of the underlying server through parallel processing, for example, will speed up particular queries. However, this approach breaks down as you add users. At the same time, most developers will opt for getting as much hardware underneath their queries as they can. The main weakness of this approach is that it leaves small and medium sized shops in the cold. High performance hardware means high performance budgets and not everyone is in a position to throw money at the problem to make it go away.

Summary Data

Of course, one of the primary ways to address a large data store is to summarize the results. Transactions become totals sales dollars by date or location. Patient visits are abstracted to treatments and occurrences. The biggest problem with this approach is that it denies the user access to the underlying facts. Without the facts, how else do you get the relationship between higher sales between diapers and beer after work but before dinner? To summarize data is to squeeze the information out of it. This works fine for certain kinds of reporting, most of which can be addressed without specific DSS server tools. At the same time, it's nice to know that as a Sybase developer, you have additional ways to solve the problem without a massive hardware upgrade or abstracting your data into summary tables.

A Server Based Solution

Let's look at what a database engine has to do to be able to effectively meet the data mining challenge.

Cardinality

As any developer knows (or soon finds out) data ranges fall into either high or low cardinality types. Gender is a low cardinality column with two or three values. (No, I'm not kidding – male, female, or null could all be legitimate values). Higher cardinality data would include columns such as State or even City. Geographic and financial data are pretty much through the roof in terms of wide range of allowable values.

Unfortunately for those of writing queries in the past, such niceties of classification don't deter users from wanting to know relationships about the data. High cardinality data is normally handled by indexes. An index on zip code even comes with the pubs database, if I remember correctly. In any case, high cardinality data has been handled with the traditional data server from the beginning.

AdaptiveIQ extends your reach into the lower cardinality values through the use of bitmap indexes.

Bitmap Indexes

The approach taken by bitmap indexes is to create an array for each unique value of a field, indicating if any particular record has a true or false value for that column.

Think of it like this: for gender, each record would have an index created with two positions in the array one each for male or female. Also for each row in the table, the position for each known value would be 0 or 1. The bitmap indexes can assume that if there is no value declared, it must be 0. Therefore, only values equal to 1 need to be stored. In searching a particular index for gender equal to female, the array explicitly lists all row id's with a true value for the female position in the array.

id	Gender
1024	Female
2048	Null
3072	Male
4096	Male
5120	Female

id	M	F	N
1024	0	1	0
2048	0	0	1
3072	1	0	0
4096	1	0	0
5120	0	1	0

FIGURE 19.1. Bitmap representation of Gender Values

Bitwise Indexing

So what does Adaptive IQ bring to the table? Bitmap indexing has been extended to higher cardinality data. While traditional bitmap indexing has worked fine for low cardinality values such as gender, it has tended to bog down when the number of allowable values increased.

As in the case with State, for example. Another advantage of the IQ approach is that bitwise indexing has been extended to include columns with other data types than just int or bit.

Another advantage to the bitwise technology built into Adaptive IQ is that it supports aggregates and grouping in queries which use the bitwise indexes.

Data Compression

One of the interesting side effects of the bitwise approach to indexing is the resulting compression which occurs. Take your basic 2k data page. Allow, say, 2 bytes for a record id. Then consider the effect of squeezing only that pointer and one bit to indicate gender or state. For each index, a 2k data page will hold hundreds of records.

Male_idx		Female_idx		Null_idx	
id	Male	id	Female	id	Null
512	1	256	1	368	1
796	1	1024	1	2048	1
3072	1	5120	1		
4096	1	7960	1		
10240	1	20480	1		

FIGURE 19.2. Compressed indexes point only to valid rows

Every physical I/O pulls in the location of only the rows which satisfy the condition of the query. But the leverage inherent in the store algorithm means that you can quickly access the data you need from a large underlying fact table. Instead of being limited to bitmap indexing on high cardinality data, this storage approach allows the application of bitmap indexing to columns with a wide range of values. This is one of the key advantages of Adaptive IQ and demonstrates why the technology has been patented by Sybase.

Hardware and Operating System Optimization

AdaptiveIQ separates query operations like sorts, bitmaps, and I/O into jobs which can be allocated to different hardware resources. The net effect of this is tremendous scalability. AdaptiveIQ running on an SMP box shows little or no degradation for the first several users and once all system resources are allocated, response is directly proportional to the number of concurrent jobs. This kind of optimization allows AdaptiveIQ to perform consistently well in environments with fluctuating demand and potentially large pools of users issuing ad hoc queries.

Integration with Replication Server

Core to the Sybase strategy for Decision Support is the ability to integrate the query tools with operational data distributed across the enterprise in non Sybase data stores. To support this, Sybase has developed the Distribution Director management console, which is a GUI tool to support moving data into Adaptive IQ. As part of this process data can be summarized or linked with other related values to best prepare the results for its ultimate use in supporting decisions through ad hoc queries.

The loading of data from either SQL or ASCII text files has been optimized for large volumes. Data load operations take advantage of all processors which means that loading and indexing can occur at rates as high as 20 GB per hour. Even a tight batch window for uploading periodic data can be accommodated at these speeds.

Integration with PowerDesigner

The Warehouse Architect module of the Powersoft PowerDesigner tool has been designed to read schemas from various non-Sybase data sources then graphically design your Adaptive IQ data warehouse. This includes all the data definition language statements needed to create your warehouse, so that even a default load of data can be immediately useful.

The self-tuning nature of the Adaptive IQ optimizer means that ad hoc queries do not need database administrators to have already thought through all of the potential indexing operations in advance. The default setup of the product means you can turn users loose on the data after a rudimentary installation process.

Integration with Sybase Central

For those of you who have persevered through command line versions of such utilities as defncopy and bcp, the move to support GUI based administration of Adaptive Server offerings will be a welcome relief. Adaptive IQ is also supported under the tool and allows creation and configuration of databases, adding users and assigning permissions, and other administrative functions within Sybase Central from a Windows workstation.

The Key Advantages

My first exposure to IQ was prior to the current Adaptive IQ release and was at a customer site where they were struggling with the entire notion of the value of a data warehouse. No server product is a magic bullet to solve business problems, but where your users know what they want and just can't get fast access to consolidated data, Adaptive IQ offers these benefits:

- Supports complex ad hoc queries without administrator intervention
- Integrates seamlessly into multi vendor database environments
- Eliminates tables scans resulting in the highest performance for all queries

- Fully relational
- Performs as much as 100 times faster than your average relational database engine on the same platform

Add to that all of the ease of administration value from Sybase Central and Distribution Director and you are looking at the Adaptive Server product that anyone could use to advantage.

From this, you should be able to see how Adaptive Server IQ can be introduced into any environment as a workable solution for scalable data mart and data warehouse applications.

CHAPTER 20

Pulling it all together:
The Adaptive Approach

In this chapter I boil down the various products and directions of Sybase into something developers can get their arms around.

From all the things we have covered in the book to date it should be clear at this point that Sybase has many irons in the fire. The company now offers 125 plus products, across three divisions, Servers, Middleware, and Tools. It seems that each month brings a new emphasis; this month, Media Server, last month, Jaguar CTS. Product names change like the wind. Watcom becomes SQL Anywhere, no, make that Adaptive Anywhere. Confusing? You bet. It seems everyone is trying to get a handle on exactly what Sybase is doing. Meanwhile, the priority at Sybase seems to be finding something to make their customer base expand. A hit product, if you will.

The natural question for a developer is this; Why should I use Sybase for my development environment? After all, the product line is confusing, the company financials are in the news (and not in a good way) and let us not forget to mention the Oracle developer buddies who keep insisting that the Sybase boat is going the way of Informix.

Well, not so fast.

First, let's look at things strictly from a developer's perspective. Sure, there are database products out there that tout themselves as a one stop solution, offering the works from tools to engines, middleware to media servers. And they say these all work together seamlessly and transparently. But hang on...does anyone truly believe that client/server development tools are actually easy to use? From anybody? I don't think so. In fact, I believe that once you get to know any given set of products, you're working with a relatively level playing field and a muddy one at that.

First let's look at the requirement.

Client/server systems are inherently complicated. They work with stacks of products with multiple versions from various vendors. They rely on platform-specific services that change from one operating system upgrade to the next. On top of this, client/server applications are used by people with backgrounds ranging from rocket science to burger flipping. Applications are expected to run on everything from top tier manufacturers' to stuff put together out of spare parts in the garage. The deployment environment is a continuum from one extreme to the other.

To meet this requirement, you need tools that let you put together durable software solutions. You are looking for an architecture that scales from notebooks to enterprise servers. If you wanted to write "bloatware" you would be looking for the most popular environment, not a high-performance tool set. And that is the key set of features that any Sybase developer is looking for from a software vendor; products that are versatile, durable, scalable and fast.

Now let's look at what Sybase offers.

This book has dealt primarily with the server side of the Sybase product line. We spent no time on development tools and there is definitely a story to tell with Power J, Jaguar, and PowerBuilder. We did spend a little time on the middleware, but overall the focus in this book has been on working with Sybase as a database engine. No doubt, part of this is a reflection of where I spend my time during development projects. But there is an underlying common denominator across every Sybase product: the unsung hero of any solution created with Sybase. I'm referring, of course, to Transact-SQL.

T-SQL: The Lingua Franca

In every age there is a common tongue used to facilitate transfer of information across peoples from different cultures. Latin comes immediately to mind, and English today is generally regarded as a must have for international trade. SQL in and of itself is crippled by the lack of fundamentally useful constructs such as If statements. This leaves the vendor implementations of SQL as the cornerstone that allows you to use relational data in a client/server application.

Write Once... Deploy Anywhere

On a practical level, object orientation is still far from the dominant model for coding applications. And the promise and potential of that world is attractive to systems folks from all walks of life. Still, there is that pesky problem of serving up data with integrity, in a relational manner to a calling application, whether it's object oriented or not.

Sybase has long called the denizens of its databases objects. In the object-oriented sense, of course, they're not. But there is still a role for the venerable stored procedure and trigger to play. With the release of Oracle 7.x, the natural advantages Sybase databases had in terms of triggers and stored procedures were neutralized. So it has become more or less passe to consider these database objects as competitive differentiators.

Passé, that is, until you consider the architectural advantages of combining T-SQL calls with Open Server and the range of Sybase database products. Using a core set of commands, you can write a stored procedure which can compile and run against data held in laptops, notebooks, NT, and Novell servers and ranging all the way up to SMP, MPP, and VLDB data stores. Write once, deploy anywhere.

Through Omni you can create catalogs of organizational data and connect to multiple production databases for periodic updates of data for your warehouse. Or you could choose to really take advantage of replication and distribute your data across the enterprise. Again, all is accomplished with a core set of SQL commands.

In terms of competitors, T-SQL has several advantages over Oracle PL/SQL. Designed later, and carrying less procedural baggage, T-SQL allows you to use extended characteristic and date functions, optimized and compiled for execution on the back end. The year 2000 was anticipated by Sybase from the outset and 00/01/01 means January 1, 2000. Date functions in T-SQL are compliant with Y2K concerns, even if you have to bypass the calling application to supply the correct result set!

With the Adaptive Anywhere T-SQL mode, you can write your stored procedures to work on any platform, mobile or stationary, 95, NT or Netware. This is not a small accomplishment, and means that you can write applications to take advantage of an existing organizational infrastructure without requiring massive upgrades or platform replacements.

At the same time, you need not keep your applications for working in a MS SQL Server 4.x, or 6.x environment. By avoiding

Microsoft's extended stored procedures, you can develop locally on your NT environment, yet be sure that your stored procs will compile and work on more powerful production Unix boxes when the time comes.

This raises the interesting question of Microsoft SQL Server 7. While the true configuration and capabilities of the Sphinx are still somewhat enigmatic, one has to admit that Sybase may have conceded custody of the SQL Server name to Microsoft, but there is no question that Sybase owns Transact-SQL.

Microsoft, on the other hand, has an announced strategy of integrating its entire product line with the Visual Basic for Applications dialect. And herein lies the true value of working with Sybase products. T-SQL is already integrated across tools, like Power J and PowerBuilder, inasmuch as they support population of screens from stored procedures. This is directly analogous to what Microsoft is doing with VB as a development language, and the ability to extend office apps such as Outlook or Access using essentially the same syntax.

This leads to the direction for Microsoft SQL Server. It makes sense for them to extend VB into their own flagship relational database product. At the same time, let's give credit where credit is due. Microsoft may be known as a firm who can over a reasonably short period of time extend and expand their products feature set. But they are not generally regarded for their expertise in producing high-performance code. They bought and paid for the rights to the Sybase optimizer version 4.2. And they did a great job of integrating a relational database engine into an Intel ready suite of back office resources. But if and when Microsoft opens up the optimizer to get it to support VBA code, they open up a can of worms. Worms they may not be in a position to stuff back into the same can. In short, expect bloated, high-feature, low-performance code waiting for the next major hardware upgrade, something not every customer can afford every year or two.

On the other hand, if Microsoft doesn't change the kernel, every core T-SQL procedure you write will work just fine on MS SQL Server as it will on any Adaptive Anywhere or Enterprise server. And let's not forget IQ, Replication or Omni servers.

Developing software solutions involves more than the writing of code, of course. There are other perspectives addressed by Sybase equally well.

Most designers of *n*-tier client/server know that the business logic of an application doesn't belong in the front end. The maintenance and enhancement of an application is much easier when you can keep the bulk of the logic in a single location. The most elegant solution proffered is to write the logic in a language like C and store it on an application server between the database engine and the client. This has turned out to be generally unwieldy.

An extension to this approach is to make your applications portable across multiple vendors by using ANSI standard SQL. Now that's painful! The logical separation of the presentation, business and data layers does not require coordination between three servers. The Adaptive approach is to populate screen forms with stored procedure calls and the result sets they return. The logic is maintained in the procedures, which can be used to ensure data integrity by locking out users from making modifications to the tables through other means than calling the proc. This is not new, of course, but let's recognize that this capability has become even more useful with the evolution of client/server systems, not less so.

Another interested party in designing client/server solutions is the systems integrator. This includes those of us who need to be able to translate a user's query into something that can be passed and parsed to a legacy or production box, regardless of its ancestry. The utility of Sybase middleware products cannot be overstated here. These products have been on the market for years and are well and truly integrated into the Adaptive back end.

Sybase is beginning to bundle server products into functional sets which recognize the reality of the multiserver world. Direct connect, which supports integration of any SQL Server version from 4.x through to 11.9 now ships with every Adaptive Server Enterprise license. Omni connect provides similar functionality by naming any number of other vendors as servers and translating SQL queries into a digestible format, returning results to the calling procedure or program. The common denominator: Transact-SQL.

Data modelers and analysts need to be sure their data have absolute integrity. Triggers and stored procedures as implemented by Sybase have supported this from the beginning. By combining Open Server calls in your triggers, you can fire off external programs to accomplish anything imaginable. The key point here is that extended stored procedures from Microsoft may be an excellent way to easily launch e-mail from database events, but the Adaptive approach gives you that and significantly more.

Administrators have a different set of concerns. A typical dba doesn't spend much time writing applications or dealing directly with end users. The recent spate of tools from Sybase to ease administration is a long overdue step in the right direction. Sybase Central plug-ins should continue to come on the market to give you a "dock" from which to run various jobs on your myriad servers. Until then, try the dbAgent application included for your use on the CD. This is a very clean example of the kinds of administrative tools which can be found for managing the Adaptive environment.

Then there is the page versus row locking argument.

Isolating a specific row to be written requires system overhead. The original Sybase SQL Server design said, let's optimize execution speed instead. Go for the quickest "in and out" of the page on which the row is located. However, certain applications in the market place have become very popular and have stressed their preference for row level locking. Personally, I think it's more than a bit strange to select a database engine on the basis of locking characteristics. The performance and scalability of the two approaches is easily tested and I don't see Sybase coming out materially worse for locking the page instead of calculating the exact beginning and end of any given row. In any case, row level locking is included with Adaptive Server Enterprise 11.9.

As covered in the chapter on the new sp_configure options, the Adaptive approach gives administrators tremendous control over the page sizes handled for any given database. Set aside row locking and look at the advantages of a 64 k page for reading large volumes of data. Sybase is the king of tunable engine parameters.

From all of these technical perspectives, Sybase offers a clearly superior toolset. The kind of people who are attracted to the Adaptive approach are those who want control over the way their programs behave and are willing to do a little extra thinking to take their application as far as it can go. On the flip side, this means that the products are not necessarily as easy to use as some, nor are they ever likely to win first prize for popularity. Capability translates into difficulty.

I believe Sybase could make some extra effort to be clear about the features and benefits of their integrated product offerings. However, the main thing I have ever looked for from Sybase was a set of products that got the job done. They have always offered that and continue to do so.

Then again, there is more to a successful product suite than technical merit. As a Sybase developer, no doubt you have been exposed to the messages of fear, uncertainty and doubt regarding the viability of the company. To clear the air, and help you get back to work feeling a bit more secure, let's look at the alternatives facing Sybase.

After reading the summary of the server and middleware products, I hope you'll agree that these tools are maturing into an integrated and functional solution set. Combined with the existing customer base, it is simply not reasonable that the products themselves would ever "go away."

What is far and away more likely is that Sybase will be acquired by a larger company.

From some Sybase developers I have talked with, this in and of itself is a source of concern. After all, investing time and considerable effort into mastering a database product set is not trivial. Mergers and acquisitions have a way of throwing a company into confusion, making product enhancements late and technical support difficult to get.

To address this concern, we came up with an acquisition scenario that is not only plausible, but it shows how Sybase customers (not to mention developers!) could be the beneficiaries of a merger. Most of the concern I've heard expressed is that as the Sybase share prices fall, they could get gobbled up by Computer Associates or some other firm interested primarily in selling maintenance licenses. The features and benefits of the Adaptive lineup are too attractive not to get snapped up in the event that current Sybase management is unsuccessful at managing the company as an independent enterprise.

To assess these possibilities, let's use a standard management consulting approach. As a systems consultant, I often have to perform a ground-up analysis of a given organization in order to make appropriate recommendations. Here we have an opportunity to perform the same kind of analysis on behalf of all of us who choose to work with the tools offered by Sybase.

Let's look at the strengths, weaknesses, opportunities, and threats Sybase incorporates and faces. This type of analysis

(SWOT) is a cornerstone of emergent strategy, which could be effectively used in this situation.

In the interests of objectivity, I'll state my biases. Having worked extensively with the technology for more than 8 years, I'd like to find a use for it beyond the nostalgic or sentimental.

Sybase Strengths

Multiplatform

From the introduction of its first SQL Servers, the quality and performance of the database engine itself differentiated Sybase from its competitors. Having successfully rearchitected the product to its current version, this is true once more. There are few organizations that can field highly competent coders capable of creating and maintaining database engines across so many different platforms. Sybase is platform independent. Quite unlike SQL Server from Microsoft...Alpha chips notwithstanding.

Scalability

As stated earlier in this book, System 10 was not readily scalable and had a lot of problems. That has unequivocally been fixed. More than that, Adaptive Anywhere, now part of the Sybase server family is scalable from Windows CE, up to SMP Unix boxes. Adaptive Server Anywhere scales, in production mind you, to 20 or more processors on some of the largest Unix boxes anywhere. When you write an N Tier application with Sybase as the backend you can rest assured – it's scalable.

Heterogeneity

Sybase is designed to peacefully coexist with more than 37 data stores. The OMNIConnect product is mature and it works. Naturally performance is not as terrific as having a Cray at your desk-side, but consider the advantages – your stored procs are translated universally, automatically, and quickly enough to get the job done. Sybase solutions exist in a multivendor world – not just at the host platform level, but where it counts – when integrating legacy systems.

Sybase Weaknesses

Marketing

As a company, Sybase has suffered chronically from critical levels of disorganization and lack of focus in a marketing sense. On a tech support level, Sybase solutions are generally intricate and complex, as a result the problems are correspondingly more difficult to solve. Bottom line, tech support is perceived as a weakness. My own experience with the organization is that it suffers a bit from the Not Invented Here Syndrome. Take the the writing of this book, for example. I gained some tremendous insight into the Sybase corporate direction from the marketing folks in Japan, and the folks working in Western Canada. I believe this helped make the book more relevant to people working with Sybase today. The individual responsible for coordinating Sybase related publications, for whatever reason, never returned my calls. As a partnering firm Sybase is weak. Pulling together multi-company solutions has not been a traditional strength of the organization, although I have seen a few Sybase reps who really make the effort.

Threats to Sybase Growth

The performance of Sybase shares on the stock market tends to influence corporate buyers who prize financial stability and popularity of a vendor. This perception may be valid from a shareholders' perspective, but it has very little to do with how well the products work. However, the need to continually appease Wall Street makes it difficult for the company to settle down and do what it does best: provide highly capable information technology products to people who know what they want to do with them. Other analysts, Gartner group in particular, seem to take joy in finding fault with the company. My own assessment is, yes there are problems, but there is no reason why Sybase should go anywhere but up.

Sybase Opportunities

Opportunities:

Life is strange, and one of the more interesting aspects is the wild card of mergers and acquisitions. One of the reasons why I wanted to address this issue here is from a developer's standpoint...what happens to my skills and applications if Sybase gets acquired?

Consider this scenario: Sybase is acquired by Lotus.

Please keep in mind that I have heard no rumors, nor do I have any inside information. But it occurred to me that there are large systems companies out there who could incorporate Sybase products to great benefit of the development community and no doubt to the shareholders as well.

With a fully integrated family of back-end server products, Lotus would be the only company in a position to offer a viable alternative to Microsoft. The Lotus SmartSuite covers all the office functions offered in MS-Office but if Lotus acquired Sybase, T-SQL could be used as the language for extending functionality in Organizer, 1-2-3, and WordPro, just as VBA is positioned within the MS-Office suite.

Replication and OMNIConnect could be used to augment Notes environments to provide synchronization of all data regardless of the data type. Adaptive Anywhere provides better performance and scalability than Approach and could be folded right into the Smart Suite as a Professional edition.

Lotus has Domino, which runs on multiple platforms, but does not have a development environment like PowerBuilder or Power J. The Dynamo team could lend some experience and perspective to the Domino group. Between cc:Mail and Domino, Lotus has the "other" product to share the mail and messaging market with Microsoft Exchange.

The combined offering Lotus Notes, Lotus Domino, Lotus Smart Suite, and Lotus Sybase could be a tremendous counterpoint to the Microsoft juggernaut. Throw in the distribution advantages to including the bundles with IBM PCs and RS/6000 servers and I think you'll agree that it would be a powerful alternative. Microsoft has clearly demonstrated its ability to dominate from the desktop up, while Lotus has tremendous success stories from the big systems on down. The clash in the middle would be fascinating.

So there you have it, at least one scenario where your investment in T-SQL in particular and Sybase products generally could pay off unexpected dividends. Of course, the Kertzman, Chen, and Gladdin team are at the helm of the Sybase ship today and their diligent efforts might still turn the company around. My point with this little scenario is simply to underscore the point that the financial or ownership issues need not adversely affect your decision to develop applications using Sybase products. It might even make things more fun.

Summary

Developing system solutions using Sybase products appeals most strongly to those developers who know what they want to accomplish and are prepared to invest the time and effort to get information technology to work at its peak. Support for this orientation has been built into every Sybase product I've touched.

The new architecture has been assembled and is shaking out to be exactly what we need: a fully integrated set of database solutions tools which allow us to build durable, versatile, scalable, and fast solutions. Maybe it's time to stop second guessing our selection of tools and get down to the business of writing superior applications. At least that's what we're going to do here at Word N Systems.

Daniel J. Worden

September, 1998

Glossary & Definition of Key Terms and Concepts

No book on client/server technology would be complete without a full definition of terms in quick reference format. The following should provide you with definitions for all of the terms used throughout this book.

aggregate function

A built-in SQL Server function which generates a single summary value from all of the rows within a column. These include AVG, SUM, MIN, MAX, ANY & COUNT.

alias

A short, temporary name declared for a table in a select statement. (i.e., select blah, blah, blah where p.pub_id = t.title_id) OR a mapping of a SQL Server login id to a database user name to allow that login to assume the users name and privileges.

allocation unit

The base measurement for database sizing. Each allocation unit equals 256 2kb pages (or half a megabyte).

ANSI

The American National Standards Institute is a standards body that is responsible (among other things) for the definition of the ANSI standard SQL, which determines the basic minimum components of the query language.

API

Applications Programming Interface. A specification and set of functions which allow third-party and custom programs to access databases and other services directly.

application generator

A software program which translates specifications into a third generation or fourth generation language syntax. PowerBuilder can be considered an application generator for T-SQL and Windows code.

application programming interface (API)

A published set of commands allowing programmers to access other programs or services from within their code. DB-Library is an API to the SQL Server.

application server

As relates to OS/2 SQL Server, an application server is an OS/2 based workstation running SQL Server which is accessible to

Novell clients under Netware Requester. NT Server is often deployed with a single application running on it.

argument

A value passed to a function or procedure necessary for it to execute (See also parameter).

arithmetic operators

The basic math operations that can be taken on numbers, including addition, subtraction, division, and multiplication. SQL Server also supports modulo operators.

attributes

Those characteristics belonging to or describing an entity in the relational model.

automatic recovery

SQL Server performs an automatic recovery on startup. This involves rolling forward any committed but unguaranteed database changes or rolling back transactions incomplete at time of systems failure.

base date

The default for SQL Server datetime fields, January 1, 1900.

base tables

The data tables on which views or a select with browse mode is based.

batch

A single set of Transact-SQL statements which are executed when terminated by an end-of-batch keyword, such as go.

browse mode

An option when issuing a select statement from within an application which affects the locking of the base tables.

built-in function

SQL Server functions which allow extra operations to be taken on strings and numbers. These include mathematical, system, string, date, text, and conversion functions. They are built into T-SQL.

cardinality

The zero-to-many, one-to-many, or many-to-many relations which are specified for an entity in an Entity-Relationship diagram.

Cartesian product

When a table join is performed, a Cartesian product is the primary calculation, yielding a number of rows equal to multiplying the number of rows in the first table by the number of rows in the second table. The joined table is made smaller than theCartesian product by eliminating rows which do not satisfy the where clause specified in the join definition.

cascading deletes

These are deletes of rows in many tables with the same key value. When a row in a table with a primary key is deleted, a cascading delete ensures there are no orphaned references to that key in other tables.

CASE tools

Computer Assisted Software Engineering tools are software products which support the disciplined practice of software development through extensive use of data modeling and code generation.

checkpoint

An operation within a transaction to ensure that all changes performed to that point are written to the database pages in the base tables.

client

A separate and distinct process or application which uses services provided by the SQL Server. Often runs on its own computer across a network from the database.

client/server architecture

A method of organizing computing resources which connects two processes, each with their own services, requirements and resources. Frequently, though not necessarily, based on a communications network with overall work sharing allocated between the client, the server and the network linking the two.

clustered index

An ordering of a database table so that the rows are physically stored in order of a particular column (i.e., department number).

column

A constituent part of a table. Tables are constructed of columns which equate to fields and rows which represent records.

command

An instruction consisting of a keyword along with mandatory and optional parameters or clauses.

compiler

The part of the database engine which generates an executable version of a query or procedure.

comparison operators

The symbols used to represent a relationship between two expressions, such as column names or variables. In SQL Server the comparision operators are equal to (=), less than (<), greater than (>), less than or equal to (<=), greater than or equal to (=>), not equal to (!=), not greater than (!>) and not less than (!<). Frequently used in where clauses, (i.e., where a.column <= b.column).

concatenation

Adding character or binary strings, column name or combinations together to form a single expression.

control-of-flow

Refers to the extensions in T-SQL which allow programming logic to be built into SQL statements. Includes IF, ELSE, WHILE, PRINT, RAISERROR, etc.

correlated subquery

The inner part of a nested query which passes its results to the outer query. This query executes once for every row to be processed by the outer query.

cursor

An extension to DB-LIB and SQL Server 10 which allows results to be stored in a structure which processes rows one at a time.

database

A separate and complete collection of tables,views, indexes, and other objects with its own name, users, storage allocations, and permission profiles than any other database on a SQL Server.

database dump

The process of transferring a copy of the contents of a SQL Server database to a separate device.

database object

A table, column, view, stored procedure, rule, trigger, index held within a database.

database owner (dbo)

The user who is assigned all controls and permissions over a particular database. Only one user can be designated as the dbo.

Data Definition Language (DDL)

The set of commands used to create tables and other database objects. Generally the output of a CASE tool, but may be created and run as a script.

Data Manipulation Language (DML)

The set of commands used to move data and database objects. T-SQL extensions such as "select into" and "order by" are examples of data manipulation language.

data modeling

The process by which a database environment is designed and defined prior to actual implementation (See logical data model and physical data model).

data type

A fundamental definition of the values allowed for a column. Each data type has its own characteristics, some which can be set by the creator of the table when the column is defined.

date function

A built-in function which operates on values stored in columns defined with the datatime data type. Displays information or manipulates date and/or time components.

DB-Library

An applications programming interface supplied by Sybase to allow applications and programs to access SQL Server databases directly.

Deadlock

An event which occurs when two transactions attempt to access a datapage which the other has locked before relinquishing the lock already held.

Default database

The database a user is automatically deemed to be in when first logged on, such as master for the systems administrator (sa).

Demand lock

Issued by a transaction waiting for read or shared locks to be relinquished when preparing for an update. The demand lock ensures no more than four shared locks allowed before the exclusive lock is granted for the write transaction.

Dirty page

A data page that has been modified but whose changes have not yet been written to disk is deemed to be dirty.

Distributed data base

An integrated set of data resources which reside on mutiple, physically segregated machines.

Domain

Refers to the range of values considered legal or valid for a particular column. The domain of human ages is 0 to 980 (if you count Methusela).

dump device

A tape or disk device specified to hold the conents of a database or transaction dump.

Embedded SQL

This refers to the process of accessing a relational database management system by surrounding SQL code within a set of programming language statements.

entities

The realworld items which have characteristics or attributes and which relate to other entities. These form the basis for the groupings of the data maintained in tables in the database.

equijoin

A straightforward joining of two tables where the values in a column on one table equal the values held in a column on the other.

error message

Messages describing the nature of a problem or complaint about an operation taken on SQL Server data. Described as a number, state and level with a text description to allow investigation for debugging purposes.

exclusive locks

A lock held on a data page when a write operation will take place on a table.

expression

Expressions are the complete statements which will execute on a SQL Server and return a value of some sort (including success or fail status). Expressions may be combined to create complex T-SQL queries and transactions. (Select * from titles is an expression whereas select by itself is a keyword.)

extent lock

A special lock maintained by SQL Server when allocating or deallocating database or index pages as the result of an operation on the table.

fatal errors

Any return status code of 19 or higher indicates a fatal error which will terminate the user's session.

field

The traditional term field meaning discrete element of data corresponds to a column value in relational databases.

foreign key

A column used as a key which depends logically on the existence of that column as a primary key in another table is considered to be a foreign key.

functions

Operations which may be taken on data. The range of functions depend on which programming environment or language is being discussed. SQL Server provides built in functions. (See built-in functions)

global variables

These system wide variables contain overall status information that may be accessed by any application or SQL Server user. Some global variables may be accessed within a transaction or application and are set for a specific session (i.e., @@error).

groups

All database users belong to a group (public by default). Permissions can be set at one time for every user within a group, speeding account setup systems administration.

guest

An identity setup option which allows any user to log in to a database to which they have not been established as a user. The guest account has restricted access and privileges associated with it.

hierarchical

A formal structure of levels. Typically refers to more traditional approaches to systems design and database software.

identifier

Unique identifiers are the name of the database object which may be up to 30 characters long, must start with a letter, # or _, contain legal symbols and may not contain spaces.

implicit conversion

For datatypes which are not identical but are compatible, SQL Server performs the conversion without being told.

inner query

In a nested query, the inner query or subquery is performed first, passing its results to the outer query.

intent lock

A read or write operation places an intent lock on a data page when other locks are already placed on the same page. The intent lock reserves the next available lock for that operation.

integrity constraint

A rules or relationship which must be enforced on a column or table to ensure data integrity is called an integrity constraint.

isql

The Sybase-supplied command line interface to SQL Server.

JAD

Joint Application Development is a process by which users and systems developers work together to define and design a system.

join

A cornerstone of relational databases, the join operation allows two separate tables to be treated as one by combining the two where a common column value matches predefined criteria (equals, not equals, greater than, less than, etc.).

kernel

The central database engine itself (the dataserver program) is the rbdms kernel which runs all of the tasks and processes of the SQL Server.

key

A column value which identifies the other columns in a table, keys are used by indexes for sorting and retrieving data.

keyword

A reserved transact SQL word or phrase used for operations on SQL Server data. (i.e., SELECT)

leaf level

Refers to the bottom level of an index. In a clustered index, the leaf level consists of the physical data as they are stored on the hard disk.

livelock

Exclusive locks for write operations may not be granted while successive shared locks for reads are in place. This is known as a livelock, which is detected automatically by the SQL Server and corrected after four new shared locks are granted.

locking

A concurrency control mechanism which manages multiple users engaging in both read and write operations on the same data.

logical database device

The name by which physical disk space is known to Sybase. This is defined with the DISK INIT command.

logical data model

The highlevel view of the entities, attributes, and relationships of a database prior to its physical implementation.

logical operators

AND/OR/NOT are the logical operators which may be used to build the desired set of expressions in a where clause. Logical operators define the select criteria by combining conditions to be met by the query.

login

The account name set for a user on the SQL Server itself. This is the first component of establishing a successful database connection. The login name need not be the same as the user name defined in a particular database.

master database

The systems database set up during the initial installation of SQL Server containing all users, databases and operation of the server as a whole.

master-detail table

A table containing high level data for which corresponding details are maintained in another table. The master table contains the primary key which links to the foreign key in the detail table.

master device

The logical device name for the disk on which the master database is installed.

messages

In SQL Server, the system communicates status information to users and applications through messages.

metadata

Data about the data. Can include dictionary definition, scope notes, formatting options, and display preferences.

modulo

An arithmetic operator which expresses division with remainders rather than decimals. (i.e., 31/3 is 10 with a remainder of 1 versus 1.3333333333...)

natural join

Where two tables can be linked by stating that the values in the columns are equal, the join is considered natural when only one of the identical columns is displayed rather than the full contents of both tables, including the redundant column.

nested queries

Multiple levels of queries are considered nested. These queries are used to retrieve first one set of data and then perform other T-SQL operations on that subset.

Net-Library

The name of the Sybase products which allow DB-Library applications to talk to network transport software and connect to SQL Server across the network

nonclustered index

This form of index stores the key values and pointers to the data pages where the rows are held.

normalization

Refers to the extent to which data are segregated or duplicated in tables. Database design defines rules for specific degrees and stages of normalization.

null

This is a unique status for a column value that does not mean zero. Null indicates that the value for that column is unknown or not yet established and does not equate to any existing value in the column.

object

A term for a database element including table, view, stored procedure, trigger, default, rule, and datatype. In object-oriented programming, an object is seen as a tightly integrated set of data and methods which has behaviors and responds to messages.

object owner

The user name which is considered the creator and has all rights to the specific object.

object permissions

The privileges or permissions provided to database users for a specific object.

operating system

The system control program for a host computer. The operating system type and version determines which SQL Server can be loaded onto the host platform.

outer join

A special join type which returns all the rows of one table and only those rows matching a where clause criteria from another. This is useful for selecting all employees for example, plus license info for those employees having parking spaces. Outer joins are specified with *= or =* to return all rows from the first or second table respectively.

outer query

Refers to the first query where that query contains a query within it.

parameter

A value which is passed to a program or stored procedure. Parameters specify names and options when running commands. For example, OPEN <filename> where filename is a parameter. Parameters may be optional or mandatory.

permission

The necessary allocation of rights or authorization to perform certain tasks.

primary key

A column or columns by which each row in a table is uniquely identified.

project

Verb. To project. A fundamental aspect of relational systems. To project over a table is to pull a subset of the table.

qualifier

A naming convention which specifies the database and/or owner of a particular object. The qualified name of the sysusers table in the master database is master.dbo.sysusers.

query

A SQL statement which selects, inserts or deletes data in the database.

referential integrity

Like normalization, referential integrity refers to the rules defined as part of the relational model. Referential integrity is the area of database practice which ensures that tables with primary keys contain rows for which other tables have foreign keys. This prevents lost or meaningless data from being proliferated through many tables.

restriction

Works with projection and is synonomous with selection. A select statment is a means of restricting the values retrieved by a query.

rollback transaction

A T-SQL extension to SQL, rollback transaction is a control of flow statement which performs an "UnDo" for all changes made within a transaction when an error or other defined condition has occurred.

row

The complete set of column values for one unique record in a relational system is considered a row. Fields and Records are referred to as Columns and Rows in Sybase.

row aggregate functions

These built-in functions create a summary row when you issue a compute sum, avg, min, max, and count within a select statement.

rule

A definition that determines the format and/or content of data entered into a specific column or user defined datatype.

sa

The systems administrator role in SQL Server. This is the root account which performs all system-wide administration and configuration functions.

savepoint

A savepoint sets up a marker to allow a rollback to undo only changes made since the last savepoint rather than from the beginning of the transaction.

scalar aggregate

A built-in function which returns a single value from a select statement without using the GROUP BY clause.

select list

The columns specified to be retrieved within the main portion of a SELECT statement.

self-join

A type of join which compares a table to itself. Useful for determining data on the basis of comparisons of column values within the same table.

severity level number

Error messages from SQL Server identify the severity of the error as part of the returned status code. Error 666 indicates armageddon.

shared lock

Select statements place shared locks on data pages which allow other queries to select data but which block write operations which require exclusive locks on pages to be affected.

sso

The systems security officer role in SQL Server Release 10.0. This role functions similiarly to sa, with specific responsibility for assigning rights and permissions.

statement

T-SQL commands and parameters are defined as statements which begin with keywords and specify the SQL operations to be performed.

statement block

The T-SQL statements which make up a single transaction.

stored procedure

T-SQL statements which have been stored as a script and compiled into an executable routine on the SQL Server.

string function

Built-in functions which perform operations on strings of characters or binary data.

subquery

An inner query or complete and legal select statement which is called from within another query.

suid

Server user id. The internal number which identifies a logged-in user.

system databases

The initial installation of SQL Server sets up three databases (more for SQL Server 10.0). The master, model, and tempdb systems databases are used as part of all ongoing user database setup and operation.

system functions

A built-in function that retrieves information from the SQL Server and systems tables.

system procedures

These stored procedures are supplied with the SQL Server to ensure that administrative tasks which affect the systems tables are performed completely and accurately.

system tables

These tables reside in the master and other databases and contain rows reflecting all users, database objects, permissions, etc. The system tables in master contain the data dictionaries about the SQL Server as a whole, while the systems tables within each database contain the data dictionary for that specific database.

table

A single complete set of columns and rows within a database.

tcp/ip

Transmission Control Program/Internet Protocol. This transport layer communications specification is used to link computers over a network. Prevalent in the Unix/Ethernet environment, but no longer restricted to this.

theta join

These joins incorporate comparison operators when specifying the join condition. Comparisons include where table 1 is equal, not equal, greater than, less than, etc. than table 2.

transaction

A set of statements which are treated as a single task and can be undone or committed according to certain conditions, such as encountering an error.

transaction log

A record of all changes made to a database. The transaction log is used in conjunction with a database dump to restore the database and replay any actions taken on the database.

trigger

A special stored procedure defined once for insert, delete and update operations on a specific table. Triggers are executed automatically rather than called like stored procedures.

type conversion function

An explicit or implicit conversion of data manipulated in a statement from one datatype to another. Formatting datetime information requires a conversion of the value to character type, for example.

update

Any change to a value within a database table can be considered an update. The update command modifies one or more column values within an existing row. Delete, insert and truncate table statements can also be considered update operations.

user-defined datatype

The Sybase-supplied datatypes can be defined to contain defaults and rules and named as unique datatypes. A postal code datatype, for example, might be based on the character datatype but include a rule to ensure that the right number of characters is entered.

variable

A variable is a logical mapping of an event, value or values to a name which can be accessed by a T-SQL program or client program. Variables may be user defined or supplied by the system.

vector aggregate

A value that is obtained through the use of an aggregate function in conjection with the GROUP BY clause.

view

A method for presenting columns from one or more tables as if they were a single, complete table. Useful for security and presenting data to users unfamiliar with joins.

view resolution

All queries accessing a view must be processed to ensure that the objects referenced by the view exist and appropriate permissions have been granted to the user of the view.

wildcard

A special character that represents any character in that position. Wildcards allow retrieval of inexact matches to within a single statement (i.e., select * from tablename).

Index